Accounting and Taxation
for Paralegals

Accounting and Taxation for Paralegals

Thomas F. Goldman, Esq.

Upper Saddle River, New Jersey 07458

Library of Congress Cataloging-in-Publication Data

Goldman, Thomas F.
   Accounting and taxation for paralegals / Thomas F. Goldman, Esq.
      p. cm.
   Includes bibliographical references and index.
   ISBN 0-13-026424-5
   1. Lawyers—Accounting. 2. Lawyers—United States. I. Title
HF5686.L35 G65 2001
657′.024′344—dc21

                                            00-053728

Executive Editor: Elizabeth Sugg
Production Editor: Linda Zuk, WordCrafters Editorial Services, Inc.
Production Liaison: Eileen O'Sullivan
Director of Manufacturing and Production: Bruce Johnson
Managing Editor: Mary Carnis
Manufacturing Buyer: Ed O'Dougherty
Cover Design Coordinator: Miguel Ortiz
Cover Design: Anthony Incione
Cover Illustration: Nikolai Punin, SIS/Images.com
Editorial Assistant: Anita Rhodes
Composition: Publishers' Design and Production Services, Inc.
Printing and Binding: Banta Company, Harrisonburg, VA

Prentice-Hall International (UK) Limited, *London*
Prentice-Hall of Australia Pty. Limited, *Sydney*
Prentice-Hall Canada Inc., *Toronto*
Prentice-Hall Hispanoamericana, S.A., *Mexico*
Prentice-Hall of India Private Limited, *New Delhi*
Prentice-Hall of Japan, Inc., *Tokyo*
Prentice-Hall (Singapore) Pte. Ltd.
Editora Prentice-Hall do Brasil, Ltda., *Rio de Janeiro*

10 9 8 7 6 5 4 3 2 1
ISBN 0-13-026424-5

Contents

Preface

This book is written in response to numerous requests from paralegals for help in preparing the tax and accounting forms that come across their desks on a regular basis. With the increasing reliance upon paralegals as members of the law office team has come increased dependence on paralegals for the preparation of forms and documents that require a basic understanding of accounting and taxation. *Accounting and Taxation for Paralegals* is designed to provide those fundamentals. Hopefully, it will retain a place on your desk as a reference work after you have completed the course.

Frequent reference is made in *Accounting and Taxation for Paralegals* to various ethical rules. Financial matters have become increasingly important in the lives of individuals, and it is important to keep in mind the ethical obligations of both the supervising attorney and the paralegal in the preparation of financial statements, tax returns, and reports to the court and beneficiaries. Although the rules of accounting may change, tax forms may vary, and court rules may become more demanding, the constant in any profession is the obligation of competence.

The material presented herein will provide you with an introduction to the fundamental concepts. But change is inevitable, particularly with regard to the preparation of tax returns. Always be certain that you are using the most current forms and following the most current laws, regulations, and guidelines.

I offer special thanks to my paralegal, Edith Hannah, for her insight and help in preparing the checklists and forms. I also owe a special debt of gratitude to my late uncle Ralph Welensky, accountant extraordinaire, for showing me that accounting records and tax returns are not numbers in isolation, but are the result of a person's life and that the records and tax returns tell the stories of individuals and their families. Finally, a debt of appreciation goes to the following reviewers for their insightful comments and suggestions: Noel McKeon, Florida Community College; Linda Cabral Marrero, Mercy College; and Laura Barnard, Lakeland Community College.

As you work with the next "shoebox" of material dropped off by a client, think of the story the records tell and you will never again think of accounting as dull and boring.

About the Author

Thomas F. Goldman is an attorney at law with a federal, state, and local practice. He graduated from Boston University with a major in Accounting and practiced accounting while pursuing a law degree from Temple University School of Law. He has lectured widely and has taught accounting, management, and paralegal courses. He is currently a Professor of Law and Management at Bucks County Community College, where he has been coordinator of Paralegal Studies.

Chapter 1

Introduction to Accounting

In This Chapter

Why Should You Learn Accounting?

Accounting courses have typically had a bad reputation with students. This is unfortunate since they are highly relevant to most students. Most of us are concerned with obtaining, using, tracking, and recording the use of money. It may be as simple as keeping track of our allowance as a child or keeping a record of our checking account transactions as an adult. Our need to set up a budget or keep track of our funds becomes more important and more involved as we get a job, set up a home, and raise a family. With employment also comes the requirement to file tax returns. This may also require keeping records for determining appropriate inclusions and deductions.

Knowing how financial records are kept can be helpful when using the documents prepared by banks, stockbrokers, and other financial institutions. If nothing else, it allows you to determine if they are accurate. Monthly checking account statements may contain errors caused by misreading of amounts shown on checks or deposits. With electronic banking, errors are not only more possible, but they can have a greater financial impact before you even become aware of the error. Until you try to use your electronic bankcard to make a purchase, you may be unaware that the bank teller incorrectly entered the amount of the deposit as $12.00 instead of $120.00 or $1,200.00. An erroneous keystroke can have a significant impact on the cardholder without cash on a Saturday night (Fig. 1-1).

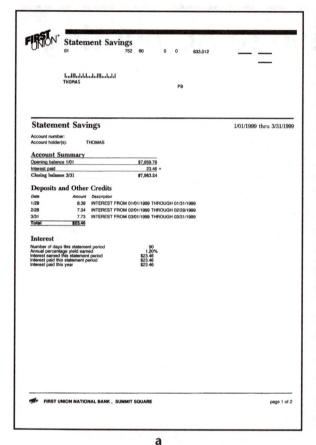

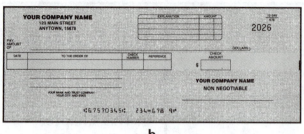

Figure 1-1   (a) Bank statement; (b) check; (c) ATM machine.

Accounting in the Law Office

In the law office working environment, your ability to understand basic financial issues makes you a more valuable member of the law office team. A law firm is a business. Unlike retail, wholesale, or manufacturing businesses that trade in goods or commodities, the law office deals in time.

Keeping track of the time spent by the lawyers and support staff on a client's case and then billing the client for the time expended is a major function of the legal support staff (Fig. 1-2). Financial account records must be accurately kept for both internal office activities and those matters related to specific clients. Expenses may be associated with a specific client or part of the overall cost of running the office. If accurate records are not kept for the law office operation, it may fail and close. When the funds involved belong to clients, errors can result in malpractice claims for improperly prepared documentation and the filing of inaccurate court documents and tax returns. At worst, it may result in the loss or misappropriation of clients' funds, which can lead to sanctions, including disbarment or even criminal prosecution.

WEEKLY TIME REPORT

ACCOUNT NUMBER	NAME OF CLIENT		HOURS WORKED								AMOUNT
			MON.	TUE.	WED.	THUR.	FRI.	SAT.	SUN.	TOTAL	
1 3 2 0 1	E. QUINN	TFG					.5			.5	1

ACCOUNT NUMBER	NAME OF CLIENT		MON.	TUE.	WED.	THUR.	FRI.	SAT.	SUN.	TOTAL	AMOUNT	2
			HOURS WORKED									3

DO NOT WRITE IN SHADED AREA BELOW

DATE	TIME START	STOP	ELAPSED	CODE	DESCRIPTION OF SERVICES PERFORMED
2/15/00	8:30	9:00	.5	OV	Meet with client to discuss P/A

CODE		NAME	
OV	D. THOMAS	CLIENT → ← STAFF MEMB.	E. QUINN

Law Office
D. Thomas & Associates
Main Street
Sacramento, CA
555-123-4567

E. Quinn
831 State Street
Newton, MA 55555

For Services Rendered:

Consultation and Preparation
of Power of Attorney

.5 hours @ $150/hour $75

a   b

Figure 1-2 (a) Time sheet; (b) client billing statement.

In addition to the internal accounting needs of the law firm is the need to understand the accounting and financial affairs of clients. Understanding accounting and financial reports and documents is essential in many areas of law today.

Family Law

In every domestic relation case, there are concerns about property settlement, support, and alimony. In today's marital climate, there is an increasing demand for full financial disclosure in prenuptial agreements. A basic understanding of the nature and the sources of the family financial information will enable you to prepare the necessary documents.

Commercial Litigation

Commercial litigation has become more complex—in no small matter because of the financial implication of contract breaches and remedies. Finding, analyzing, and presenting financial matters increasingly falls on the litigation paralegal.

Litigation

Even in the simplest of litigation matters, a measure of damages will need to be computed. Calculations of how much wages were lost, what the future losses will be, and the current or present value may need to be computed or reviewed for accuracy.

Maintaining Financial Information

Law firms, like any other business, have numerous forms of financial obligations. Utility bills, employees, and taxes have to be paid on a regular basis. Accurate records need to be maintained to determine which costs are chargeable to individual clients. Office operations frequently involve record keeping for clients' funds in the form of escrow accounts. Records of the various receipts and disbursements are regularly used to prepare the tax returns, including quarterly and annual employee withholding and employer taxes, income tax returns, and informational tax returns, such as reports for nonemployee compensation to independent contractors (e.g., court reporters).

When a systematic system is used on a regular basis, the completion of the financial reports is simplified. By using a standard system of accounting, lawyers, bookkeepers, paralegal, and secretarial personnel can all use the same system, contributing information of charges and revenues that are useable for all concerned, including the outside accountants and auditors.

Reconstructing Financial Information

In many cases, clients will deliver piles of financial documents and expect the law office to sort, classify, and organize the seemingly unrelated pieces of paper into tax returns, estate tax returns, and documents with which settlements and major decisions will be made. Knowing how to attack the piles of paper can save time, stress, and frustration.

Accounting as the Language of Business

ACCOUNTING The analyzing, recording, classifying, summarizing, and interpreting of financial transactions

Accounting is frequently referred to as the language of business. Anyone with an interest in financial matters uses accounting terminology. Some of the terms are well known (e.g., cash, gross, accrued). Others, while frequently used, are not necessarily used with the precision of accounting professionals, such as the terms debit and credit. A knowledge of the correct usage of the terminology makes the job of the law office professional easier by permitting accurate conversation and discussion in matters involving money with clients, bankers, stockbrokers, the court, and other law office professionals. Every profession and occupation has a lexicon of terms and phrases that has developed to enable those working in the field to communicate with each other. Some of the terms include words that have evolved over a long period of time to have a very specific meaning today. Terms like *point* may mean a gesture to a trial lawyer, although to the banker or mortgage banker, it usually refers to a percentage of interest charged. In working with clients who work in different fields, as well as other support suppliers, it is important to be sure of how words are being used in financial matters.

Terminology and Understanding

Every business, occupation, and profession have a language of their own. Lawyers use words in specific ways, not to confuse or hide behind language, but to mean specific things. Legal terminology is generally found in court decisions. To avoid confusion and litigation, lawyers use these words as they have been interpreted. Accountants use language in the same way. Accountants are concerned with monetary issues and tax matters. They are also concerned with accurately describing financial issues by using words and phrases that will be understood by the readers of the statements they prepare. Unlike lawyers, who usually look to local or state interpretation, accountants in the private sector follow a set of descriptions and interpretations set by the Financial Accounting Standards Board, whose members are nominated from the national sponsoring organizations, including the American Accounting Association, American Institute of Certified Public Accountants, Financial Analysts Federation, Financial Executives Institute, National Association of Accountants, and the Securities Industry Association.

Accounting as the Source of Information

It seems that, ultimately, every case and most issues in the law office involve monetary or financial issues. These may be as simple as calculating the cost of repairs for property damage in a tort action or as complex as a pension plan analysis in a divorce case. Somewhere in the middle are the cases involving a determination of assets and expenses, and allocations among different parties. All of this information comes from accounting records—formal and informal. The family checking account is an informal source of the expenses, assets, and financial allocations for a family. The business ledgers, journals and computerized accounting system provide the sources and uses of funds for a business. To understand how the records are created in a traditional accounting system permits one to understand more complex accounting systems as well. It is necessary to understand the source of the accounting entry and how the financial information is processed to make maximum use of the information available.

What Is Accounting?

Accounting has been traditionally defined as analyzing, recording, classifying, summarizing, and interpreting financial transactions. Less traditionally, it is the keeping track of monetary transactions in such a fashion that one can understand what happened and the keeping track of information so that it can be understood and used in the future. Since the records may be looked at and used by others, such as tax preparers and financial institutions in making loan decisions, it is useful to follow a common set of rules that are well understood by those involved in the use of this information. Within the United States, this common set of rules, developed by the Financial Accounting Standards Board **(FASB)**, is known as the Generally Accepted Accounting Principles **(GAAP)**.

FASB   Financial Accounting Standards Board

GAAP   Generally Accepted Accounting Principles

ANALYZING
Determining the effect and significance of a financial transaction

Analyzing. Each transaction must be looked at to determine the effect and significance to the individual or business entity. Each time cash is spent, a check is written, or an obligation is incurred, there are financial implications for the individual, business, or other entity.

RECORDING
Entering the financial transactions in the journals and ledgers

Recording. This part of the accounting process is frequently thought of as bookkeeping. Monetary transactions are recorded in some form. The form of **recording** may be as informal as keeping a checkbook or as involved as keeping a complete set of journals and ledgers. The size of the organization and the uses of the data in the future will determine the most appropriate methods to be used. In the law office, the tracking of monetary transactions can take on new obligations when the transactions involve clients' funds. Accurate recording in a manner and form that will allow others to understand the transactions is essential. The nature of local court rules and ethical obligations frequently will dictate the nature of the records to be kept. Even the law firm's own records need to be kept very carefully to ensure that tax returns can be properly prepared and filed in a timely fashion to avoid ethical violations.

CLASSIFYING
Sorting financial information into appropriate groups

Classifying. The recorded financial information must be sorted into appropriate groupings based upon the accounting use of the information contained in the various financial statements normally prepared. These statements include the following: the income statement, which is a statement of the income and expenses during a fiscal period; the balance sheet, which is a statement of the assets and liabilities of the business or financial entity; and the statements of owner's equity, which show the increases and decreases in the claims of the owners to the assets of the business or financial entity.

Accountants frequently prepare the list of accounts for use in a particular financial entity. This is known as a chart of accounts. Individual monetary transactions can then be sorted by a standard set of account titles for ease in preparing financial reports.

SUMMARIZING
Organizing the financial information into useful and meaningful statements

Summarizing. Once the transactions have been analyzed and recorded by appropriate classifications, they can then be summarized into useful and meaningful statements, such as the income statement, balance sheet, and owner's equity statements, mentioned above, and which will be further discussed later in this book.

INTERPRETING
Determining the relationships between the financial transactions and the accounts on the financial statements

Interpreting. The most important of all the accounting functions is the interpretation of financial statements. Based on the relationship among certain account items on the financial statements, decisions can be made and policies established for future operations.

Understanding the Rules

If everyone followed the generally accepted accounting principles and accounting procedures, the life of the paralegal would be much easier. Unfortunately, clients are not always organized in their financial affairs. It is more common to have a client drop off a container full of financial information. It may be a checkbook, a shoebox of receipts, or a filing box full of all manner of relevant and irrelevant paperwork of a financial nature (Fig. 1-3). From this raw data, it becomes the paralegal's job to analyze, classify, and summarize the financial information for interpretation by the attorney or, more frequently, for the preparation of tax returns and court reports. By understanding the basic rules of accounting, these jobs can be done by different members of the office, because everyone will be using the same terminology and procedures.

Receipts Old tax returns Cancelled checks Bank books Stock broker reports Wage statements Bills—paid and unpaid	<u>Decedents Estates</u> Court accounting Prepare gift tax returns Prepare estate tax return <u>Family Law</u> Prepare support request <u>Tort Law</u> Damage estimate Loss of income calculations

Figure 1-3 The shoebox approach to accounting.

 **Ethical Issue**

All professionals are subject to some ethical rules or guidelines. The paralegal or legal assistant needs to have a firm understanding of the ethical guidelines and state regulations, which vary by state or jurisdiction, that define acceptable conduct and ethical responsibilities. Among the relevant ethical guidelines are the **American Bar Association Code of Professional Responsibility (ABA)**, the **American Bar Association Guidelines for the Utilization of Legal Assistant Services**, and the ethics guidelines or codes of professional responsibility of professional associations, such as the **National Association of Legal Assistants (NALA)** and the **National Federation of Paralegal Associations (NFPA) Model Code of Ethics and Professional Responsibility (Model Code)**.

NFPA Model Code:
EC1.1 (a) A paralegal shall achieve competency through education, training, and work experience.

CHAPTER SUMMARY

Everyone has an interest in some financial matter. Within the law office, the interest is more than just casual. Keeping track of the financial affairs of the firm is important to its overall success. In the law firm, keeping track of funds belonging to clients is critical. Everyone in the firm needs to understand the financial records involved in operating the firm and in handling the funds belonging to clients. It may be a simple matter of calculating an interest payment or performing a more complex calculation necessary to prepare an accounting for the court or the tax return for an estate.

To be able to discuss financial matters with other professionals, including accountants, bankers, financial advisors, and other legal professionals, it is necessary to speak the same language. With an understanding of the accounting process, it is easier to reconstruct necessary financial information and understand why certain procedures are followed.

GLOSSARY

Accounting   The analyzing, recording, classifying, summarizing, and interpreting of financial transactions

Analyzing   Determining the effect and significance of a financial transaction

Classifying   Sorting financial information into appropriate groups

FASB   Financial Accounting Standards Board

GAAP   Generally Accepted Accounting Principles

Interpreting   Determining the relationships between the financial transactions and the accounts on the financial statements

Recording   Entering the financial transactions in the journals and ledgers

Summarizing   Organizing the financial information into useful and meaningful statements

REVIEW QUESTIONS

1. Does the paralegal or legal assistant have an ethical obligation to study accounting?
2. Why is it important for the paralegal or legal assistant to understand accounting terminology?
3. What problems can be caused by not keeping accurate internal law firm records?
4. Explain how poorly kept records can result in a malpractice claim?
5. Define the term *accounting*.
6. What is meant by the Generally Accepted Accounting Principles?
7. How can a keystroke error adversely affect a credit card holder?
8. How does understanding accounting make a paralegal a more valuable member of the law office team?
9. How can poorly kept accounting records of a law office affect its survival?
10. What is the advantage of using a standardized system of accounting?

Chapter 2

Accounting: The Concepts

In This Chapter

Why Study the Concepts of Accounting?

The concepts of accounting can be thought of as the rules of accounting. These are the accounting profession's equivalent of the lawyer's use of the rules of court and the use of legal decisions or precedent in analyzing cases and the preparation of documents. The basic concepts and principles provide a common set of guidelines so everyone can understand the basics of what is being prepared and discussed. These also help in preparing and using the information by giving a reference point for understanding what was intended and what is needed by others who will be reviewing and using the information.

The Entity Concept

ENTITY CONCEPT
The treatment of each financial entity separately from all other financial entities

The **entity concept** requires that we separate each financial entity and treat it for accounting purposes independent from any other financial entity. Each person for accounting and tax purposes can be considered as a financial entity. Each business for accounting and tax purposes is also a financial entity. All businesses are owned, either by individuals or by other business entities. For accounting purposes, the individual business owner's personal finances must be kept separate from the business finances (Fig. 2-1).

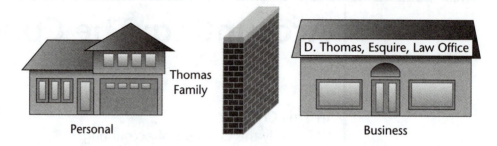

Figure 2-1   For accounting purposes, the individual business owner's personal finances must be kept separate from the business finances.

In effect, we build a wall around each entity. By separating each entity, we can then look at the success or failure of the business operation. By separating the two entities, we can look at the monetary contributions to the business operation of the owner, not as income for determining success, but as an investment. From the owner's personal finance perspective, the question is whether this was a good investment in terms of the return for the monetary investment.

A person may own a small business, such as a one-person law office. For accounting purposes, there are two economic entities, the personal economic entity (e.g., Daniel Thomas) and the business economic entity (e.g., Daniel Thomas, Esquire, Law Office). Two sets of records should be maintained—one for each entity. To determine the success or failure of the law office operation, it is necessary to separate the financial transactions of the individual with regard to his or her personal life and the business. The questions that need to be answered to determine business success might include the following: Is the business generating enough income without personal contribution by the owner, or, are the expenses solely those of the business? If the day came to sell the business to a new owner, the prospective owner would want to be able to see *only* what the business generated in the form of sales and incurred in the form of expenses, without the commingling of the personal resources or expenses of the owner. If we treat the business as a *separate economic entity* from the owner, this is possible.

Just as each person and each business is an economic entity, a family can be thought of as an economic entity separate from the individual members of the family. In family law situations, this is the way the courts look at the financial issues in making support decisions. Within a family, each person is an individual entity, and the collective family is also an entity. Individual members of the family may have personal assets, personal obligations and debts, and individual personal bank accounts that are not shared with the family unit, in essence, an individual entity. The family as an entity may have the family assets, the family home, family furnishings, family debts, such as the home mortgage and the obligations for household upkeep, and a communal or family bank account for family needs (Fig. 2-2).

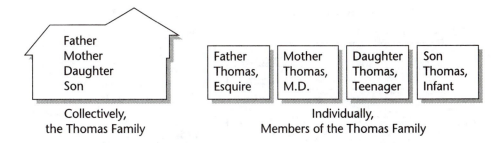

Figure 2-2   A business must be treated as a separate economic entity from the owner.

In the same manner as a person has his or her own assets and obligations on a personal level, he or she may also have a separately owned business, such as a law practice with its own separate business assets, obligations, and bank accounts.

In the area of estates and trusts, it is important to separate and identify the various economic entities involved. In a decedent's estate, the lifetime financial transactions of the decedent need to be separated from the post-death transactions for purposes of preparing the last lifetime tax return and the estate tax return for all the lifetime transactions (Figs. 2-3 and 2-4). Each beneficiary's financial interests, while being handled by the fiduciary, must be kept separate for reporting purposes to the beneficiary, the court, and the taxing agencies.

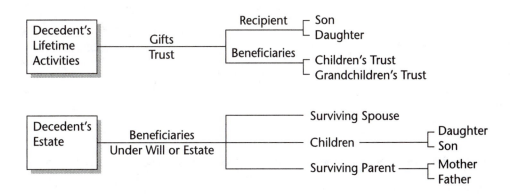

Figure 2-3   The lifetime financial transactions of a decedent need to be separated from the post-death transactions for the purposes of preparing the last lifetime tax return and the estate tax return for all the lifetime transactions.

Forms of Business Ownership

To better understand the entity concept, one can look at the forms business entities can take. Traditionally, there are three basic forms of business ownership: the sole proprietorship, the partnership, and the corporation. Each form of ownership is a legal financial entity (Fig. 2-5).

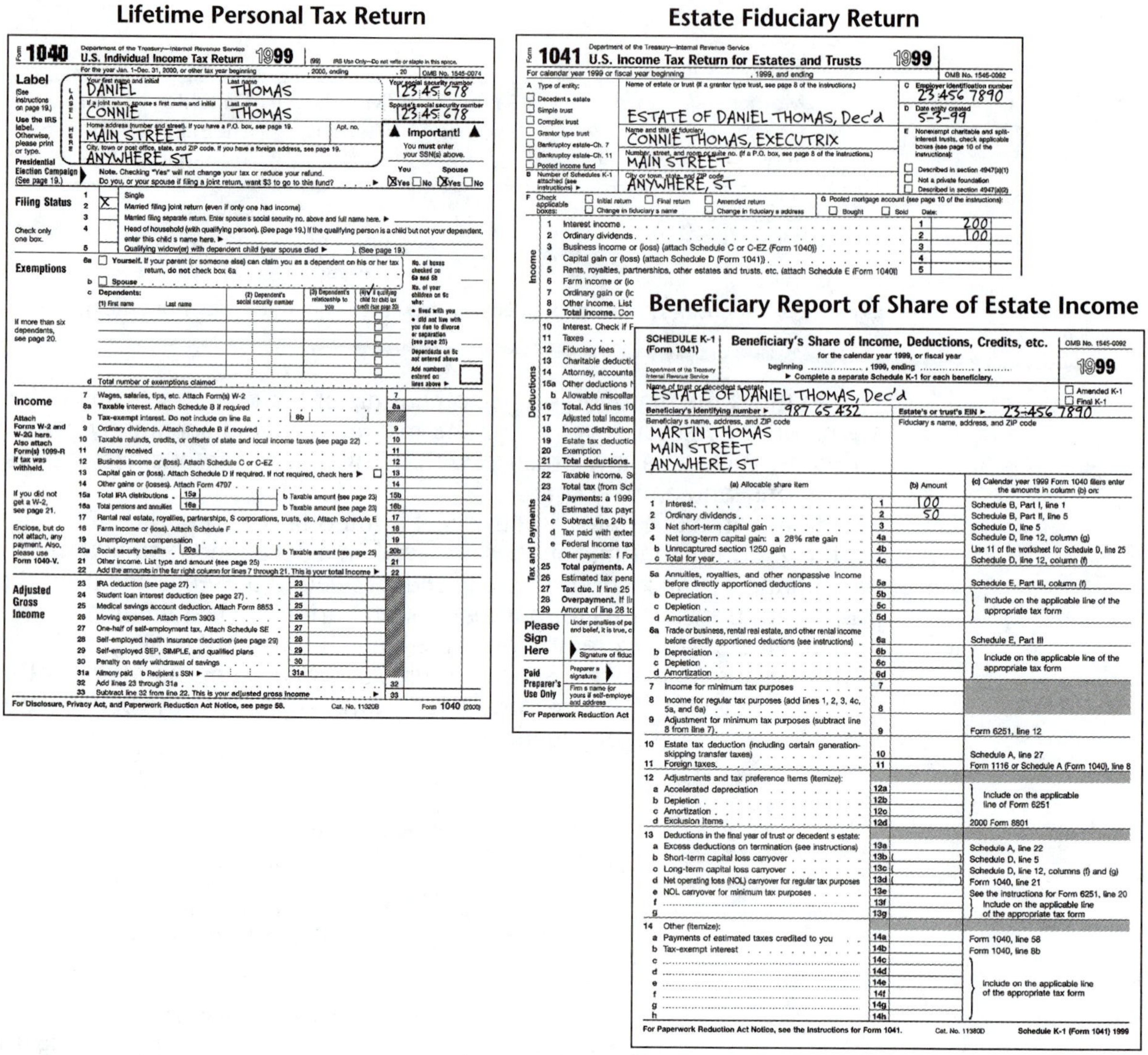

Lifetime Personal Tax Return

Estate Fiduciary Return

Beneficiary Report of Share of Estate Income

Figure 2-4 Decedent's lifetime tax return: Form 1040, and fiduciary forms 1041 and 1041-K1.

SOLE PROPRIETORSHIP
A business entity owned by one person

Without any legal formality, anyone setting up a business by him or herself is considered a **sole proprietor**. Ideally, this includes the establishment of a separate bank account for business activities. For federal and some state tax purposes, a separate tax schedule—the schedule C—is prepared, showing the revenue of the business and the expenses of the business in generating the revenue. Because the sole proprietorship is personal to the owner, the business terminates upon the death or legal incapacity of the owner.

PARTNERSHIP   A business entity owned by two or more persons

A **partnership** is two or more individuals who agree to work together as co-owners of a business without any other formalities except a verbal or written agreement on sharing profits and losses; these individuals

Sole Proprietor

D. Thomas

Partnership

D. Thomas & Partner

Corporation

D. Thomas, Corporation

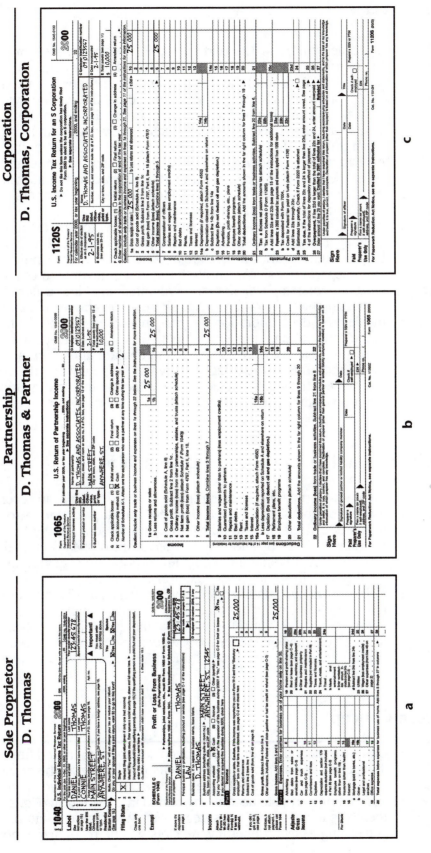

Figure 2-5 Tax returns for various forms of ownership: (a) sole proprietorship (1040 Schedule C), (b) partnership (1065), and (c) corporation (1120S).

are called partners. The partnership is considered a separate entity from the partners. This business entity lasts as long as the individuals or the partners wish or until the death of any one of them. Since these are personal forms of ownership with unlimited liability on the owners, they last only as long as all or any one of the partners desires or until all or any one of the partners dies or becomes legally incompetent. In recognition of this separate legal entity, for federal tax purposes, a separate tax return is prepared and filed showing only the partnership revenue and partnership loss. The net profit or loss is then transferred to the individual partner's own tax return in the ratio agreed to between the partners.

To avoid the limited life and unlimited liability issues, many businesses take advantage of the laws that allow for the creation of an artificial legal entity called a corporation. A corporation is a creation of legislation that varies from state to state. One or more individuals can create a separate business entity that has the advantage of limited liability, ease of ownership transfer, and unlimited legal life. Unless the individual owners of the corporation, called shareholders, agree to be responsible for the debts of the corporation, they are free of any liability for the obligations of the corporation. The ownership interests, or shares, can be freely transferred, unless restricted by law or shareholder agreements. Unlike natural individuals, this artificial legal entity has perpetual life; the deaths or legal disability of the shareholders has no effect on the continuation of the corporation as an entity.

Variations on the Traditional Forms of Ownership

LIMITED LIABILITY CORPORATION An artificial legal entity created by legislation; incorporates features of traditional corporations and unincorporated forms of ownership

Two new forms of ownership have become popular in recent years. The limited partnership and the **limited liability corporation**. These are forms of ownership and business operation created by the states to encourage business by allowing combinations of the traditional forms of unincorporated ownership with the corporation's advantages of limited liability and, in some cases, taxation advantages.

From an accounting point of view, these are all separate economic entities. The same rules of accounting apply, although the names of some of the accounts may vary. The principal difference is the tax-reporting obligation. Depending on the form of ownership and the variation, a different set of state and federal tax returns and informational returns must be filed.

Going Concern Concept

GOING CONCERN CONCEPT Unless otherwise set up for a limited period of time, business entities are presumed to continue in operation into the future

Unless an economic entity has been set up for a limited function or a limited period of time, such as for a seasonal business, the entity will, for accounting purposes, be treated as if it will continue in business from accounting period to accounting period into the future (Fig. 2-6). Normally, the costs incurred will be spread over the estimated life of the revenue-generating assets. Generally, receipts will be recognized, not necessarily

Figure 2-6   The entity is presumed to continue into the future.

when received, but rather in the period or periods in which the goods or services are delivered.

Accrual Method versus Cash Method

CASH METHOD
Recording of transactions only when cash is paid or received, independent of when earned

One of the fundamental accounting concepts is that of matching revenues with related expenses. Two basic methods are used by accountants to try to achieve some level of accuracy in matching up the revenue received with the costs that were incurred to create this revenue (Fig. 2-7). The **cash method** is generally used when all expenses are paid in the same financial period as the income they generate. The annual cost of an insurance policy would be expensed against the revenue for the time period covered by the policy.

Method	Year 2000	Year 2001	Year 2002
Cash Basis	$3,000	—	—
Accrual Basis	$1,000	$1,000	$1,000

Figure 2-7   Cash method versus the accrual method.

ACCRUAL METHOD
Recognizing income and expenses when they actually occur or are incurred, regardless of when the actual cash is paid or received

When expenses are prepaid or income is spread over more than one financial period, the **accrual method** of accounting is generally used. The accrual method keeps a record of expenses and applies the portion used in the different time period. For example, a three-year fire insurance policy may be paid in a lump sum in year one, but have value in the next two years by providing coverage in each of those years. It would not be an accurate reflection of profitability to charge against one year's revenue; expenses paid in that year will be of value in future years.

Occasionally, revenue may be received in one year for work to be performed over a multiyear period. Again, it is not accurate to include the income only in the year of receipt. Expenses will be incurred in each of the years and the recognition of the income should also be spread over the years involved. In this way, the financial statements of the enterprise—the entity—will be more accurately shown.

The Cost Principle

Most things have a cost and a value. These may not be the same. A truck may cost $10,000, but have a value to the owner of more or less than the monetary cost. During snowstorms, a vehicle with a snowplow is of great value to the owner and probably to anyone else desperate to get their parking lot plowed. The same snowplow will be worth much less in the summer during a drought. Land, building, equipment, and other assets have a cost in dollars and a value to the owner. It is a generally accepted accounting principle that assets and services be recorded on the books of the entity at their cost at the time of purchase, otherwise referred to as their **historical cost**, and not their value. As long as the business holds the assets, these are listed at their historical cost. At the time of disposal, any gain or loss is recognized and recorded in the accounting records. For example, a snowplow bought by the business for $10,000 during the middle of a snowstorm is sold three months later. What is the value at the time of disposal? The **fair market value** is the price a willing buyer would pay a willing seller, neither buyer nor seller being under compulsion to buy or sell. Vehicles typically have a number of values: the list price, the price actually paid, the retail used vehicle price, the wholesale used vehicle price, and, possibly, the auction price. Which is to be used? All are speculative until the actual sale is made. For going concerns, the value will remain the historical price until the actual sale is completed and the proceeds from the sale are received or recorded as a receivable.

HISTORICAL COST
The cost of an asset at the time of acquisition or purchase

FAIR MARKET VALUE
The price that a willing buyer would pay a willing seller with neither being under any obligation to buy or sell

Valuation for Litigation and Estate Purposes

There are many situations where a current value is used. In litigation, it is frequently necessary to determine the value of the damages sustained. This may be the cost to replace an asset. In a fire loss, this may be the current construction cost of the building and the contents. In an automobile accident case, it may be the cost to repair the vehicle or, in the case of a total loss, the estimated value at the time of the accident. In estate matters, taxes will generally be assessed on the value of the assets on the date of death or an alternate valuation date. In these cases, we are concerned with the current value as opposed to the historical cost used by going concerns. These current values are frequently provided from appraisers and auctioneers with expertise in the property involved or, for publicly traded securities, the last or closing price on the date in question.

The Accounting Equation

ACCOUNTING EQUATION Assets equal liabilities plus owner's equity. All of the assets have claims against them by creditors or by the owners.

Things of Value *equal* Claims of Outsiders *plus* Claims of Owners

ASSETS *equal* **LIABILITIES** *plus* **EQUITY**

Accounting is based on the concept that every "thing of value" belongs to someone, either to an outsider in the form of someone to whom money is owed, or to the owners of the entity, whether an individual, a

ASSETS Things that have value

LIABILITIES Claims of outsiders to the assets of the entity

EQUITY The value of the assets of an entity reduced by the value of the claims of outsiders; the residual claims of the owners to the assets of the entity

partner, or a shareholder. At times, there may be claims against the assets by both outsiders, such as creditors, and by the individual owner or shareholders. Since the claims may not be against a specific thing of value, known as an **asset**, but against a portion of all the assets, we summarize these claims of outsiders under the classification of **liabilities**. The assets less these liabilities are the claims of the owners, called **equity**, or **owner's equity**. Equity is the value of all the assets reduced by the liabilities. This is illustrated by the following examples.

Assume a person has cash of $100 and no debts or outstanding bills

Things of Value	=	Claims of Outsiders	+	Claims of Owners
↓		↓		↓
Asset	=	Liabilities	+	Equity
$100		0	+	$100

The assets and the equity are equal (Fig. 2-8).

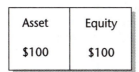

Figure 2-8 Accounting equation blocks showing assets and equity of equal value.

If a long distance telephone call is made costing $25

Things of Value	=	Claims of Outsiders	+	Claims of Owners
↓		↓		↓
Asset	=	Liabilities	+	Equity
100		25	+	75

The claim against the asset of $100 is a liability of $25 leaving equity of $75, the difference after all claims of outsiders (Fig. 2-9).

Asset	Liability $25
$100	Equity $75

Figure 2-9 Accounting equation blocks showing a liability of $25.

Accounting Systems

ACCOUNTING SYSTEM Computer or manual methods for the recording of financial transactions

Keeping track of the various assets and claims of creditors and the resulting equity of the owner requires a system. The accounting information may be recorded using various types of manual systems or automated or computerized systems. The simplest manual system is a checkbook in which all deposits of revenue are recorded and in which all disbursements

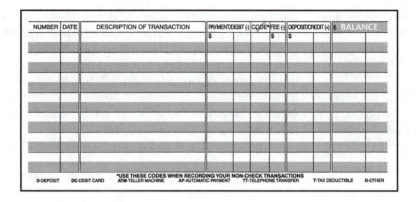

NUMBER	DATE	DESCRIPTION OF TRANSACTION	PAYMENT/DEBIT (-)	CODE*	FEE (-)	DEPOSIT/CREDIT (+)	$ BALANCE
			$		$	$	

*USE THESE CODES WHEN RECORDING YOUR NON-CHECK TRANSACTIONS

D-DEPOSIT   DC-DEBIT CARD   ATM-TELLER MACHINE   AP-AUTOMATIC PAYMENT   TT-TELEPHONE TRANSFER   T-TAX DEDUCTIBLE   O-OTHER

Figure 2-10   A check register.

are made by check (Fig. 2-10). The obvious advantage is the simplicity of everything being recorded in one place. With few transactions, this is a fairly workable system. However, as the volume of transactions increases, and the need to prepare reports and records increases, it become more difficult and time consuming to summarize the transactions.

Many forms of computerized accounting systems are currently in use in law offices, from the simple computer checkbook programs such as Quicken (Fig. 2-11) to the more elaborate multi-report-generating systems, such as Peachtree. The advantage of the computerized systems is

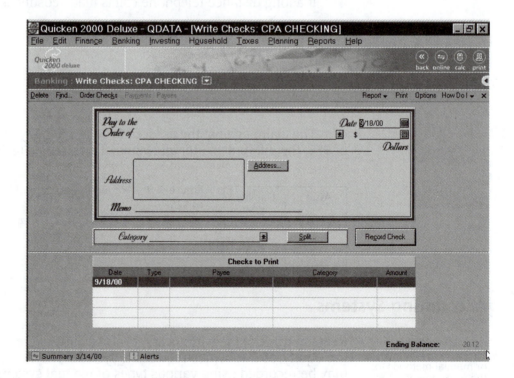

Figure 2-11   Screen shot of Quicken software.

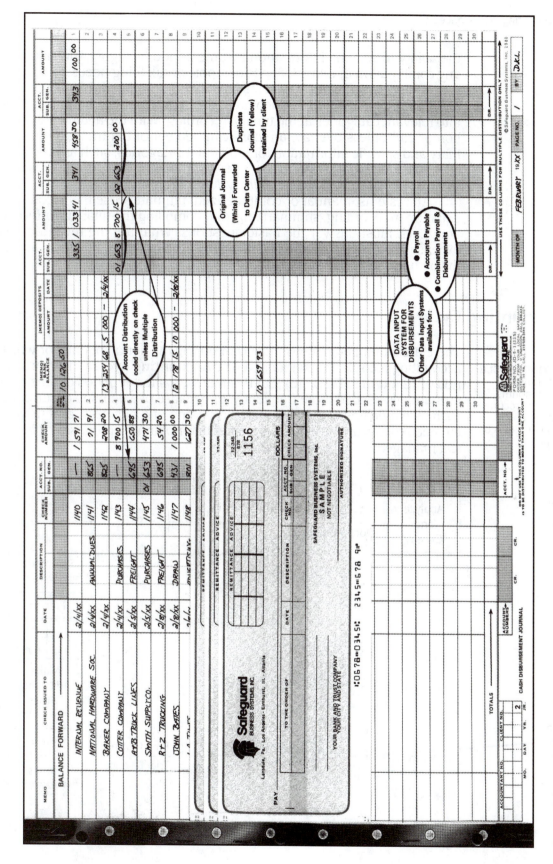

Figure 2-12 A Safeguard Business Systems one-write cash disbursement journal.

the ability to sort the information by time period, category, individual, or any combination of items for special report or tax filing needs.

A number of manual systems have been developed that expand the checkbook register into multicolumn sheets for sorting the information into relevant categories at the time of recording. With the addition of a carbon or carbonless overlay, a record can be kept of the transaction summary and specific information for individual categories, such as individual clients or individual suppliers, or expense or income categories. These are sometimes referred to as *one-write systems* (Fig. 2-12).

All systems, manual or computerized, ultimately use the accounting equation in recording, summarizing, and compiling the financial information. Each must answer the basic questions: What are the revenues and expenses, and what are the claims against the assets of outsiders and of the owners?

The Accounting Cycle

ACCOUNTING CYCLE
A period of time, generally 12 months, for which financial records are maintained of inflows and outflows of financial matters

There are a number of steps that occur during the period of time for which accounting records are maintained. The **accounting cycle** is usually a period of 12 months (Fig. 2-13). But this may be a shorter period of time if information is needed more frequently, or because of a defining occurrence, such as the death of an individual, the closing of a business, or if there is the need for accurate periodic statements for planning purposes or financial management.

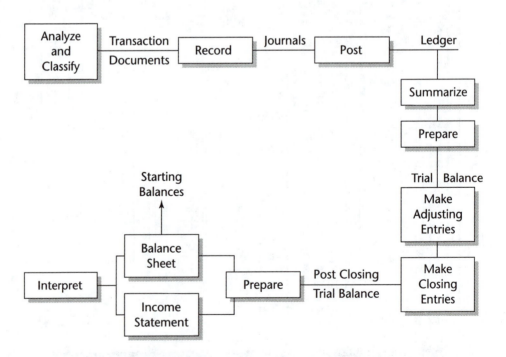

Figure 2-13   The accounting cycle.

CALENDAR YEAR
A 12-month period
starting on January 1
and ending on
December 31

FISCAL YEAR   Any
consecutive twelve-
month period starting in
any month other than
January of each year

SHORT YEAR   An
annual accounting
period of less than
twelve months

For tax filing purposes, the accounting period for individuals is normally the **calendar year**. Many businesses also use the calendar year for
business income tax return filing. However, some corporations may
use a different period of time, a **fiscal year** (e.g., July 1 to June 30). For
federal tax purposes, the period cannot exceed 12 months. The difficulty
in these cases is the need to also file some returns such as employee
withholding returns, and reports, on a **calendar year** of January 1 to
December 31.

The accounting period may also be shortened. In the case of the
death of an individual during the year, the individual's last lifetime return
will be for a shorter period of time than 12 months, known as a **short
year**. In this situation, an estate is created that may also have to file a return for financial matters occurring after death, but before distribution of
the deceased's assets to the beneficiaries. Most typical are interest and
dividends on assets owned at the time of death, but may also include
business income from rents and other business sources. Again, an accounting cycle starts and continues until finalization of the estate, during
which tax returns will need to be filed not more than every 12 months
(Fig. 2-14).

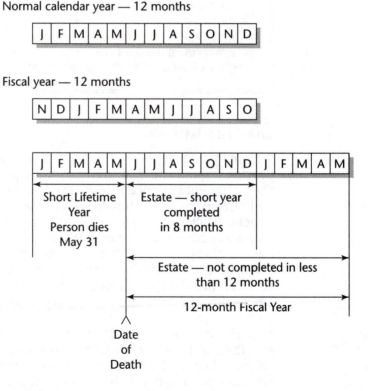

Figure 2-14   Calendar year versus fiscal year.

☑ Checklist of Steps During the Accounting Cycle

During the accounting cycle:

____ Analyze and classify each transaction

____ Record journal entries in a general journal

____ Post from the journal to the ledger

At the end of the accounting cycle:

____ Summarize

____ Prepare a trial balance

____ Working papers

____ Adjust entries

____ Close entries

____ Prepare post-closing trial balance

____ Prepare the financial statements

____ Interpret the statements

⚖ Ethical Issue

> **ABA Model Code:**
>
> Canon 9. A lawyer should avoid even the appearance of professional impropriety.
>
> Ethical Consideration EC9-5. Separation of the funds of the client from those of the lawyer not only serves to protect the client, but also avoids even the appearance of impropriety, and therefore, commingling of such funds should be avoided.

CHAPTER SUMMARY

Accounting concepts are the rules of accounting. The individual concepts provide a guideline and framework for performing the accounting functions. The entity concept provides that we separate each financial entity and treat each separately from all other financial entities. Unless the financial entity is set up for a limited time, the assumption is made that the entity will continue in operation into the foreseeable future. All of the financial transactions of the entity are recorded and maintained at their historical cost. All financial entities have assets, liabilities, and equity. Assets are the things of value, the liabilities are the claims of outsiders against these assets, and equity is the difference between the assets and liabilities.

The accounting cycle is typically a period of 12 months. The 12 months may be a calendar period from January 1 to December 31 or a fiscal period of any other 12 consecutive months. In unusual circumstances, such as a termination of business or death of an individual owner, the accounting cycle may be less than the normal 12 months.

GLOSSARY

Accounting cycle   A period of time, generally 12 months, for which financial records are maintained of inflows and outflows of financial matters

Accounting equation   Assets equal liabilities + owner's equity; all of the assets have claims against them by creditors or by the owners

Accounting system   Computer or manual methods for the recording of financial transactions

Accrual method   Recognizing income and expenses when they actually occur or are incurred, regardless of when the actual cash is paid or received

Assets   Things that have value

Calendar year   A twelve-month period starting on January 1 and ending on December 31

Cash method   Recording of transactions only when cash is paid or received, independent of when earned

Entity concept   The treatment of each financial entity separately from all other financial entities

Equity   The value of the assets of an entity reduced by the value of the claims of outsiders; the residual claims of the owners to the assets of the entity

Fair market value   The price that a willing buyer would pay a willing seller with neither being under any obligation to buy or sell

Fiscal year   Any consecutive twelve-month period starting in any month other than January of each year

Going concern concept   Unless otherwise set up for a limited period of time, business entities are presumed to continue in operation into the future

Historical cost   The cost of an asset at the time of acquisition or purchase

Liabilities   Claims of outsiders to the assets of the entity

Limited liability corporation   An artificial legal entity created by legislation; incorporates features of traditional corporations and unincorporated forms of ownership

Partnership   A business entity owned by two or more persons

Short year   An annual accounting period of less than twelve months

Sole proprietorship   A business entity owned by one person

REVIEW QUESTIONS

1. Why is it important to maintain separate records for the individual and the business?
2. Is it acceptable practice to maintain one checking account for business and personal affairs?
3. Can unearned fees be deposited in the business checking account?
4. Commingling of funds violates what accounting concept?
5. How is the family entity different from the individual members?
6. What are the differences between the different forms of business ownership?
7. How would the payment for a three-year insurance policy be different under the cash basis from the accrual basis?
8. What is the difference between cost and value?
9. What is the usual time period for the accounting cycle?
10. How do the American Bar Association's ethics rules emphasize the accounting entity concept?

Chapter 3

The Building Blocks of Accounting

In This Chapter
Why Study the Building Blocks of Accounting?
Building Blocks of Accounting
Permanent and Temporary Accounts
Debits and Credits
Using T Accounts
Double-Entry Accounting
Sources of Financial Information
Ethical Issue

Why Study the Building Blocks of Accounting?

The basic concepts of accounting apply to every financial entity. For every asset, there is a claim by someone, whether it is an outside creditor, the owner of the business, a beneficiary of an estate or trust, or the government claiming a tax. Understanding this basic foundation makes it easier to understand the accounting information that is prepared by others. It also makes a little easier the reconstruction of records for courts, clients, and tax purposes. Ultimately, all the financial information must fit somewhere; understanding the building blocks of accounting makes the task easier (Fig. 3-1).

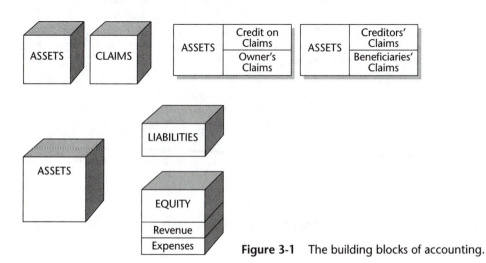

Figure 3-1 The building blocks of accounting.

Building Blocks of Accounting

In its simplest form, accounting builds on the accounting equation

ASSETS equal **LIABILITIES** plus **Equity**

or

$$A = L + E$$

Another way of expressing the accounting equation is

ASSETS minus **LIABILITIES** equals **Equity**

or

$$A - L = E$$

The remaining questions are centered on keeping track of the information in an organized way and defining what items fit into the accounting categories. Keep in mind that the ultimate purpose of the accounting exercise is to be able to keep track of financial matters and obtain the necessary information for preparing financial reports, tax returns, and court filings with the least effort and greatest accuracy.

All accounting transactions fit into one of the three accounting categories shown below.

Assets: things of value
Liabilities: claims of outsiders
Equity: claims of owners or beneficiaries

Each category contains individual accounts, such as the asset's account (cash), the liabilities account (accounts payable), and the equity account (owner's capital, or as it's also known, owner's equity). Initially, you need to decide into which category a transaction fits.

Assets are things of value; some are obvious, such as cash and accounts receivable. They may be tangible (things you can see and touch), such as buildings and equipment, or intangible (legal obligations and rights), such as prepaid rent and insurance. Liabilities are claims against the assets of the entity by outsiders, such as trade suppliers, banks, utility companies, and the landlord for unpaid rent.

These things of value, or assets, less the claims of outsiders, or liabilities, belong to the owner or owners, or equity. Or,

ASSETS minus LIABILITIES equals EQUITY

$$A - L = E$$

Some of the more common individual accounts in each category are listed below.

Assets	**Liabilities**	**Equity**
Cash	Accounts Payable	Owner's Capital
Accounts Receivable	Notes Payable	
Supplies		
Furniture		

Examples of the accounting equation categories and classification are shown below.

Transaction 1. The owner, in setting up the business, opens a checking account and deposits $1,000.

ASSETS	equal	**LIABILITIES**	plus	**EQUITY**
+ $1,000	=			+ $1,000

Assets increase and the owner's equity increases.

The accounts are cash and owner's investment or owner's capital.

ASSETS	equal	**LIABILITIES**	plus	**EQUITY**
Cash + $1,000	=		+	Owner's Capital + $1,000

Transaction 2. Office supplies costing $200 are delivered to the business on 30 days credit.

ASSETS	equal	**LIABILITIES**	plus	**EQUITY**
+ $200	=	+ $200		

The assets increase and the claim of the creditor in the form of an account payable increases.

ASSETS	equal	**LIABILITIES**	plus	**EQUITY**
Supplies + $200	=	Account Payable + $200		

Transaction 3. The account payable for the office supplies is paid.

ASSETS	equal	**LIABILITIES**	plus	**EQUITY**
– $200	=	– $200		

The assets are decreased and the liabilities are decreased.

ASSETS	equal	**LIABILITIES**	plus	**EQUITY**
Cash – $200	=	Account Payable – $200		

Transaction 4. A telephone-answering machine is purchased for $100 in cash.

ASSETS   equal   **LIABILITIES**   plus   **EQUITY**

+ $100   =

− $100

The assets are increased by the new asset and decreased by the use of another asset.

ASSETS   equal   **LIABILITIES**   plus   **EQUITY**

Equipment + $100

Cash   − $100

Transaction 5. The owner withdraws $400 in cash from the business.

ASSETS   equal   **LIABILITIES**   plus   **EQUITY**

− $400   =   − 400

The assets are decreased and the equity of the owner is decreased.

ASSETS   equal   **LIABILITIES**   plus   **EQUITY**

Cash − $400   =   Owner's Capital −400

In each of the transactions, the accounting equation must remain in balance, and the value of each side of the equation must be equal.

The examples shown above are the five basic forms that a transaction can have. In each case, two entries are made. Each entry either increases or decreases an account balance. The net result is that the new total of assets equals the total of the liabilities and the owner's equity.

In summary:

		ASSETS equal		**LIABILITIES** plus **EQUITY**	
Transaction					
1.	Cash	+ $1,000 =		Owner's Capital + $1,000	
2.	Supplies	+ 200 =	Account Payable + 200		
3.	Cash	− 200 =	Account Payable − 200		
4.	Equipment	+ 100			
5.	Cash	− 100			
6.	Cash	− 400 =		Owner's Capital − 400	
Total		$ 600 =	0 +	$ 600	

Permanent and Temporary Accounts

The accounts in the three primary categories are further divided into two groups: permanent accounts and temporary accounts. The accounts that continue from period to period are called *permanent* accounts because they show the running balances from the beginning of the business until the business is terminated. The other group of accounts are called *temporary* because they are only used during the accounting period. Temporary accounts always start the accounting period with a zero balance; the balance at the end of the accounting period is transferred to a permanent account, and the account is reset to zero for the start of the next period.

Permanent Accounts

The permanent accounts are those that have balances that carry over from period to period. These include the asset accounts, the liability accounts, and the equity accounts. These are the accounts found on the balance sheet (Fig. 3-2).

Balance Sheet
D. Thomas, Esquire

December 31, 2000

ASSETS		LIABILITIES	
Current Assets		**Current Liabilities**	
Cash	$300	Accounts payable	$0
Accounts receivable (less doubtful accounts)	0		
Supplies	200		
Total Current Assets	$500	**Total Current Liabilities**	___
Fixed Assets		**Long-term Liabilities**	
Equipment		Other long-term liabilities	0
(less accumulated depreciation)	100	**Total Long-term Liabilities**	$0
		Owner's Equity	
		D. Thomas, Capital;	$600
		Retained earnings	0
Total Net Fixed Assets	$100	**Total Owner's Equity**	$600
TOTAL ASSETS	$600	**TOTAL LIABILITIES & EQUITY**	$600

Figure 3-2   Sample balance sheet.

PERMANENT ACCOUNT Accounts whose balance carry over from one accounting cycle to the next

These categories of items, assets, liabilities, and equity are known as the **permanent accounts**. The permanent accounts are the three general classifications of accounts that will continue to exist or, in accounting terms, remain open, from period to period as long as the business continues. Within each of these three general account classifications are the specific individual accounts, such as cash, accounts payable and owner's equity, that will carry over from period to period. Accounts are the detailed records of changes for a specific individual item, such as the individual asset account cash.

Assets. Assets are things that have value. They include personal property, such as furniture, automobiles, and stocks, and, of course, cash, and real property, buildings, and land. They also include some things that are not tangible but have value, such as patents and the right to collect money, such as promissory notes, bonds (both corporate and government), and accounts receivable from customers and clients.

Liabilities. Liabilities are amounts owed to others. They are promises to pay tomorrow for things and services received in the past. They include accounts payable for goods and services received, debts, such as credit card debt and bank debt in the form of mortgages on buildings, loans payable, and taxes owed.

Equity. Equity or owner's equity is the difference between the value of the assets and the liabilities. It is what is left over from the assets after all the claims of outsiders—the liabilities—have been satisfied. This amount belongs to the owners. In its simplest form it is represented by the accounting equation as

ASSETS minus LIABILITIES equals EQUITY.

This equity can be divided into two classes, investment by the owners and retained earnings, the profits and losses from operations.

Figure 3-3 shows the possible combination of changes in the permanent accounts.

Figure 3-3 Table of combinations.

	Assets	Liabilities	Equity
1.	+		+
2.	+	+	
3.	+ −		
4.	−	−	
5.		+ −	
6.	−		−

To illustrate:

1. Assets increase: cash increases by $100.00

    Equity increase: owner's equity increases by $100.00

The owner invests money to start the business, D. Thomas—Law Office.

D. Thomas takes $100.00 from his personal bank account and puts it into the new law office account.

	Assets	=	Liabilities	+	Equity
1.	$100	=		+	$100

2. Assets increase: supplies increase by $50.00

Liabilities increase: accounts payable increase by $50.00

The owner, D. Thomas, buys supplies using a credit card for $50.00.

	Assets	=	Liabilities	+	Equity
1.	$100	=		+	$100
2.	$50	=	$50		

3. Assets increase: equipment increases by $15.00

Assets decrease: cash decreases by $15.00

The owner buys an answering machine for cash.

	Assets	=	Liabilities	+	Equity
1.	$100	=		+	$100
2.	$50	=	$50		
3.	$15				
	($15)				

4. Assets decrease: cash decreases by $50.00

Liabilities decrease: accounts payable decrease by $50.00

The owner pays $50.00 of the credit card bill for the supplies bought on credit.

	Assets	=	Liabilities	+	Equity
1.	$100	=		+	$100
2.	$50	=	$50		
3.	$15				
	($15)				
4.	($50)	=	($50)		

5. Liabilities decrease: accounts payable decreases by $25.00

Liabilities increase: note payable increases by $25.00

The owner asks for extended payment of the account payable, agreeing to pay it next year and gives a promissory note.

	Assets	=	**Liabilities**	+	**Equity**
1.	$100	=		+	$100
2.	$50	=	$50		
3.	$15				
	($15)				
4.	($50)	=	($50)		
5.			($25)		
			$25		

6. Equity decreases: owner's equity decreases by $10.00

Assets decrease: cash decreases by $10.00

The owner withdraws $10.00 from the business account for personal use.

	Assets	=	**Liabilities**	+	**Equity**
1.	$100	=		+	$100
2.	$50	=	$50		
3.	$15				
	($15)				
4.	($50)	=	($50)		
5.			($25)		
			$25		
6.	($10)	=		+	($10)
	$90	=		+	$90

Temporary Accounts

Some accounts are used during the accounting cycle to keep track of information that will be transferred to other permanent accounts at the end of the period. These are the revenue and the expense accounts, collectively called the **temporary accounts**. The summary of the revenue and expense accounts is either profit or loss. Ultimately, the profit or loss of a business will either increase or decrease the equity of the owner, that is, the claims of the owner on the assets of the business. For convenience, temporary accounts—revenue and expense accounts—are the accounts found on the income statement, that is, the statement showing the revenue and expenses for a specific period of time (Fig. 3-4).

TEMPORARY ACCOUNT Accounts that start the accounting cycle with a zero balance and whose balance at the end of the year is transferred to a permanent account

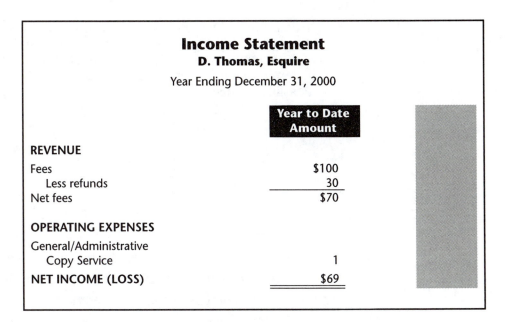

Figure 3-4   Sample income statement.

REVENUES
Increases in the owner's equity resulting from the delivery of services and goods

EXPENSES
Decreases in the owner's equity caused by an outflow of the assets of the entity in the delivery of services and goods

Revenues. **Revenues** are increases in the owner's equity from the delivery of services and goods. They are the amounts received from carrying out the primary activity of the entity by a professional from the rendering of services or a business from the sale of merchandise.

Expenses. **Expenses** are decreases in the owner's equity caused by an outflow of the assets of the entity while performing the primary activity of delivering of services and the sale of goods.

The revenue accounts increase the equity while the expense accounts decrease the equity of the owner. Revenues reduced by expenses will equal profit while excess of expenses over revenues will result in a loss. The temporary accounts are those used to keep track of the revenue and expenses during the accounting period. The temporary accounts are opened up at the beginning of the accounting period and closed at the end of the accounting period and are, therefore, in an accounting sense, temporary accounts, open only during an account period (usually one year) and not carried over from year to year.

The temporary accounts are used to determine what revenue is recognized as earned in an accounting period and to recognize what related expenses are being incurred to generate that revenue. At the end of the period, the difference between the revenue and the expense accounts is the profit or loss of the business. Each accounting period starts off with zero balances for the revenues and the expenses. At the end of the period, if revenues exceed expenses, there is a profit, but if there are more expenses than revenues, there is a loss.

This profit or loss ultimately belongs to the owners. In a profitable year, the owner's equity will increase, in a bad year, it will decrease. At the end of the accounting cycle, the net balance from the temporary accounts is transferred to the owner's equity account.

Possible changes in the temporary accounts

	Revenue	Expense
1.	+	
2.	–	
3.		+
4.		–

1. Revenue increases: received a fee for services rendered
2. Revenue decreases: refunded a fee previously recorded
3. Expense increases: paid the electric bill
4. Expense decreases: received a rebate on previously paid bill

1. Revenue increases.

| Cash increases | $100.00 |
| Legal fees increase | $100.00 |

Received a fee of $100.00 for preparing a will.

	Assets	**=**	**Liabilities**	**+**	**Equity**
1.	$100	=		+	$100 Revenue

2. Revenue decreases.

| Fees decrease | $30.00 |
| Cash decreases | $30.00 |

Agreed to refund a portion of the fee from the preparation of the will.

	Assets	**=**	**Liabilities**	**+**	**Equity**
1.	$100	=		+	$100 Revenue
2.	($30)	=		+	($30) Expense

3. Expense increases.

| Copy expense increases | $10.00 |
| Cash decreases | $10.00 |

Pay the cost of photocopying the will for the client.

	Assets	=	Liabilities	+	Equity
1.	$100	=		+	$100 Revenue
2.	($30)	=		+	($30) Expense
3.	($10)	=		+	($10) Expense

4. Expense decreases.

Cash increases $9.00

Copy expense decreases $9.00

Received a refund from a copy center for overcharge by new employee.

	Assets	=	Liabilities	+	Equity
1.	$100	=		+	$100 Revenue
2.	($30)	=		+	($30) Expense
3.	($10)	=		+	($10) Expense
4.	$ 9	=		+	$ 9 Expense
	$69	=			$69

In this example, our owner, D. Thomas, Esquire, made a profit for the period of $69.00.

In the accounting equation, at the end of the period, any profit will increase the owner's equity and any loss will decrease the owner's equity. If there is a profit, there will be an increase in the assets or a decrease in the liabilities of the business, while a loss will result in the loss of assets or an increase in the liabilities of the business. In terms of the accounting equation, the sides remain equal. For example, at the beginning of the year:

$$\textbf{Assets} = \textbf{Liabilities} + \textbf{Equity}$$
$$\$100 \quad = \quad \$25 \quad + \quad \$75$$

If a profit of $30 is made during the year, then, at the end of the year:

	Assets	=	Liabilities	+	Equity	or	Assets	=	Liabilities	+	Equity
	$100		$25	+	$75		$100		$25	+	$75
	30				30		5		(25)	+	30
Total	$130	=	$25	+	$105	or	$105	=	$0	+	$105

Assets increase *or* liabilities decrease or there is a combination of an asset increase and a liability decrease.

If a loss is incurred during the year of $15, then at the end of year:

	Assets	=	**Liabilities**	+	**Equity**	or	**Assets**	=	**Liabilities**	+	**Equity**
	$100	=	$25	+	$75	or	$100	=	$25	+	$75
	(15)				(15)						15			(15)
Total	$85	=	$25	+	$60	or	$100	=	$40	+	$60

Assets decrease or liabilities increase or there is a combination of an asset increase and a liability decrease.

Debits and Credits

The terms *debit* and *credit* are the accountant's way of indicating an increase or decrease in an account. In the simplest terms, these are entries made in the left column—the debit side—and the right column—the credit side. The use of the terms debit and credit are as much a part of accounting for the left and right sides of the column, as the use of the terms port and starboard are parts of boating terminology for the left and right sides of a boat.

DEBIT   The left side of the accounting equation

CREDIT   The right side of the accounting equation

LEFT = **DEBITS**   RIGHT = **CREDITS**

All accounts have a left side and a right side. One side for increases and one side for decreases.

The accounting equation can also be looked at as having a right side and a left side.

LEFT   RIGHT

ASSETS   equal   LIABILITIES plus EQUITY

To increase asset accounts, we put the entry or amount on the left side. To increase liability or equity accounts, we put the entry or amount on the right side.

Asset		Liability		Equity	
Increase	Decrease	Decrease	Increase	Decrease	Increase

In the same way, we can decrease the value of an item by putting the amount on the opposite side of the equal sign in the accounting equation. For example, buying a fax machine for $100 cash. To decrease cash, we can put the amount on the right side and to increase the new asset account—fax machine—we put the increase on the left side, and the equation still balances.

```
        Asset        Asset
        Cash          Fax
   ─────────┬──   ──┬─────────
            │$100  $100│
```

ASSETS = LIABILITIES + EQUITY
+$100
−$100

Using T Accounts

As you can see, for every entry on the left, or a debit, there is an entry on the right, or a credit. This can be represented by a large T on which we enter the debits and the credits. The economic entity can also be represented by a big T with the assets listed on the left and the liabilities and equity on the right.

```
   ──────────────┬──────────────────
     Assets      │ Liabilities + Equity
```

Because we place the assets on the left or debit side, we can say that to increase the assets in value, we will place the value on the debit side and any decrease must then be on the credit side. If we set up a T account for an asset, this is an easy way to keep track of the entries.

```
        Cash
     ───────┬───────
        +   │   −
```

Liabilities are normally on the right side of the big T, so we will increase this value by placing increases on the right, or credit, side and decreases on the left, or debit side. If you remember that every asset has a claim against it by either a creditor or by the owner, you can see that for every increase in an asset on the left, there will an increase in the claim of a creditor—in the form of a liability—or of an owner—as equity—unless we are merely exchanging assets, in which case, an asset increases and an asset decreases, but even so, there is a debit and a credit.

In reconstructing financial records, it is frequently useful to set up a series of T accounts when information is obtained or discovered. There will always be a debit and a credit, or a combination of debits and credits, that balance. Usually, you can figure out a least one side of the equation (usually the asset side) and then you can figure out who has the claim or right to the asset on the other side.

Using T accounts with the temporary accounts of revenues and expenses are easy when you remember that the profits are considered equity, so any increase in profit or revenue is an entry on the right or credit side and any loss of expense is a decrease in the owner's equity and so will go on the debit side.

Double-Entry Accounting

DOUBLE ENTRY ACCOUNTING   The system requiring that the accounting equation always be equal in each financial transaction recorded

Each financial transaction will affect at least two accounts, these accounts may be in the same category, as when cash is paid for another asset. **Double-entry accounting** is the process of making a record of the financial transaction, listing the effect of the transaction on the individual accounts, and showing the increases and decreases on the related individual accounts. For example, buying a fax machine for cash would require an entry decreasing the asset category Cash account and increasing the asset category Fax Machine account.

Double-entry accounting provides a process for ensuring that every financial transaction balances in the accounting equation. The process provides a procedure that ensures that when all of the individual transactions are summarized, they will balance (there will be an equal amount of debits and credits).

In many organizations, the financial management functions are divided, one person or group handles cash receipts, another, payables, and a third, the maintenance of the ledgers. Since the rules for entry are the same, increases and decreases in individual accounts will be uniformly recorded. By separating the handling of cash and its entry from the entry of the account to which it relates, such as the accounts receivable of a client, there is a separation of function that leads to internal control. Instead of one person being responsible for the total transaction entry, two or more people are involved. In the summary process, unless each has made the correct entry, the account will not balance, and this will raise an issue that will be looked into by someone else.

Sources of Financial Information

There are many sources of information that can be used to determine the needed accounting entries, for example, checks, invoices, bank statements, and credit card slips. It is useful to look at each form of input for accuracy and authenticity. It is not uncommon for the financial records to be reviewed or audited by an outsider. Businesses frequently will engage the services of a firm of independent auditors to guarantee that the records and statements prepared from the business's internal records are accurate. Generally, this is a task performed by certified public accountants, or CPAs. They perform routine checks on the records and the underlying back-up documentation to ensure that outsiders can rely on the financial statements. Banks will frequently require an independent outside audit of a company record as part of the loan-making process.

Every taxpayer, individual, partnership, and corporation lives in the constant fear of an audit by the taxation authority. It may be the local or state sales tax department, or the federal Internal Revenue Service. What these auditors are looking at, at least initially, is the reliability and accuracy of the accounting records. If the underlying documentation for an entry is reliable, it is generally accepted. If the documentation is absent or questionable, at least some doubt is created in the mind of the auditor. It is, therefore, important from the beginning to ensure that the underlying documents support the entries in the journals and ledgers.

 Ethical Issue

ABA Model Code:

The comment to Guideline 1 provides as follows:

An attorney who utilizes a legal assistance services is responsible for determining that the legal assistant is competent to perform the tasks assigned, based on the legal assistance education, training, and experience . . .

Based on the guideline comments what are the obligations of the supervising attorney when assigning accounting activities to the legal assistant?

CHAPTER SUMMARY

All financial transactions involve assets and claims. These claims may come from a creditor, an owner, or a beneficiary of a trust or an estate. The basic building block of accounting is the accounting equation—Assets equal Liabilities plus Equity. These three classifications can be further divided into permanent accounts and temporary accounts. Permanent accounts are those maintained from accounting cycle to accounting cycle. Temporary accounts are those opened at the beginning of the accounting cycle and then closed at the end of the accounting cycle; the balance at the end of the accounting cycle is transferred in the form of profit or loss, or gain or loss, into a permanent equity account. Financial transactions are divided into permanent accounts—the assets, liabilities, and equity—and temporary accounts. During the accounting cycle, the temporary accounts are used to keep track of revenues and expenses for that accounting cycle.

GLOSSARY

Credit   The right side of the accounting equation

Debit   The left side of the accounting equation

Double entry accounting   The system requiring that the accounting equation always be equal in each financial transaction recorded

Expenses   Decreases in the owner's equity caused by an outflow of the assets of the entity in the delivery of services and goods

Permanent account   Accounts whose balance carry over from one accounting cycle to the next

Revenues   Increases in the owner's equity resulting from the delivery of services and goods

Temporary account   Accounts that start the accounting cycle with a zero balance and whose balance at the end of the year is transferred to a permanent account

REVIEW QUESTIONS

1. All financial transactions fit into what three categories?
2. What are the five basic forms that all financial transactions can have in accounting?
3. What is meant by the term *permanent accounts*?
4. What are the main classifications of the temporary accounts?
5. Which accounts start out each accounting cycle with a zero balance?
6. Complete the following:
   a. Assets equal Liabilities plus _____
   b. Assets minus Liabilities equal _____
   c. Assets minus _____ equal Liabilities
7. What is the effect of an increase in the revenue account on the owner's equity?
8. What is the function of the temporary accounts?
9. At the end of the accounting period, what is an excess of expenses over revenue?
10. In a T account, on which side is an entry made to record an increase in revenue?

Chapter 4

Financial Statements: The Pictures of a Business

In This Chapter
Why Study about Financial Statements?
Balance Sheet
The Income Statement
Service Business versus Merchandising Business
Owner's Equity
The Tax Return
Ethical Issue

Why Study about Financial Statements?

Financial statements are the financial pictures of a business. They show what the business owns: its assets; what claims are being made by outsiders—its creditors—against the assets; and the value of what is actually owned by the owner, its owner's equity. They also show the financial history of the operation of the business over a period of time, or the revenues and expenses.

These statements of ownership, claims, and operations are used to communicate financial information about the business or financial entity. Financial statements are also the pictures of business and financial health that are looked at by outsiders, including bankers, lenders, potential buyers, and potential business partners.

Comparing the statements of operations from year to year may show a pattern demonstrating the business growth or decline. Analysis of the details can lead to an understanding of the business's strengths and weaknesses and reveal areas that need change. For example, is revenue in the major area of activity decreasing? Is the trend towards a different source of income that needs more attention? Are the individual expense items consistent with the level of revenue? The summarized information may also be used for the preparation of tax returns, reports to the court, beneficiaries of estates and trust, and for clients.

Balance Sheet

BALANCE SHEET
A statement of financial position at a specific moment and time showing the assets, liabilities, and equity

The **balance sheet** is a snapshot of a business at a specific moment in time (Fig. 4-1). It is also referred to as the *statement of financial position*. It shows, as of a specific moment in time, the assets, the liabilities, and the owner's equity of the entity. It is a detailed description of the accounting equation (Fig. 4-2).

Figure 4-1 The balance sheet is a snapshot of a business at a specific moment in time.

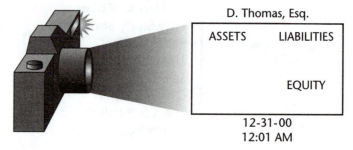

D. Thomas, Esq.

ASSETS	LIABILITIES
	EQUITY

12-31-00
12:01 AM

D. Thomas, Esquire
Balance Sheet
As of December 31, 2000

Assets		**Liabilities**	
Current Assets		**Current Liabilities**	
Cash		Accounts Payable	
Accounts Receivable			
Total Current Assets	_____	**Total Current Liabilities**	_____
Long-term Assets		**Long-term Liabilities**	
Prepaid Insurance		Notes Payable	
Equipment		**Total Long-term Liabilities**	_____
Total Long-term Assets	_____	**Total Liabilities**	_____
		EQUITY	
		D. Thomas-Equity	
Total Assets	══════	**Total Liabilities & Equity**	══════

Figure 4-2   Sample balance sheet.

Classifications on the Balance Sheet

Traditionally, the assets and liabilities sections of the balance sheet are divided into classifications and grouped under the classification of current or

CURRENT ASSETS
Assets in the form of cash and near-cash items expected to be converted to cash within the coming year

long term. **Current assets** are those in the form of cash—bank and checking accounts—and those assets expected to be converted into cash within the coming year, such as the amount of accounts receivable due within the coming year and the portion of the prepaid assets, such as insurance, that will be used up in the coming year. Accounts receivable not due until future periods and the noncurrent portion of prepaid assets are then listed as long-term assets.

CURRENT LIABILITIES
Financial obligations due within one year

The portion of accounts and notes payable within the current year are listed under the **current liabilities** classification. If a note or other obligation will be paid over a number of years, such as a mortgage, the portion due in the current year is usually listed as a current liability and the balance due in future years as a long-term liability.

The Income Statement

INCOME STATEMENT
A statement of the revenues and expenses for a financial entity over a period of time

The **income statement** is a report of the revenue and expenses for an entity over a period of time. It can be viewed as a motion picture covering a time period, recording all the financial activities during this time period (Fig. 4-3). Typically, a business will prepare an income statement for the year. It may be a calendar year covering January 1 to December 31 (Fig. 4-4). It may also be for a fiscal year, a 12-month period with a different starting and ending date, such as July 1 to June 30.

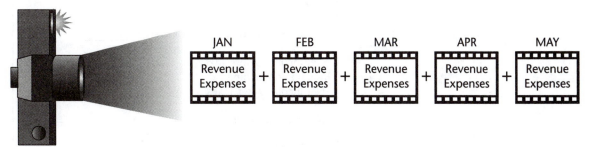

Figure 4-3   The income statement is like a motion picture of a business covering a period of time.

It is also very common to prepare quarterly returns, or returns covering a three-month period. These are frequently prepared to assist the business in determining the amounts to be paid in taxes for the profit from operations on a quarterly basis.

Service Business versus Merchandising Business

A law office generates revenue from the billing for time spent on a case. Supplies and materials are not a major factor in the generation of revenue. Clients are usually only billed for the actual out-of-pocket costs of things like copies, postage, and telephone calls. In reviewing a client's income statements and balance sheets, inventory may be a major item. A client in the retail business generates revenue from the sale of inventory.

Figure 4-4 Sample income statement.

D. Thomas, Esquire
Income Statement
For the Year Ending January 1, 2001

Revenue
Fee Income
    Less refunds
Net Fees   _____

Expenses
General/Administrative
    Advertising
    Depreciation
    Salaries and wages
    Employee benefits
    Payroll taxes
    Insurance
    Rent
    Utilities
    Furniture and equipment
    Office supplies
    Travel and entertainment
    Postage
    Equipment maintenance
    Interest

Total General/Administrative Expenses _____

Net Income Before Taxes   _____
    Taxes on income   _____
Net Income After Taxes   _____

Net Income (Loss)   =======

Depending on the type of merchandise, the value of the inventory may represent a significant investment. Manufacturers may also have a significant investment in inventory. For the manufacturer, this inventory may be partially in raw materials waiting to be processed and in finished goods waiting to be shipped to customers.

For businesses where inventory is a major item, a separate calculation is made in the income statement to determine the **cost of goods sold**, or the cost of the items sold during the accounting period.

COST OF GOODS SOLD   For a business where inventory is a major item, the cost of the merchandise sold during the accounting cycle

Cost of Goods Sold Statement

Beginning inventory	$140
Plus purchases	35
Total available during the period	$175
Less ending inventory	50
Cost of goods sold	$125

Owner's Equity

OWNER'S EQUITY
The claims of the owners against the assets of the business

A statement of **owner's equity** may also be prepared to show the increase from profitable operations or reduction from operating losses, as well as any additional investments or withdrawals by the owner.

In a sole proprietorship, these changes in the owner's equity accounts will be summarized at the end of the year in one account, Owner's Equity.

Sole Proprietor Equity Statement

D. Thomas, Esquire Statement of Owner's Equity	
Balance at beginning of period	$ 0
Plus additional investment	100
Profit for the period	99
Less withdrawals by owner	30
Loss for the period	____
Balance at the end of the period	$169

In a partnership, the amount of the individual partner's investment in the partnership, the amount each partner withdraws from a partnership, and the individuals' share of profits may not be equal. Each of the partners may have initially invested different amounts and, during the year, withdrawn different amounts. So, even if the sharing of profit and loss is equal among all partners, the amounts in their individual accounts will vary. It is necessary, then, to keep a record of the changes and balances of each partner. For federal partnership tax return purposes, a schedule will have to be prepared (Fig. 4-5).

Partnership Reconciliation Form

	Capital Account at Beginning of Year ($)	Capital Contributed during the Year ($)	Partners' Share of Income and Loss ($)	Withdrawals and Distributions ($)	Capital Account at the End of the Year ($)
Partner A	1,000	$200	500	800	900
Partner B	1,000	100	300	900	500
Totals	2,000	300	800	1,700	1,400

SHAREHOLDERS
The owners of a corporation

The owners of a corporation are called **shareholders** or stockholders. The ownership of the corporation is divided into shares represented by stock certificates. The corporation is different from a sole proprietorship or partnership in a number of ways: it has unlimited life, limited liability, and the profits and losses from operation do not automatically flow through to

| SCHEDULE K-1
(Form 1065)
Department of the Treasury
Internal Revenue Service | **Partner's Share of Income, Credits, Deductions, etc.**
▶ See separate instructions.
For calendar year 2000 or tax year beginning _____ , 2000, and ending _____ , 20 ___ | OMB No. 1545-0099
20**00** |

Partner's identifying number ▶ 123456789	Partnership's identifying number ▶ 09 ⋮ 012345
Partner's name, address, and ZIP code D. THOMAS MAIN STREET ANYWHERE, ST	Partnership's name, address, and ZIP code D. THOMAS AND ASSOCIATES MAIN STREET ANYWHERE, ST

A This partner is a ☒ general partner ☐ limited partner
☐ limited liability company member
B What type of entity is this partner? ▶ INDIVIDUAL
C Is this partner a ☒ domestic or a ☐ foreign partner?
D Enter partner's percentage of: (i) Before change or termination (ii) End of year
Profit sharing . . . . % 62.5 %
Loss sharing . . . . % 62.5 %
Ownership of capital . . . . . . % 50 %
E IRS Center where partnership filed return: PHILA

F Partner's share of liabilities (see instructions):
Nonrecourse . . . . $ ....
Qualified nonrecourse financing . . $ ....
Other . . . . $ ....
G Tax shelter registration number . . ▶ ....
H Check here if this partnership is a publicly traded partnership as defined in section 469(k)(2) . . . . . ☐
I Check applicable boxes: **(1)** ☐ Final K-1 **(2)** ☐ Amended K-1

J   Analysis of partner's capital account:

(a) Capital account at beginning of year	(b) Capital contributed during year	(c) Partner's share of lines 3, 4, and 7, Form 1065, Schedule M-2	(d) Withdrawals and distributions	(e) Capital account at end of year (combine columns (a) through (d))
1000	200	500	(800)	90

	(a) Distributive share item		(b) Amount	(c) 1040 filers enter the amount in column (b) on:
Income (Loss)	**1** Ordinary income (loss) from trade or business activities . . .	1	500	See page 6 of Partner's Instructions for Schedule K-1 (Form 1065).
	2 Net income (loss) from rental real estate activities	2		
	3 Net income (loss) from other rental activities	3		
	4 Portfolio income (loss):			
	a Interest	4a		Sch. B, Part I, line 1
	b Ordinary dividends	4b		Sch. B, Part II, line 5
	c Royalties	4c		Sch. E, Part I, line 4
	d Net short-term capital gain (loss)	4d		Sch. D, line 5, col. (f)
	e Net long-term capital gain (loss):			
	(1) 28% rate gain (loss)	4e(1)		Sch. D, line 12, col. (g)
	(2) Total for year.	4e(2)		Sch. D, line 12, col. (f)
	f Other portfolio income (loss) (attach schedule)	4f		Enter on applicable line of your return.
	5 Guaranteed payments to partner	5		See page 6 of Partner's Instructions for Schedule K-1 (Form 1065).
	6 Net section 1231 gain (loss) (other than due to casualty or theft) .	6		
	7 Other income (loss) (attach schedule)	7		Enter on applicable line of your return.
Deductions	**8** Charitable contributions (see instructions) (attach schedule) . .	8		Sch. A, line 15 or 16
	9 Section 179 expense deduction	9		See pages 7 and 8 of Partner's Instructions for Schedule K-1 (Form 1065).
	10 Deductions related to portfolio income (attach schedule) . . .	10		
	11 Other deductions (attach schedule)	11		
Credits	**12a** Low-income housing credit:			
	(1) From section 42(j)(5) partnerships for property placed in service before 1990	12a(1)		
	(2) Other than on line 12a(1) for property placed in service before 1990	12a(2)		Form 8586, line 5
	(3) From section 42(j)(5) partnerships for property placed in service after 1989	12a(3)		
	(4) Other than on line 12a(3) for property placed in service after 1989	12a(4)		
	b Qualified rehabilitation expenditures related to rental real estate activities	12b		
	c Credits (other than credits shown on lines 12a and 12b) related to rental real estate activities	12c		See page 8 of Partner's Instructions for Schedule K-1 (Form 1065).
	d Credits related to other rental activities	12d		
	13 Other credits	13		

For Paperwork Reduction Act Notice, see Instructions for Form 1065.   Cat. No. 11394R   Schedule K-1 (Form 1065) 2000

Figure 4-5   Form 1065, Schedule K-1: Partner's Share of Income, Credits, Deductions, etc.

the owners to be reported on their personal tax returns. With the exception of the small business corporation, also known as the subchapter S corporation, corporations are independent legal entities and separate tax-paying entities. Shareholders of ordinary corporations may receive dividends, which are reported on personal returns. Earnings and losses are reflected in the owner's equity section of the balance sheet (Fig. 4-6).

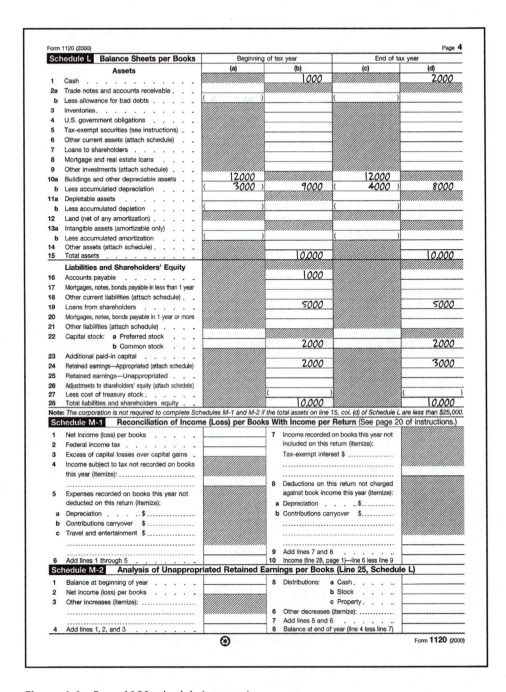

Figure 4-6   Form 1120 schedule L, page 4.

The Tax Return

In some sense, tax returns can be thought of as financial statements. The rules for inclusion and deduction of items are based, not on the generally accepted accounting principles, but on the tax code, whether federal, state, or local. Some lenders, particularly mortgage lenders, look on the tax return as a statement of income in making the lending decision and in considering the borrower's ability to pay the mortgage. Some items that appear on the financial statement do not appear on the tax return, or appear in a different amount. The cost of club dues and entertaining ex-

---

SCHEDULE C
(Form 1040)

Department of the Treasury
Internal Revenue Service (99)

Profit or Loss From Business
(Sole Proprietorship)

▶ Partnerships, joint ventures, etc., must file Form 1065 or Form 1065-B.
▶ Attach to Form 1040 or Form 1041.   ▶ See Instructions for Schedule C (Form 1040).

OMB No. 1545-0074

2000

Attachment
Sequence No. **09**

Name of proprietor: D. THOMAS

Social security number (SSN): 123 45 6789

A Principal business or profession, including product or service (see page C-1 of the instructions) LAW

B Enter code from pages C-7 & 8

C Business name. If no separate business name, leave blank. D. THOMAS

D Employer ID number (EIN), if any

E Business address (including suite or room no.) ▶ MAIN STREET
   City, town or post office, state, and ZIP code ANYWHERE, ST

F Accounting method: (1) ☒ Cash   (2) ☐ Accrual   (3) ☐ Other (specify) ▶ ....

G Did you "materially participate" in the operation of this business during 2000? If "No," see page C-2 for limit on losses ☐ Yes ☐ No

H If you started or acquired this business during 2000, check here ▶ ☐

Part I Income

1	Gross receipts or sales. **Caution.** If this income was reported to you on Form W-2 and the "Statutory employee" box on that form was checked, see page C-2 and check here ▶ ☐	**1** 100
2	Returns and allowances	**2**
3	Subtract line 2 from line 1	**3**
4	Cost of goods sold (from line 42 on page 2)	**4**
5	**Gross profit.** Subtract line 4 from line 3	**5**
6	Other income, including Federal and state gasoline or fuel tax credit or refund (see page C-2)	**6**
7	**Gross income.** Add lines 5 and 6 ▶	**7** 100

Part II Expenses. Enter expenses for business use of your home **only** on line 30.

8	Advertising	**8**	19 Pension and profit-sharing plans	**19**
9	Bad debts from sales or services (see page C-3)	**9**	20 Rent or lease (see page C-4):	
10	Car and truck expenses (see page C-3)	**10**	a Vehicles, machinery, and equipment	**20a**
11	Commissions and fees	**11**	b Other business property	**20b**
12	Depletion	**12**	21 Repairs and maintenance	**21**
13	Depreciation and section 179 expense deduction (not included in Part III) (see page C-3)	**13**	22 Supplies (not included in Part III)	**22**
			23 Taxes and licenses	**23**
			24 Travel, meals, and entertainment:	
14	Employee benefit programs (other than on line 19)	**14**	a Travel	**24a**
15	Insurance (other than health)	**15**	b Meals and entertainment	
16	Interest:		c Enter nondeductible amount included on line 24b (see page C-5)	
a	Mortgage (paid to banks, etc.)	**16a**	d Subtract line 24c from line 24b	**24d**
b	Other	**16b**	25 Utilities	**25**
17	Legal and professional services	**17**	26 Wages (less employment credits)	**26**
18	Office expense	**18**	27 Other expenses (from line 48 on page 2)	**27**

28	**Total expenses** before expenses for business use of home. Add lines 8 through 27 in columns ▶	**28**
29	Tentative profit (loss). Subtract line 28 from line 7	**29** 99
30	Expenses for business use of your home. Attach **Form 8829**	**30**
31	**Net profit or (loss).** Subtract line 30 from line 29.	
	• If a profit, enter on **Form 1040, line 12,** and **also** on **Schedule SE, line 2** (statutory employees, see page C-5). Estates and trusts, enter on Form 1041, line 3.	**31** 99
	• If a loss, you **must** go to line 32.	
32	If you have a loss, check the box that describes your investment in this activity (see page C-5).	
	• If you checked 32a, enter the loss on **Form 1040, line 12,** and **also** on **Schedule SE, line 2** (statutory employees, see page C-5). Estates and trusts, enter on Form 1041, line 3.	32a ☐ All investment is at risk.
	• If you checked 32b, you **must** attach **Form 6198.**	32b ☐ Some investment is not at risk.

For Paperwork Reduction Act Notice, see Form 1040 instructions.   Cat. No. 11334P   Schedule C (Form 1040) 2000

Figure 4-7 Form 1040, schedule C.

penses may appear in the full amount on the financial statement. On the federal tax return, the only amount that would be shown is a portion of the entertainment expense and none of the nondeductible club dues (Fig. 4-7).

Ethical Issue

> **ABA Model Code:**
> DR9-102(B)(3): Maintain complete records of all funds, securities, and other properties of a client coming into the possession of the lawyer and render appropriate accounts to his client regarding them. . . .

CHAPTER SUMMARY

The financial statements of a business present the activity and financial position of the financial entity. The income statement presents the revenues and expenses of the entity over a specific period of time, or the accounting cycle. The balance sheet shows the financial position of the entity at a specific moment in time. With the use of standard terminology, and by following generally accepted accounting principles, the statements can be readily understood by those needing to review the financial affairs of the entity, whether owners, creditors, or potential investors.

GLOSSARY

Balance sheet   A statement of financial position at a specific moment and time showing the assets, liabilities, and equity

Cost of goods sold   For a business where inventory is a major item, the cost of the merchandise sold during the accounting cycle

Current assets   Assets in the form of cash and near-cash items expected to be converted to cash within the coming year

Current liabilities   Financial obligations due within one year

Financial statements   The financial pictures of a business

Income statement   A statement of the revenues and expenses for a financial entity over a period of time

Owner's equity   The claims of the owners against the assets of the business

Shareholders   The owners of a corporation

REVIEW QUESTIONS

1. Is it proper to have one set of records for accounting purposes and another for tax purposes?
2. How are financial statements like pictures of a business?
3. Why is a balance sheet like a snapshot?
4. Why is the income statement like a motion picture?
5. What is the difference between a service business and merchandising business for accounting purposes?

6. What types of items increase or decrease owner's equity?
7. What is the difference between a corporation and a partnership?
8. How is a tax return like a financial statement?
9. What obligation does an attorney have to keep records of clients' funds and property?
10. Is there an equivalent to the cost of goods sold statement for a law office? Explain.

Chapter 5

Keeping the Records: Journals and Ledgers

In This Chapter
Why Study about Journals and Ledgers?
Chart of Accounts
The General Journal and Ledger
Special Journals and Ledgers
Posting
Ethical Issue

Why Study about Journals and Ledgers?

Journals and ledgers are the places where individual financial transactions are recorded. Traditionally, financial records were recorded on paper sheets and kept in binders called ledgers and journals. These hard-copy documents were divided into the journals, or chronological listing of transactions, which were then transferred to the individual accounts, or ledger sheets.

Today many of these records are computerized. Transactions are entered from original sources, such as check-writing or accounts payable programs, and automatically sorted into the individual ledgers. Understanding the transaction flow and the traditional terminology will help in understanding the layout and internal sorting in the computerized methods. Ultimately, the information will be available in a chronological sequence and in individual accounts, just as was provided by the old fashioned bookkeeping system.

Chart of Accounts

CHART OF ACCOUNTS A listing of all the names of the accounts used in a particular financial entity

A **chart of accounts** is a listing of the names of all the accounts a business will use in preparing its financial statements. The details and account titles will be based on the information needs of the owners. In a professional practice, expense accounts might include costs of attending a required continuing education course and be listed under the category, Seminars. Revenues might be broken down by the individual who generated the fee. These accounts might be called Fees—Partner, Fees—Associate, or Fees—Paralegal.

D. Thomas Law Office

CHART OF ACCOUNTS

1000	ASSETS
1100	Cash
1110	Petty Cash
1200	Clients Escrow Account
1300	Costs Advanced for Clients
1400	Office Supplies
1510	Prepaid Insurance—Premises Liability
1520	Prepaid Insurance—Professional Liability
1600	Office Equipment
1600.1	Accumulated Depreciation—Office Equipment
2000	LIABILITIES
2100	Accounts Payable
2200	Clients Escrow Funds
2310	Employee Withheld Tax Payable—Federal
2320	Employee Withheld Tax Payable—State
2340	Social Security Tax Payable—FICA
2350	Social Security Tax Payable—Medicare
2360	Federal Unemployment Tax Payable
2400	Note Payable
3000	EQUITY
3100	D. Thomas Capital
3200	D. Thomas Drawing
3300	Income Summary
4000	REVENUE
4001	Legal Fees
5000	EXPENSES
5100	Computer Service
5210	Insurance Expense—Premises Liability
5220	Insurance Expense—Professional Liability
5300	Library Update
5410	Payroll Tax
5500	Professional Fees
5600	Rent
5700	Salary
5810	Supplies
5820	Telephone
5830	Utilities
5900	Miscellaneous

Figure 5-1 Chart of accounts.

In setting up a chart of accounts, it is frequently useful to consider the individual account information necessary for preparing tax returns. A good listing of expense titles can be taken from the Schedule C of the federal form 1040. These accounts are divided into the permanent and temporary account categories—Assets, Liabilities, Equity, Revenues, and Expenses (Fig. 5-1).

One of the advantages of using a standard chart of accounts is to maintain consistency in the sorting of financial transactions into the categories that will be used in statements and tax returns, as well as maintaining consistency from period to period.

The General Journal and Ledger

General Journal

The **general journal** is a chronological listing of all of the financial transactions of a business (Fig. 5-2). The general journal is an original source of all of the financial information. When properly maintained, it contains the date, accounts, amount of the transaction, and a brief description of the transaction itself. More frequently than not, in many small offices or businesses, the general journal is not maintained. In these situations, the checking account records are used as the original source of financial information. These may be in the form of checkbook journals, computerized checkbook records, such as Quicken or Peachtree accounting systems, or of just the check stubs or second copies of the checks themselves.

DATE		DESCRIPTION	POST REF.	DEBIT	CREDIT
2001					
JAN 4		Cash	1100	100.—	
		D. Thomas – Capital	3100		100.—
		Initial Investment			
	5	Office Supplies	1400	50.—	
		Accounts Payable	2100		50.—
		Purchase Office Supplies on Credit			
	5	Office Equipment	1600	15.—	
		Cash	1100		15.—
		Purchase Answering Machine			
FEB 16		Account Payable	2100	25.—	
		Cash	1100		25.—
		Paid on Account			
	16	Account Payable	2100	25.—	
		Note Payable	2400		25.—
		Extend Payment terms by issuing a			
		Promissory Note due in one year			
	27	D. Thomas — Drawing	3200	10.—	
		Cash	1100		10.—
		Withdraw cash for personal use			

General Journal — Page 1

Figure 5-2   Ledger sheet from the general journal.

Ledger

A **ledger** is generally maintained for each of the accounts listed in the business's chart of accounts (Fig. 5-3). These generally include the assets, liabilities, revenues, expenses, and equity accounts. While businesses may not have a formal chart of accounts, they all, at some point, will need to summarize the information from the general journal or checking account statement to determine revenues, losses, and account balances.

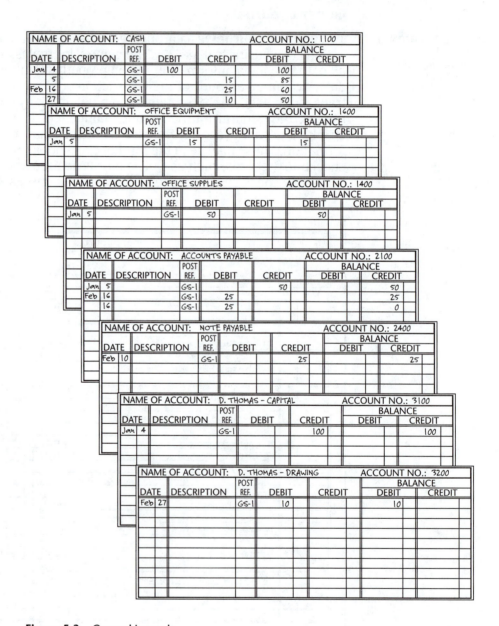

Figure 5-3   General journals.

Special Journals and Ledgers

SPECIAL JOURNALS
A journal used for recording frequently made entries containing the same combination of accounts

Special journals are frequently used to record one specific type of transaction. In the professional office, this may include the cash receipt journal. There is always a debit to cash and a credit to fee income. In other cases, there may be a sales journal, purchases journal, and cash disbursement journal. As with the general journal, the amounts for individual accounts will be posted to the ledger. In the case of cash, the total instead of the individual amounts may be posted.

1. The owner, in setting up the business, opens a checking account and deposits $1,000 on March 1.

   In a T account format:

Cash		Capital (equity)	
$1,000			$1,000

2. Office supplies costing $200 are delivered to the business on 30 days credit on March 15.

Supplies		Account Payable	
$200			$200

3. The account payable for the office supplies is paid on April 3.

Cash		Account Payable	
	$200	$200	

4. A telephone answering machine is purchased for $100 cash on May 15.

Cash		Equipment	
	$100	$100	

5. The owner withdraws $400 in cash from the business on June 1.

Cash		Capital (equity)	
	$400	$400	

In a cash disbursements journal, these entries would appear as shown in Figure 5-4.

Cash Disbursements Journal								
DATE 2001			POST REF.	OTHER ACCOUNT DR.		ACCOUNT PAYABLE DR.		CASH CR.
Apr	3						2 0 0	2 0 0
May	15	OFFICE EQUIPMENT	1600	1 0 0				1 0 0
Jul	1	OWNER'S CAPITAL	3100	4 0 0				4 0 0
				5 0 0		2 0 0		7 0 0

Figure 5-4 Cash disbursements journal.

The journal items are posted to the individual ledger accounts and would appear as shown in Figure 5-5.

An informal special journal found in many offices is the petty cash envelope (Fig. 5-6). The petty cash fund is usually established to provide a quick source of cash for the payment of small amounts when it is not practical to issue a check. For example, paying the mail carrier postage due, reimbursing an associate for parking at the courthouse, or reimbursing the charge to photocopy docket entries for a case. The individual accounts, such as postage, auto expense, and cost advanced for a client, are listed with the appropriate account numbers from the chart of accounts. The individual amounts may be posted to the appropriate ledger, and the total of cash disbursed entered at a later date, such as when the petty cash fund is reimbursed. Generally, a separate entry is made in the ledger account, Petty Cash, for the amount of the initial sum set up for petty cash. The entries are then made to the individual accounts when the petty cash is replaced (Fig. 5-7).

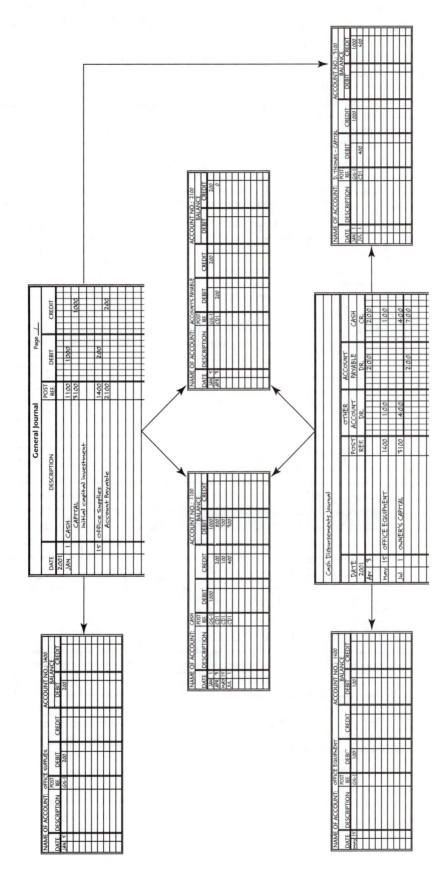

Figure 5-5 Journal–Ledger map.

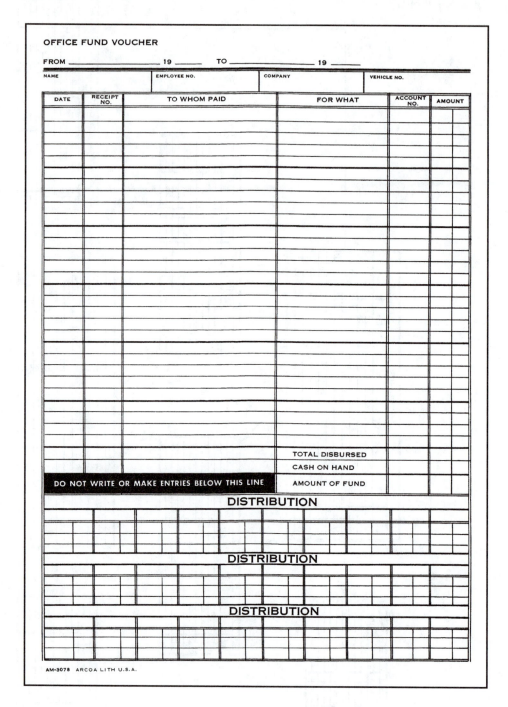

Figure 5-6   Petty cash envelope.

General Journal				Page 3	
DATE	DESCRIPTION	POST REF.	DEBIT		CREDIT
2001					
Aug. 15	Supplies		20		
	Cost Advanced — Client Jones		40		
	Auto Expense to Courthouse		15		
	Banking Expense — Courthouse		5		
	CASH				80
	Record petty cash expenses and				
	replenish petty cash fund				

Figure 5-7   General journal page showing petty cash entries.

Among the most important accounting functions in the law office is the maintenance of accurate client financial records. This includes the identification of funds received as advances against costs to be disbursed, refundable retainers for fees to be earned, and money received on behalf of a client for settlement of suits and sales of real estate. Keeping a record of client financial items may be accomplished by using a special journal–ledger sheet combination. As the amounts received are entered in the cash receipts journal, a client ledger card is also prepared with the same information (Fig. 5-8).

In an automated system (Fig. 5-9), the same information can be obtained by use of references to the client and the nature of the entry used when recording the deposit or disbursement (Fig. 5-10).

In the traditional accounting system, the client ledger entries are made from the general journal. Each of the amounts received from individual clients would be posted to that client's individual ledger account.

All Coverage Insurance

Vincent Matthews vs. _____

R.A. Healy

CASE OR FILE NO. 1701

CLIENT LEDGER

DATE	NAME	CHECK OR RECEIPT NUMBER	CASE NUMBER	TRUST FUNDS		COSTS		RECEIVED	FEES		FEE BALANCE	TRUST BALANCE	COST ADVANCE BALANCE
				RECEIVED	DISBURSED	RECOVERED	ADVANCED		DATE BILLED	CHARGED			
											BALANCES FORWARDED		
											-0-	-0-	-0-
2/4	Vincent Matthews		1701	50 00					1			50 00	
2/18	Crest Photo Service	1915	1701		20 00				2			30 00	
4/3	County Court Clerk	2005	1701		18 50				3			11 50	
4/13	City Bank	2999	1701	Loan Repay			785 00		4				785 00
4/13	City Hospital	3000	1701	Physical Exam			75 00		5				860 00
4/14	All Coverage Ins. (Matthews Settlement)		1701	10000 00					6	2500 00	2500 00	10011 50	
4/14	Healy & Myers	2023	1701		3360 00				7			6651 50	
4/14	Vincent Matthews Transfer ($3360)		1701			860 00		2500 00	8		-0-		-0-
4/15	V. Matthews	2024	1701		6651 50				9			-0-	
		+							10				
									11				
									12				
									13				
									14				
									15				
									16				
									17				
									18				
									19				
									20				
									21				
									22				

© Safeguard Business Systems, Inc. 1989
REORDER FROM YOUR LOCAL SAFEGUARD DISTRIBUTOR.
IF THE NUMBER HAS BEEN MISPLACED CALL 1-800-521-2422

SYSTEM QUESTIONS?
CALL YOUR SAFEGUARD DISTRIBUTOR

THE LAST (BOTTOM MOST) FIGURE IN EACH COLUMN REPRESENTS A CURRENT ACCURATE BALANCE FOR THIS CLIENT MATTER AS OF THE LAST ENTRY.

Safeguard Business Systems
Form No. ACL-6

SAFEGUARD AMBASSADOR LINE®

Figure 5-8 Safeguard client accounting system.

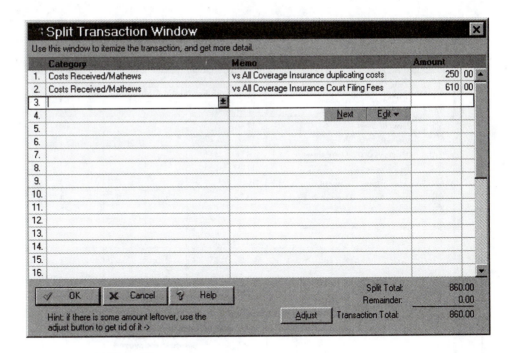

Figure 5-9   Example of entry in Quicken.

Posting

POSTING   The
process of transferring
the financial
information from the
journals to the ledgers

Posting is the process of transferring the financial information from the journals to the individual ledger accounts (Fig. 5-11). In the computer world, this is sometimes referred to as sorting. All of the transactions for the same account are transferred in chronological order into the ledger for the specific account.

DATE	NAME/RECEIVED FROM	CASE NUMBER	A TRUST FUNDS RECEIVED	B COSTS RECOVERED	C MISC. CHARGES	D FEES RECEIVED		E FEES CHARGED	F FEE BALANCE
4/4	Paul M. Jones	1818	150 00				1		
4/4	Thomas Corrian	1819	200 00				2		
4/4	H. E. Atlas	1820	1100 00				3		
4/5	John A. Swart	1821	350 00				4		
4/6	Walter Field	1822	225 00				5		
4/12	Stanton Lewis (Aiken settlement)	1376	5000 00				6	1250 00	1250 00
4/14	All Coverage Ins. (Matthews Settlement)	1701	10000 00				7	2500 00	2500 00
4/14	John Adams Transfer	1615				250 00	8		250 00
4/14	Lewis Aikens Transfer (#1510)	1376		320 00		1250 00	9		-0-
4/14	Robert Johnstone Xerox				9 00		10		
4/14	Vincent Matthews Transfer (#3360)	1701		860 00		2500 00	11		-0-
							12		
							13		
							14		
							15		
							16		
							17		
							18		
							19		
							20		
							21		
							22		
							23		
							24		
							25		
	PAGE TOTALS →		17025 00	1180 00	9 00	4000 00		3750 00	4000 00
	PREVIOUS PAGE TOTALS TO DATE →		11050 00	1610 00	45 00	5000 00		5000 00	F
	TOTALS TO DATE →		28075 00	2790 00	54 00	9000 00		8750 00	
			A	B	C	D		E	

Chronological listing of all:
• trust received
• cost recovered
• miscellaneous charges
• fees charged and received

Safeguard
Form No. ACRF-6   (CRF)

PROOFS FOR PAGE TOTAL LINE ONLY

TRUST ACCOUNT PROOF: K + A = G*
COST PROOF: L + C = B = H*
FEES PROOF: J + E = D = F*
TRUST DEPOSIT PROOF: A = M + O
GENERAL DEPOSIT PROOF: B + D = N + P

* ASSUMES COLS. J, K & L ARE INDEED USED FOR PREVIOUS BALANCE, NOT FOR EXTRA DISTRIBUTION

Safeguard Business Systems, Inc. 1989

SAFEGUARD AMBASSADOR LINE

CASH RECEIPTS AND FEES CH

Figure 5-10 Cash receipts journal sheet.

	(MEMO) BALANCES		(MEMO) PREVIOUS BALANCES			1 TELE CHARGES	2 PHOTO CHARGES	3	4	CURRENCY RECEIVED		DEPOSITS TRUST ACCOUNT		DEPOSITS GENERAL ACCOUNT		
	G TRUST BALANCE	H COST ADVANCE BALANCE	J PREVIOUS FEE BALANCE	K PREVIOUS TRUST BALANCE	L PREVIOUS COST BALANCE					M TRUST	N GENERAL	REF.	O AMOUNT	REF.	P AMOUNT	
1	150 00			-0-								55-231	150 00			1
2	200 00			-0-								60-178	200 00			2
3	1300 00			200 00						1100 00						3
4	350 00			-0-								3-3	350 00			4
5	225 00			-0-						225 00						5
6	5000 00		-0-	-0-								3-88	5000 00			6
7	10011 50		-0-		11 50							56-66	10000 00			7
8			500 00											50-34	250 00	8
9		-0-	1250 00		320 00									50-34	1570 00	9
10		119 00			110 00		9 00									10
11		-0-	2500 00		860 00									50-34	3360 00	11
12																12
13																13
14																14
15																15
16																16
17																17
18																18
19																19
20																20
21																21
22																22
23																23
24																24
25																25
	17236 50	119 00	4250 00	211 50	1290 00	-0-	9 00			1325 00	-0-		15700 00		5180 00	
	G	H	J	K	L	45 00				50 00	-0-		11000 00		6610 00	
						45 00	9 00			1315 00	-0-		26700 00		11790 00	
						1	2	3	4	M	N		O		P	

Entries prove that all client ledgers are in balance.

Complete audit trail for all deposits to the trust account and the general account.

SE (MEMO) JOURNAL BALANCE
BALANCE FIGURES ARE FOR
ND DO NOT REFLECT AN ACTUAL
.. ONLY THE BANK BALANCE AND
ALANCES ARE VALID.

ALIGN RIGHT EDGE OF
CLIENT LEDGER HERE

SYSTEM QUESTIONS?
CALL YOUR SAFEGUARD DISTRIBUTOR

IARGED JOURNAL

REMEMBER: RECORD ALL TRUST AND
GENERAL ACCOUNT BANK DEPOSITS HERE
AND IN THE DEPOSIT COLUMNS OF THE
TRUST AND GENERAL DISBURSEMENT JOUR-
NALS.

MONTH OF APRIL 19 XX PAGE NO. 3 BY CJA

RECORD OF BANK DEPOSITS			
TRUST ACCOUNT		GENERAL ACCOUNT	
DATE	AMOUNT	DATE	AMOUNT
4/4	1450 00	4/4	5180 00
4/14	15575 00		

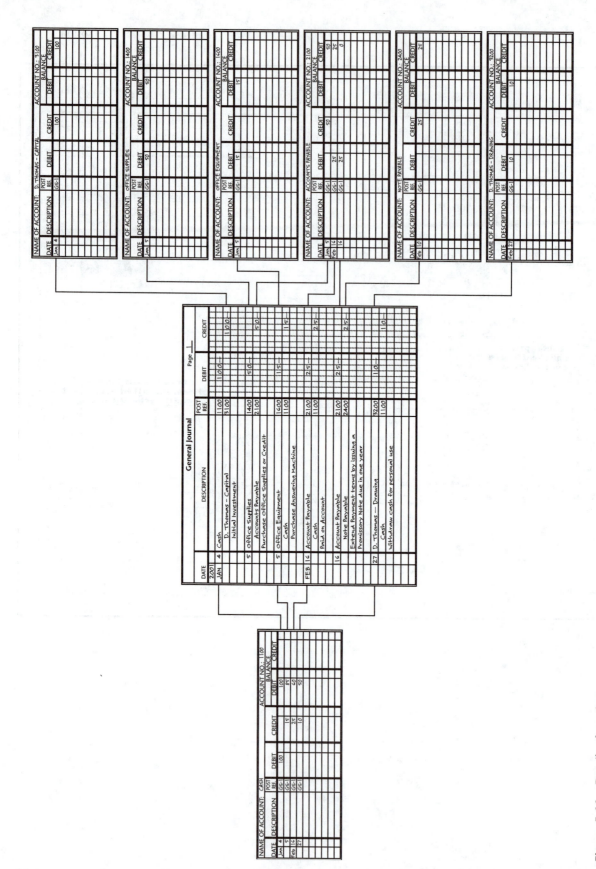

Figure 5-11 Details of posting.

 **Ethical Issue**

> **NFPA model code**
>
> EC-1.2(e): A paralegal shall be scrupulous, thorough, and honest in the identification and maintenance of all funds, securities, and other assets of a client and shall provide accurate accounting as appropriate.

CHAPTER SUMMARY

The financial transactions on a financial entity are systematically recorded in journals and ledgers. All of the financial transactions are initially recorded in the general journal in chronological order. The individual entries are then posted, or transferred, to the ledgers, which are the individual accounts. The ledgers are divided into three permanent categories and two temporary categories. The permanent accounts are the assets, liabilities, and owner's equity accounts. The temporary accounts are divided into revenue accounts and expense accounts.

GLOSSARY

Chart of accounts   A listing of all the names of the accounts used in a particular financial entity

General journal   A chronological listing all of the financial transactions of a business

Ledger   The individual account records for each of the permanent and temporary accounts

Posting   The process of transferring the financial information from the journals to the ledgers

Special journals   A journal used for recording frequently made entries containing the same combination of accounts

REVIEW QUESTIONS

1. What is recorded in the general journal?
2. In what order is the general journal maintained?
3. What is the advantage of using a chart of accounts?
4. What do the ledgers contain?
5. What is the function of a special journal?
6. What is the source of information found in the ledger accounts?
7. What is the process of posting?
8. Into how many categories is the ledger divided?
9. What is the advantage in using special journals?
10. What is the purpose of a general journal?

Chapter 6

Adjusting and Closing Entries and Preparation of Statements

In This Chapter

Why Study about Adjusting and Closing Entries and Statement Preparation?
Using Worksheets
Trial Balance
Adjusting Entries
Closing Entries
Preparing the Financial Statements

Why Study about Adjusting and Closing Entries and Statement Preparation?

At the end of an accounting cycle, whether it is at the end of a year, the end of a fiscal period, or with the occurrence of a specific event, such as the closing of a business or the death of an individual, the financial records must be adjusted to reflect a proper matching of income and expense items in the appropriate time period. The preparation of the statements is a process with a number of steps. First, the basic accounting equation items are summarized. Then, any necessary adjustments are made to reflect needed modifications in accounts that were not made in a normal transactional basis. Finally, entries are made that have the effect of closing out the fiscal period and setting up the accounts for the new accounting or fiscal period.

In preparing the end-of-period adjusting and closing entries and the financial statements, most accountants use a worksheet. The worksheet is a rough draft of the entries and statements. Using the multicolumn worksheet helps the preparer see all of the accounts in one place and, by the use of the various columns, be sure that everything balances before making the final general journal entries and postings to the ledgers.

D. Thomas, Esquire
For the Year Ending December 31, 2001

Account	Trial Balance Debit	Trial Balance Credit	Adjustments Debit	Adjustments Credit	Adjustment Trial Balance Debit	Adjustment Trial Balance Credit	Income Statement Debit	Income Statement Credit	Balance Sheet Debit	Balance Sheet Credit
Cash	$1,500.00				$1,500.00				$1,500.00	
Office Supplies	500.00			$100.00(a)	400.00				400.00	
Prepaid Insurance	1,200.00			300.00(b)	900.00				900.00	
Office Equipment	3,600.00				3,600.00				3,600.00	
Accumulated Depreciation—Office Equipment		$0.00		300.00(c)		$300.00				$300.00
Accounts Payable		800.00				800.00				800.00
D. Thomas, Capital		5,000.00				5,000.00				5,000.00
D. Thomas, Drawing										
Fees		1,000.00				1,000.00		$1,000.00		
Office Supplies Expense			$100.00(a)		100.00		$100.00			
Insurance Expense			300.00(b)		300.00		300.00			
Depreciation Expense—Office Equipment			300.00(c)		300.00		300.00			
	$6,800.00	$6,800.00	$700.00	$700.00	$7,100.00	$7,100.00	$700.00	$1,000.00	$6,400.00	$6,100.00
Net Income							300.00			300.00
							$1000.00	$1,000.00	$6,400.00	$6,400.00

Figure 6-1 Example of a ten-column worksheet.

Using Worksheets

WORKING PAPERS
A collection of
worksheets used by the
accountant

Accountants and bookkeepers use a number of different forms of worksheets, from the single-column listing of accounts to the multicolumn form used at the year's end to prepare financial statements. The purpose of the worksheet and **working papers**, as the collection of worksheets is referred to by accountants, is to help organize the information about an account or group of accounts in an informal manner that allows the preparer to see the whole picture in one place. In the law office, some of these worksheets are used to collect the information to be transferred to tax returns. In an estate, it is common to work from a collection of documents and papers. Worksheets are frequently set up for the different assets, such as savings bonds, insurance policies, stocks, and other items, to be inventoried and reported to the beneficiaries and tax authorities. The worksheet for the year-end statement preparation is a rough draft of the journal entries necessary to adjust and close the accounts and prepare the balance sheet and income statement. Spread out over a multicolumn worksheet, it is easier to see if every thing is in balance, as all the information appears in one place (Fig. 6-1).

Trial Balance

TRIAL BALANCE   A
summary of all the
accounts, temporary
and permanent, with
their balances

The **trial balance** (Fig 6-2) is a summary of the accounts with their balances. It is a listing of all the accounts and their balances as of a specific point in time, generally the end of an accounting period, such as the end of the year. Some businesses use a shorter accounting period for internal purposes and may prepare monthly or even weekly trial balances.

D. Thomas, Esquire		
Trial Balance		
December 31, 2001		
Cash	$1,500.00	
Office Supplies	500.00	
Prepaid Insurance	1,200.00	
Office Equipment	3,600.00	
Accumulated Depreciation—		
Office Equipment		
Accounts Payable		800.00
D. Thomas, Capital		5,000.00
D. Thomas, Drawing		
Fees		$1,000.00
	$6,800.00	$6,800.00

Figure 6-2   Example of a trial balance.

The first test of the trial balance is determining whether the debits and credits equal one another. In double-entry accounting, all of the accounts should balance: debits equal credits. If the debits and credits are not equal, an error may exist in the accounts that will need to be corrected before any further action is taken. Some of the more common mistakes are mechanical in nature: copying the wrong amount, transferring the wrong amount when posting from the journal to the ledger, reversing a number, and math errors in adding the columns.

Adjusting Entries

In the normal course of business, many transactions occur that result in changes to the asset, liability, and equity accounts. In the normal daily activity of a business, account balances are changed, and entries are made in the books to reflect these changes. For example, the Cash account is reduced when cash is used to pay for the purchase of supplies, such as paper for the copy machine. The account, Supplies, is increased to reflect the purchase.

Cash	Supplies
$500	$500

Accounts, like Supplies, are *not* changed on a transactional basis each time paper is taken from the supply closet and used. At the end of the year, the value of the paper supplies used will need to be recorded as an expense, and the value of the paper supplies available for the beginning of the next period will need to be updated to the current value for this asset.

Supplies	Supplies Expense
$100	$100

Some assets lose value by virtue of their use, obsolescence, destruction, or other loss, which also has to be recorded. Equipment wears out and has a reduced value to the business as a result. Computers may become obsolete and have no value in the future. Other assets may have been lost or stolen during the year.

ADJUSTING ENTRY Entries made to recognize the use of assets during the accounting cycle

The purpose of making **adjusting entries** is to recognize the use of these assets during the accounting period in the operation of the business and to adjust the balances in the accounts to reflect the current value and the amounts to be charged as expenses against current period revenue.

Office Equipment	Accumulated Depreciation of Office Equipment	Depreciation Expense of Office Equipment
$3,600	$300	$300

Some assets, such as prepaid insurance, are adjusted to show the portion of the prepaid amount used and the balance left to be used in the future. Portions of income items or revenues, such as prepaid retainers, need to be adjusted to show what has been earned during the period and what amount remains as an obligation to the client.

Prepaid Insurance		Insurance Expense
$1,200	$300	$300

Depreciation

DEPRECIATION An expense in the income statement that spreads the cost of an asset over its useful life

Assets, such as copy machines, computers and office furniture, wear out over a period of time. The amount of use is called **depreciation**. The amount of depreciation, or usage, is an expense that should be reflected in the income statement for the period of time involved. While there are many methods for calculating depreciation and a number of different arguments for the appropriate time that an asset is useful, generally, the time period allowable by the federal government for income tax purposes is used. For example, a copy machine with a five-year useful life has one fifth of its value charged each year.

first year:	20% of cost charged as expense
second year:	20% of cost charged as expense
third year:	20% of cost charged as expense
fourth year:	20% of cost charged as expense
fifth year:	20% of cost charged as expense
Total,	100%

In a pure cash basis accounting system, there would be no need to adjust these expense items, they would be recorded as an expense at the time the payment was made. Some items are treated on a cash basis, while others are adjusted. If the amounts of the expenses are not material (i.e., so small in amount that the treatment on a cash basis will not distort the financial results of operation), they may be expensed immediately. If the amount is significant, such as with the purchase of specialty items, or if the desire is to allocate expenses precisely, then adjustment will be made under the accrual basis.

UNADJUSTED TRIAL BALANCE The trial balance before any adjustments

At the end of the accounting period, a trial balance is prepared showing the balance of the accounts. This is the **unadjusted trial balance**; the accounts are unadjusted for the amounts of the prorations, depreciation, and other allocations for use, obsolescence, loss, and amounts earned. The purpose of making the adjusting entries at this time is to update the values of the affected accounts. The new balances will be carried into the new period, so they should reflect the amounts unused or unearned as of the beginning of the new period.

Some items are calculated based on the time periods involved. Assume an asset has a five-year or 60-month life (5 years × 12 months per year = 60-month life). The portion used up during the period will be the number of months in the current period (12 months for the year or three months for a quarter of the year) out of the total. For example, three months of 60 months is five percent (3/60 = 1/20 or 5%). The same method may be used for items, such as annual insurance policies, where there is a portion of days not months. If we assume a 360-day year and we have used 60 days, the reduction in the value of the insurance in the new period will be 60 out of 360 equals one sixth times the premium paid. The value carried into the new period will be 300 days worth or 300 of 360, or five sixths of the premium.

Other items are not as routine, such as supplies used during the period. If the amount shown in the supplies account is the total of the purchases for the year, it may be necessary to carry into the next period what is left. This is frequently referred to in some businesses as taking inventory, or seeing what is still on hand. The formula used is the same for merchandise and things like supplies.

Beginning inventory	$ 0
Plus purchases	500
Total available	$500
Less ending inventory	400
Amount used or withdrawn	$100

There must be an offsetting entry to make the accounts balance. So far, we have looked at the correction of the asset accounts only. But there must be a balancing entry for each of the adjustments. The items used to generate income are charges against revenues or expenses.

By using a worksheet, we can see the account and the unadjusted balances and then make the adjustments item by item. It is customary to label each adjustment with a lower-case letter showing the debit and the related credit or credits. When the number of adjustments grows, labeling makes finding the information and correcting potential errors easier. It is also a way of making a list of the necessary journal entries that will be made in the actual journals and ledgers. The worksheets are just working papers, the actual entries must still be made in the official records, that is, the journal and ledger (Fig. 6-3).

After the adjustments are made on the worksheet and the debits and credits balanced, the adjustments can be recorded in the general journal (Fig. 6-4).

Closing Entries

CLOSING ENTRY
Entries made to close the temporary accounts and transfer the balances to the permanent accounts

Closing entries are a process for moving the balances of temporary accounts to permanent accounts at the end of the accounting cycle. Every business starts off the accounting period with a zero balance in the temporary accounts, its revenue (income) accounts, and its expenses accounts. During the period, entries are made to reflect the amounts earned and the expenses related to the generation of the income. At the end of the period, adjusting entries are made to reflect amounts earned and expenses

D. Thomas, Esquire
For the Year Ending December 31, 2001

	Trial Balance		Adjustments	
Cash	$1,500.00			
Office Supplies	500.00			$100.00(a)
Prepaid Insurance	1,200.00			300.00(b)
Office Equipment	3,600.00			
Accumulated Depreciation— Office Equipment				300.00(c)
Accounts Payable		$ 800.00		
D. Thomas, Capital		5,000.00		
D. Thomas, Drawing				
Fees		1,000.00		
Office Supplies Expense			$100.00(a)	
Insurance Expense			300.00(b)	
Depreciation Expense— Office Equipment			300.00(c)	
	$6,800.00	$6,800.00	$700.00	$700.00

Figure 6-3   Example of an adjusted trial balance.

General Journal   Page __4__

DATE 2001		DESCRIPTION	POST REF.	DEBIT	CREDIT
DEC	31	Supplies Expense		100	
		Supplies			100
		(to adjust supplies and record expense)			
		Insurance Expense		300	
		Prepaid Insurance			300
		(to adjust insurance and record expense)			
		Depreciation Expense—Office Equipment		300	
		Accumulated Depreciation—Office Equipment			300
		(to record depreciation expense on office equipment)			

Figure 6-4   Adjusting journal entries.

incurred, such as the portion of equipment used up or the portion of the premium on a multiperiod or one-year insurance policy. These adjusting amounts are entered in the temporary accounts in the adjustment process.

After the completion of the adjusting entries, the temporary account will reflect the total amount of revenue and the total amount of expenses. Unless the revenue exactly equals the expenses for the period, the totals of the temporary account will not balance. An additional entry is needed to bring the temporary account into balance. Since the profit or loss will belong to the owner, the balancing entry will be made to an equity account.

Revenue
Fees

Expenses
Insurance
Supplies
Depreciation

DATE 2001		DESCRIPTION	POST REF.	DEBIT	CREDIT
DEC	31	Income Summary		700	
		Supplies Expense			100
		Insurance Expense			300
		Depreciation Expense			300
		(to close Expenses for the Period)			
		FEES		1000	
		Income Summary			1000
		(to close Revenue for the Period)			
		Income Summary		300	
		D. Thomas, Capital			300
		(to close Income Summary and add profit to			
		Capital Account)			

General Journal   Page 5

Figure 6-5 Closing journal entries.

During the accounting period, revenue is generated and expenses are incurred.

Revenue minus Expenses equals Profit or (Loss)

At the end of the accounting period, the two items—Revenue and Expenses—are compared, if the revenue is greater than the expenses, a profit is shown; if expenses are greater than income, a loss is shown. The income or the loss of the business operation belongs to the owners. If there is a profit, the owner's equity increases. If there is a loss, the owner's equity decreases. The closing entries are the entries used to close the revenue and expense accounts (Fig. 6-5). We then transfer the balance of income or loss to the equity account of the owner and set up the revenue and expenses account with a zero balance for the next accounting period.

Income Summary	
$700	$1,000
$300	

Preparing the Financial Statements

The financial statements, income statement, balance sheet, and statement of equity (Fig. 6-6) can be prepared from the worksheet.

D. Thomas, Esquire		
Income Statement		
For the Year Ending December 31, 2001		
Income		
Fees		$1,000.00
Expenses		
Office Supplies Expense	$100.00	
Insurance Expense	300.00	
Depreciation Expense—		
Office Equipment	300.00	
Total Expenses		700.00
Net Profit		$ 300.00

a

Figure 6-6 (a) Income statement.

D. Thomas, Esquire
Balance Sheet
December 31, 2001

Assets
Current Assets
   Cash $1,500.00
   Office supplies   400.00
   Prepaid insurance   900.00
Total Current Assets $2,800.00

Long-term Asset
   Office equipment $3,600.00
   Less accumulated depreciation   300.00   3,300.00
Total Long-term Assets   3,300.00
Total Assets $6,100.00

Liabilities
Accounts Payable $ 800.00

Total Liabilities $ 800.00

Owner's Equity
D. Thomas, Capital   5,300.00

Total Liabilities and Owner's Equity $6,100.00

b

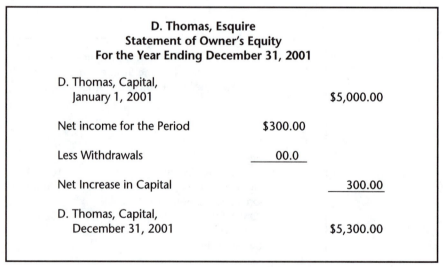

D. Thomas, Esquire
Statement of Owner's Equity
For the Year Ending December 31, 2001

D. Thomas, Capital,
  January 1, 2001 $5,000.00

Net income for the Period $300.00

Less Withdrawals   00.0

Net Increase in Capital   300.00

D. Thomas, Capital,
  December 31, 2001 $5,300.00

c

Figure 6-6   (b) balance sheet; (c) statement of owner's equity.

CHAPTER SUMMARY

A basic concept of accounting is to match expenses with revenues. Adjusting entries are used to recognize the use of assets during the accounting period. Where items have been paid for in advance, it becomes necessary to determine the amount actually used during the current accounting cycle. For supplies that have been prepaid, it is easy to count what has been used and adjust the Permanent Supplies account to show what will be available in the next accounting period. The amount used in the current accounting period is charged as an expense. Depreciation is the amount charged as an expense for the use of assets, such as machinery and equipment, and buildings that have a multiyear life.

Closing entries are those made to transfer the balances of temporary accounts—revenue and expenses—to the permanent accounts at the end of the accounting cycle. The temporary accounts start each accounting cycle with a zero balance after the closing entries are made.

GLOSSARY

Accounting cycle   A period of time for which financial statements are prepared

Adjusting entry   Entries made to recognize the use of assets during the accounting cycle

Closing entry   Entries made to close the temporary accounts and transfer the balances to the permanent accounts

Depreciation   An expense in the income statement that spreads the cost of an asset over its useful life

Trial balance   A summary of all the accounts, temporary and permanent, with their balances

Unadjusted trial balance   The trial balance before any adjustments

Working papers   A collection of worksheets used by the accountant

REVIEW QUESTIONS

1. What is the difference between the trial balance and the adjusted trial balance?
2. What is the first test of trial balance accuracy?
3. What is the purpose of the adjusting entries?
4. What is the purpose of the closing entries?
5. What is depreciation?
6. What adjustments are made in a cash accounting system?
7. What is the purpose of the income summary?
8. What effect does an excess of expenses over revenues have on the owner's equity?
9. Why is a worksheet helpful in making adjusting and closing entries?
10. Why are some items, such as supplies, not charged on a transactional basis?

Chapter 7

Applications in the Law Office

In This Chapter

Why Study Accounting Applications in the Law Office?

To anyone working in a law office, there seem to be an endless number of forms that need to be completed. Many of these are financial in nature. In the family law practice, it may be the statement of income and expenses for use in determining support. In the real estate practice, it will include the statement of receipts and disbursements or the settlement sheet. Even in the general practice, it will include the monthly checking account reconciliation of the office business accounts and client escrow accounts. The common element of these forms is that, in some way, they must balance. Expenses cannot exceed income. The bank balance must equal the book balance. In each case, there is a starting point, whether it is the prior balance or a zero balance. Knowing where to start and having a plan of action will make the task easier and provide a trail to finding any errors. Many of the activities also require an understanding of the methods used to split amounts among accounts or parties, such as the proration of taxes between a buyer and seller, or the split of interest income between a lifetime tax return and the estate tax return.

Calculations in the Law Office

Prorations

PRORATION The process of allocating amounts between different entities or accounting cycles

The two most frequently used calculations are the **proration** calculations and the "find the missing amount" calculations. The proration calculations are generally in allocating an amount between different accounting periods or different entities. Real estate settlement will usually require a sharing of items, such as taxes, rents, and utility payments, between the buyer and the seller. These may be annual amounts, such as an annual tax payment, or a monthly amount, such as a prepaid utility bill. These prorations are also frequently referred to as adjustments on the real estate settlement sheet. The concept is the same.

$$\frac{\text{Number of Months}}{\text{Total Months}} \times \text{Amount to Be Shared}$$

For example, assume a tax bill covers 12 months from January 1 to December 31. The bill is for $1,200. The transaction was on April 30. The seller has already paid the tax bill and wants to recover the amount he prepaid so that the buyer will have to pay for the period of May 1 to December 31. If we assume equal months of the same number of days the amount owed is as follows:

$$\frac{8 \text{ months}}{12 \text{ months}} \times \$1,200$$

Or, the buyer's share is

$$\frac{8 \text{ Months}}{12 \text{ months}} \times \$1,200 = \$800$$

and the seller's share is

$$\frac{4 \text{ months}}{12 \text{ months}} \times \$1,200 = \$400.$$

If we want to be totally accurate, we can use the total actual number of days and not use the 30-day month. For example, the number of days from January 1 to April 30 equals 120.

January = 31 days
February = 28 days (except leap years)
March   = 31 days
April   = 30 days

The number of total days from January 1 to December 31 equals 365.

January   = 31 days
February   = 28 days (except leap years)
March   = 31 days
April   = 30 days
May   = 31 days
June   = 30 days
July   = 31 days
August   = 31 days
September = 30 days
October   = 31 days
November = 30 days
December = 31 days

Or,

$$120/365 \times \$1{,}200 = \$394.52 \text{ as the seller's share}$$
$$245/365 \times \$1{,}200 = \$805.48 \text{ as the buyer's share}$$
$$365/365 \times \$1{,}200 = \$1{,}200.00 \text{ as the total amount}$$

Depending on whether you represent the buyer or the seller, and on the amount of time involved, you may want more or less accuracy in the calculation.

If the calculation is for a monthly amount, the method is the same. For example, a property has a tenant who pays $600 per month. The property is sold on the tenth of the month and the tenant has not paid the rent yet. The seller is entitled to the rent for the first ten days and the buyer for the balance of the month. If the month is April, then the calculation is

$$\frac{10}{30} \times \$600 = \$200 \text{ as the seller's share}$$

If the month is February and the 30-day month is not assumed then

$$\frac{10}{28} \times \$600 = \$214.28568 \text{ as the seller's share.}$$

Since we need to limit the amounts to whole pennies, we will use the rounding convention that says if the third decimal is five or more to round up, if four or less to round down. In this case, .285, the third decimal is five or greater, so the amount becomes .29.

From the buyer's side,

$$\frac{18}{28} \times \$600 = \$385.7142, \text{ or as the third decimal is four or less,}$$
the amount is .71.

Seller	$214.29
Buyer	385.71
Total rent	$600.00

Occasionally, the amount to be prorated covers an odd period of time (e.g., the 13th of January to the 28th of March). We count the total days on the calendar as follows:

```
January 13 to 31 = 19 days
February 1 to 28 = 28 days
March 1 to 28    = 28 days
Total days       = 75 days
```

Depending on the amount of money involved, a question might be raised as to the inclusion of the day of the settlement, March 28. If the transaction is deemed concluded at the end of the day, the day belongs then to the seller; if concluded at the beginning of the day, then to the buyer. In larger transactions, this may be found in the agreement of sale or contract.

Interest Calculations

Interest is calculated in the same manner as follows:

1. determine the amount to be divided;

2. calculate the total days involved; and

3. calculate the number of days to be shared or calculated.

Calculating interest is based on the formula

Interest equals the Principal Amount times the Rate times the Time involved,

or, I = PRT.

For example, if interest is six percent (.06) for one year, and the principal amount is $1,000, the total interest for a one-year period is

$$.06 \times \$1,000 \times 1 \text{ Year} = \$60.$$

Or, if the time is from January 13 to March 28, then, as we have seen, the total number of days involved is 75. The total days in a year is 365, so

$$\frac{.06 \times 75}{365} \times \$1000 = \frac{75}{365} = .0254794,$$

or, .06 × .0254794 × $1,000 = 12.3287, rounding up, $12.33.

Account Reconciliation

Checking Account

The **checking account reconciliation** is the easiest and most frequently performed task. Good accounting and business practice is to prepare a monthly statement. Bank rules and regulations generally require that any errors or discrepancies are reported to the bank promptly or the customer waives the right to have the error corrected.

The purpose of the reconciliation is to verify the accuracy of the disbursements and deposits as shown on the office records with the accuracy of the bank in handling and processing the checks and deposits. There are many reasons why the two sets of records may not match or balance.

The most frequent error in manual systems is not entering the same amount on the deposit slip or on the check as is entered in the check register. For banks, the most common errors are the human errors in the keystroking of the amounts shown on the deposit slip or the attached checks into the computer system. These are the errors that can be discovered by a visual comparison of the documents (Fig. 7-1).

The checks, and sometimes the deposit slips returned from the bank, will show the amounts entered. On checks it is the amount shown on the lower right under the signature line. This amount should be the same as the amount written on the check. Because it may be entered by hand, the keystroke amount may be in error. The amount shown on the check in numbers may be different than the amount shown in words, resulting in the application of the Uniform Commercial Code rule that states when there is a conflict between the numerals and the words, the words take precedence over numbers.

Less obvious, but more difficult to detect, is the increasing frequency of differences caused by intentional alteration of instruments or misrepresentation in securing payment of the negotiable instrument. It is not uncommon to find that a check has been altered, either as to the amount or as to the payee. Also increasingly common is the falsification of signatures of both drawers and of payees. Forgery of a drawer's signature invalidates

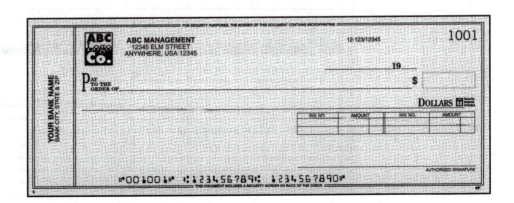

Figure 7-1   Check with magnetic coding.

the negotiable instrument and, if promptly presented to the bank, the fraudulently obtained funds will be returned. Verification of the endorsee's signature is not as easy, but the burden is usually on the bank, if questionable. In both cases, a timely report is essential and monthly reconciliation will bring the issue to light in a timely fashion (Fig. 7-2).

Steps in the reconciliation process are as follows:

1. Sort checks by number

2. Compare canceled (returned) checks against the bank statement

Bank Reconciliation

Month _____

Name _____   Bank Acct. _____

Balance per Bank Statement
   Deposits After Statement Date
   Transfers into Account After Statement Date
   Charges Recorded After Statement Date
   Outstanding Checks   _____
Adjusted Balance per Bank Statement   _____

Balance per Checkbook or Ledger   _____

Difference   _____

Deposits After Statement Date   Total

Description	Date	Amount	Description	Date	Amount

Transfers into Account After Statement Date   Total

Description	Date	Amount	Description	Date	Amount

Charges Recorded After Statement Date   Total

Description	Date	Amount	Description	Date	Amount

Outstanding Checks   Total

Description	Number	Amount	Description	Number	Amount

Figure 7-2   Bank reconciliation form.

3. Compare bank statement amounts with the check register
4. List those checks and deposits from the check register not recorded on the bank statement (uncleared items)
5. Balance bank amount with the business check register

Adjusting Entries from the Bank Reconciliation. There are two bank actions that may result in the two amounts being different: bank charges for the month's activity and the payment of interest on the account by the bank. These require entries to bring the accounts into balance.

To record the bank charges:

	Debit	Credit
Bank charge	$15.00	
Cash		$15.00

To record the interest received:

Cash	$3.25	
Interest income		$3.25

Occasionally, loans or other expense payments will be automatically deducted from the account. For example:

To record the automatic repayment of a loan to the business:

Loan payable	$1,000.00	
Interest expense (on loan payable)	$12.00	
Cash		$1,012.00

Where utility bills are automatically deducted from the checking account:

Utility expense	$234.00	
Cash		$234.00

For automatic deposits or wire transfers not previously reported:

Cash	$500.00	
Fee income		$500.00

Petty Cash

Most offices have some form of petty cash account (Fig. 7-3). It may be nothing more than an envelope with a small amount of cash in which receipts are kept or notations made on the outside, or formal systems involving a checking account. In any event, the amounts chargeable to a client or deductible as an expense must be recorded, and funds replenished.

Petty Cash Reconciliation February, 2001		Client Cost Add.	General Expenses	Auto Parking	Postage	Supplies
Beginning	$1,000					
Disbursement						
Filing fees						
E. Quind	60	60				
E. Hannah	30	30				
G. Hains	30	30				
Courthouse parking	40			40		
Postage due	7				7	
Paper—Copy	24					24
Copy service	120		120			
TOTALS	$ (311)	120	120	40	7	24
Reimbursement	311					
Ending	$1,000					

Figure 7-3 Petty cash form.

Trust Account Reconciliation March 2000						
	Balance Beginning of Period			$		
Plus	Receipts					
	Total					
Less	Disbursements					
Plus	Disbursements Outstanding					
	Ending Balance—Bank			$		
Date	Receipts			Amount	Recorded	Not Recorded
	Description					
	Total Receipts					
	Receipts Not on Statement					
Date	Disbursements					
	Total Disbursements					
	Disbursements Outstanding					
	Check #	Amount				
	Total Disbursements Outstanding					

Figure 7-4 Trust account reconciliation form.

Trust Account Reconciliation

The reconciliation of a Trust or Escrow account is the same process as bank reconciliation. The amounts shown on the internal records must be compared and any differences explained (Fig. 7-4).

Civil Practice: Fee and Costs Billing

HOURLY RATE A fee system based upon a charge for each hour of service performed

CONTINGENT FEE A fee system based on a percentage of the amount collected on behalf of a client, usually as a result of litigation

In a civil litigation practice, fees may be calculated on an **hourly rate**, a **contingent fee**, or a combination of the two. The time records for each member of the firm must be obtained, either from the hard copies of time slips or the computer printout of hours spent working on the case. The

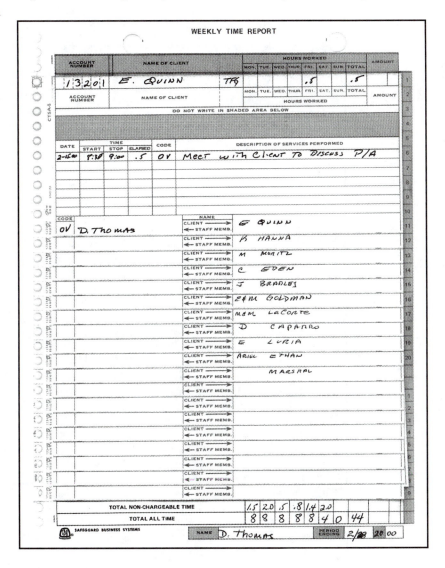

Figure 7-5 Individual attorney totals.

actual time may be reported to the client chronologically, with all activity by each person who worked on the file integrated with all the others, or they may be listed separately by the individual. The difficulty is in calculating the correct amount for each person at his or her respective hourly rate. It is not unusual to have a senior partner bill at one rate, a junior partner at another, and a paralegal at a third rate. It is good practice to calculate the total for each billable person separately, and then collectively (Fig. 7-5). The totals of the individuals, of course, must equal the total of all (Fig. 7-6). Therefore, the comparison acts as a check on the mathematical accuracy.

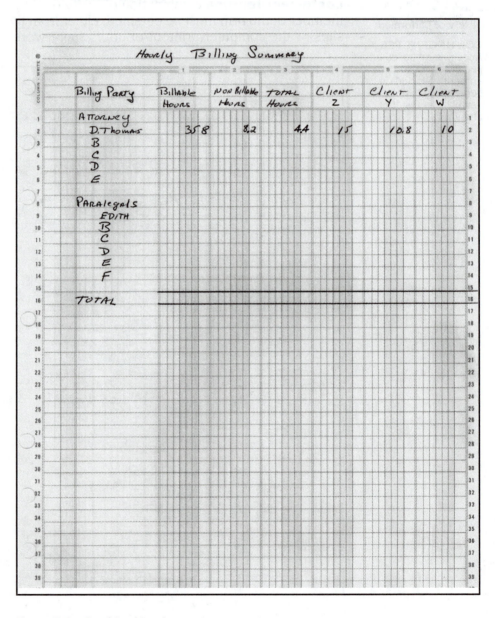

Figure 7-6   Combined invoice.

```
              SMITH V. JONES & ROE AIR CONDITIONING
                   DATE OF ACCIDENT: 04-23-91
                  SETTLEMENT DISBURSEMENT SHEET

GROSS SETTLEMENT:                                        $18,000.00

LESS:  Out-of-Pocket Costs:

     04/14/93 Prothonotary
                Filing Fees          $ 80.50
     04/16/93 Sheriff
                Service Fees           42.80
     06/11/93 Sheriff of Bucks
                Service Fees           38.00
     08/02/93 Postmaster
                Address Information     3.00
     09/30/93 Sheriff
                Service Fees           42.80
     06/07/95 R.R.S.
                Record Copy Service    37.10
     07/27/95 3D Printing
                Copy of Photographs    15.24
     01/19/96 Knipes-Cohen Associates
                Deposition Transcript 119.96        379.40


NET SETTLEMENT:                                          $17,620.60

LESS:

     Attorney's Fees 40% of
     Gross Settlement pursuant to
     Fee Agreement dated 06/27/91
     copy attached.

     Reduced to 1/3 of Net
     Recovery per Thomas F. Goldman                     5,873.34


NET DISBURSEMENT TO CLIENTS:                             $11,747.26
                                                        ===========

We hereby acknowledge and agree to the disbursements as outlined
above.

Date:_____          _____


Date:_____          _____
```

Figure 7-7   Tort case disbursement sheet showing contingent fee calculation.

Real Estate Applications

Loan Applications

The loan application for a mortgage or other business or personal loan usually requires the preparation of a personal financial statement. Lenders usually have their own forms. These forms generally resemble a personal balance sheet (i.e., what assets do you have, what do you owe, and what is your equity; Fig. 7-8). As with business balance sheets, the values are as of a moment in time. It is usually easiest to complete as of the first of the month. Bank and other financial institutions provide end-of-month statements and creditors usually issue bills on a monthly basis.

Real Estate Settlement

Depending on local practice and whether there is a mortgage involved in the transaction, either a summary of receipts and disbursements will be prepared or an approved HUD-1 (Housing & Urban Development) or RESPA (Real Estate Settlement Procedures Act) form will be completed (Fig. 7-9). In many cases, the real estate agent or broker prepares a good-faith estimate of the closing costs at the time of the initial agreement-of-sale execution. Since the closing costs are, in part, dependent on the actual day of the settlement, you may need to prepare a new closing cost statement with correct prorations and interest calculations. The individual amounts paid or received may be different for the buyer and the seller, but the total of the funds passing through the settlement will be the same, with any excess deposits from the buyer being refunded.

Prorations in real estate are usually computed using a 360-day year and a 30-day month. Some government lending programs, such as the FHA (Federal Housing Administration) and VA (Veterans' Administration), may require more exact method and use a 365-day year. The calculations are based on the end of the day, with the seller being responsible for the day of settlement. Local custom and contract terms can vary the obligation.

Real Estate Refinance

The refinance of a mortgage or a property is the creation of a new mortgage and the satisfaction of an old mortgage. The parties are the mortgagor (the property owner) and the mortgagee (the financial institution putting up the mortgage money). The same forms can be used as with the original settlement, except that the balance is the funds provided and the mortgage and costs paid by the property owner.

Residential Loan Application

MORTGAGE APPLIED FOR	☐ Conventional ☐ FHA ☐ VA ☐	Amount $	Interest Rate %	No. of Months	Monthly Payment Principal & Interest $	Escrow/Impounds (to be collected monthly) ☐ Taxes ☐ Hazard Ins. ☐ Mtg. Ins. ☐
Prepayment Option						

Subject Property

Property Street Address	City	County	State	Zip	No. Units

Legal Description (Attach description if necessary)				Year Built

Purpose of Loan: ☐ Purchase ☐ Construction-Permanent ☐ Construction ☐ Refinance ☐ Other (Explain)

Complete this line if Construction-Permanent or Construction Loan ☞	Lot Value Data	Original Cost	Present Value (a)	Cost of Imps. (b)	Total (a + b)	ENTER TOTAL AS PURCHASE PRICE IN DETAILS OF PURCHASE.
	Year Acquired $	$	$	$		

Complete this line if a Refinance Loan		Purpose of Refinance	Describe Improvements [ ] made [ ] to be made	
Year Acquired / Original Cost $	Amt. Existing Liens $			Cost: $

Title Will Be Held In What Name(s)	Manner In Which Title Will Be Held

Source of Down Payment and Settlement Charges

This application is designed to be completed by the borrower(s) with the lender's assistance. The Co-Borrower Section and all other Co-Borrower questions must be completed and the appropriate box(es) checked if ☐ another person will be jointly obligated with the Borrower on the loan, or ☐ the Borrower is relying on income from alimony, child support or separate maintenance or on the income or assets of another person as a basis for repayment of the loan, or ☐ the Borrower is married and resides, or the property is located, in a community property state.

Borrower				Co-Borrower			
Name		Age	School Yrs ___	Name		Age	School Yrs ___
Present Address	No. Years ___ ☐ Own ☐ Rent			Present Address	No. Years ___ ☐ Own ☐ Rent		
Street				Street			
City/State/Zip				City/State/Zip			
Former address if less than 2 years at present address				Former address if less than 2 years at present address			
Street				Street			
City/State/Zip				City/State/Zip			
Years at former address	☐ Own ☐ Rent			Years at former address	☐ Own ☐ Rent		
Marital Status ☐ Married ☐ Separated ☐ Unmarried (incl. single, divorced, widowed)	DEPENDENTS OTHER THAN LISTED BY CO-BORROWER NO. AGES			Marital Status ☐ Married ☐ Separated ☐ Unmarried (incl. single, divorced, widowed)	DEPENDENTS OTHER THAN LISTED BY BORROWER NO. AGES		
Name and Address of Employer	Years employed in this line of work or profession? ___ years			Name and Address of Employer	Years employed in this line of work or profession? ___ years		
	Years on this job ___ ☐ Self Employed*				Years on this job ___ ☐ Self Employed*		
Position/Title	Type of Business			Position/Title	Type of Business		
Social Security Number ***	Home Phone	Business Phone		Social Security Number ***	Home Phone	Business Phone	

Gross Monthly Income				Monthly Housing Expense**			Details of Purchase	
Item	Borrower	Co-Borrower	Total	Rent	$ PRESENT	PROPOSED	Do Not Complete If Refinance	
Base Empl. Income	$	$	$	First Mortgage (P&I)		$	a. Purchase Price	$
Overtime				Other Financing (P&I)			b. Total Closing Costs (Est.)	
Bonuses				Hazard Insurance			c. Prepaid Escrows (Est.)	
Commissions				Real Estate Taxes			d. Total (a + b + c)	$
Dividends/Interest				Mortgage Insurance			e. Amount This Mortgage	( )
Net Rental Income				Homeowner Assn. Dues			f. Other Financing	( )
Other† (Before completing, see notice under Describe Other Income below.)				Other:			g. Other Equity	( )
				Total Monthly Pmt.	$	$	h. Amount of Cash Deposit	( )
				Utilities			i. Closing Costs Paid by Seller	( )
Total	$	$	$	Total	$	$	j. Cash Reqd. For Closing (Est.)	$

Describe Other Income

	NOTICE:† Alimony, child support, or separate maintenance income need not be revealed if the Borrower or Co-Borrower does not choose to have it considered as a basis for repaying this loan.	Monthly Amount
▷ B—Borrower C—Co-Borrower		$

If Employed In Current Position For Less Than Two Years, Complete the Following

B/C	Previous Employer/School	City/State	Type of Business	Position/Title	Dates From/To	Monthly Income
						$

These Questions Apply To Both Borrower and Co-Borrower

If a "yes" answer is given to a question in this column, please explain on an attached sheet.

	Borrower Yes or No	Co-Borrower Yes or No		Borrower Yes or No	Co-Borrower Yes or No
Are there any outstanding judgments against you?	___	___			
Have you been declared bankrupt within the past 7 years?	___	___			
Have you had property foreclosed upon or given title or deed in lieu thereof in the last 7 years?	___	___	Are you a U.S. citizen?	___	___
Are you a party to a law suit?	___	___	If "no," are you a resident alien?	___	___
Are you obligated to pay alimony, child support, or separate maintenance?	___	___	If "no," are you a non-resident alien?	___	___
Is any part of the down payment borrowed?	___	___	Explain Other Financing or Other Equity (if any).		
Are you a co-maker or endorser on a note?	___	___			

*FHLMC/FNMA require business credit report, signed Federal Income Tax returns for last two years; and, if available, audited Profit and Loss Statement plus balance sheet for same period.
**All Present Monthly Housing Expenses of Borrower and Co-Borrower should be listed on a combined basis.
***Optional for FHLMC
FHLMC 65 Rev. 10/86

L 18–10/86

Fannie Mae Form 1003 Rev. 10/86

(continues)

Figure 7-8 Loan documentation: residential loan application.

This Statement and any applicable supporting schedules may be completed jointly by both married and unmarried co-borrowers if their assets and liabilities are sufficiently joined so that the Statement can be meaningfully and fairly presented on a combined basis; otherwise separate Statements and Schedules are required (FHLMC 65A/FNMA 1003A). If the co-borrower section was completed about a spouse, this statement and supporting schedules must be completed about that spouse also. ☐ Completed Jointly ☐ Not Completed Jointly

Assets		Liabilities and Pledged Assets				
		Indicate by (*) those liabilities or pledged assets which will be satisfied upon sale of real estate owned or upon refinancing of subject property				
Description	Cash or Market Value	Creditors' Name, Address and Account Number		Acct. Name If Not Borrower's	Mo. Pmt. and Mos. Left to Pay	Unpaid Balance
Cash Deposit Toward Purchase Held By	$	Installment Debts (Include "revolving" charge accounts)			$ Pmt./Mos.	$
		Co.	Acct. No.			
Checking and Savings Accounts (Show Names of Institutions (Account Numbers) Bank, S & L or Credit Union		Addr.				
		City			/	
		Co.	Acct. No.			
Addr.		Addr.				
City		City			/	
Acct. No.		Co.	Acct. No.			
Bank, S & L or Credit Union		Addr.				
		City				
Addr.		Co.	Acct. No.			
City		Addr.				
Acct. No.		City				
Bank, S & L or Credit Union		Co.	Acct. No.			
		Addr.				
Addr.		City			/	
City		Other Debts including Stock Pledges				
Acct. No.					/	
Stocks and Bonds (No./Description)						
		Real Estate Loans Co.	Acct. No.			
		Addr.				
		City				
Life Insurance Net Cash Value Face Amount $		Co.	Acct. No.			
		Addr.				
Subtotal Liquid Assets		City				
Real Estate Owned (Enter Market Value from Schedule of Real Estate Owned)		Automobile Loans Co.	Acct. No.			
Vested Interest in Retirement Fund		Addr.				
Net worth of Business Owned (ATTACH FINANCIAL STATEMENT)		City				
		Co.	Acct. No.			
Automobiles Owned (Make and Year)		City				
Furniture and Personal Property		Alimony/Child Support/Separate Maintenance Payments Owed to			/	
Other Assets (Itemize)						
		Total Monthly Payments			$	
Total Assets	A $	Net Worth (A minus B) $			Total Liabilities	B $

SCHEDULE OF REAL ESTATE OWNED (If Additional Properties Owned Attach Separate Schedule)

Address of Property (Indicate S if Sold, PS if Pending Sale or R if Rental being held for income)	Type of Property	Present Market Value	Amount of Mortgages & Liens	Gross Rental Income	Mortgage Payments	Taxes, Ins. Maintenance and Misc.	Net Rental Income
		$	$	$	$	$	$
TOTALS →		$	$	$	$	$	$

List Previous Credit References

B—Borrower C—Co-Borrower	Creditor's Name and Address	Account Number	Purpose	Highest Balance	Date Paid
				$	

List any additional names under which credit has previously been received _____

AGREEMENT: The undersigned applies for the loan indicated in this application to be secured by a first mortgage or deed of trust on the property described herein, and represents that the property will not be used for any illegal or restricted purpose, and that all statements made in this application are true and are made for the purpose of obtaining the loan. Verification may be obtained from any source named in this application. The original or a copy of this application will be retained by the lender, even if the loan is not granted. The undersigned ☐ intend or ☐ do not intend to occupy the property as their primary residence.

I/we fully understand that it is a federal crime punishable by fine or imprisonment, or both, to knowingly make any false statements concerning any of the above facts as applicable under the provisions of Title 18, United States Code, Section 1014.

_____ Date _____ Borrower's Signature   _____ Date _____ Co-Borrower's Signature

Information for Government Monitoring Purposes

The following information is requested by the Federal Government for certain types of loans related to a dwelling, in order to monitor the lender's compliance with equal credit opportunity and fair housing laws. You are not required to furnish this information, but are encouraged to do so. The law provides that a lender may neither discriminate on the basis of this information, nor on whether you choose to furnish it. However, if you choose not to furnish it, under Federal regulations this lender is required to note race and sex on the basis of visual observation or surname. If you do not wish to furnish the above information, please check the box below. (Lender must review the above material to assure that the disclosures satisfy all requirements to which the Lender is subject under applicable state law for the particular type of loan applied for.)

Borrower: ☐ I do not wish to furnish this information
Race/National Origin:
☐ American Indian, Alaskan Native ☐ Asian, Pacific Islander
☐ Black ☐ Hispanic ☐ White
☐ Other (specify):_____
Sex: ☐ Female ☐ Male

Co-Borrower: ☐ I do not wish to furnish this information
Race/National Origin:
☐ American Indian, Alaskan Native ☐ Asian, Pacific Islander
☐ Black ☐ Hispanic ☐ White
☐ Other (specify):_____
Sex: ☐ Female ☐ Male

To Be Completed by Interviewer

This application was taken by:
☐ face to face interview
☐ by mail
☐ by telephone

_____ Interviewer   _____ Name of Interviewer's Employer

_____ Interviewer's Phone Number   _____ Address of Interviewer's Employer

FHLMC Form 65 Rev. 10/86   REVERSE   Fannie Mae Form 1003 Rev. 10/86

Figure 7-8 Continued.

92

RESPA

Final Rules & Regulations

Real Estate Settlement Procedures Act as of May 1, 1996

PART 3500—APPENDIX C

Appendix C to Part 3500—Sample Form of Good Faith Estimate

[Name of Lender]\1\

The information provided below reflects estimates of the charges which you are likely to incur at the settlement of your loan. The fees listed are estimates—the actual charges may be more or less. Your transaction may not involve a fee for every item listed.

The numbers listed beside the estimates generally correspond to the numbered lines contained in the HUD - 1 or HUD - 1A settlement statement that you will be receiving at settlement. The HUD - 1 or HUD - 1A settlement statement will show you the actual costs for items paid at settlement.

Item\2\	HUD - 1 or HUD - 1A	Amount or range
Loan origination fee	801	$XXXX
Loan discount fee	802	$XXXX
Appraisal fee	803	$XXXX
Credit report	804	$XXXX
Inspection fee	805	$XXXX
Mortgage broker fee	[Use blank line in 800 Section]	$XXXX
CLO access fee	[Use blank line in 800 Section]	$XXXX
Tax related service fee	[Use blank line in 800 Section]	$XXXX
Interest for [X] days at $XXXX per day	901	$XXXX
Mortgage insurance premium	902	$XXXX
Hazard insurance premiums	903	$XXXX
Reserves	1000 - 1005	$XXXX
Settlement fee	1101	$XXXX
Abstract or title search	1102	$XXXX
Title examination	1103	$XXXX

(continues)

Figure 7-9   RESPA Final Rules and Regulations, pages 1–2, and RESPA HUD-1 form, pages 1–2.

Item\2\	HUD - 1 or HUD - 1A	Amount or range
Document preparation fee	1105	$XXXX
Attorney's fee	1107	$XXXX
Title insurance	1108	$XXXX
Recording fees	1201	$XXXX
City/County tax stamps	1202	$XXXX
State tax	1203	$XXXX
Survey	1301	$XXXX
Pest inspection	1302	$XXXX
[Other fees—list here]		$XXXX

Applicant

Date

Authorized Official

These estimates are provided pursuant to the Real Estate Settlement Procedures Act of 1974, as amended (RESPA). Additional information can be found in the HUD Special Information Booklet, which is to be provided to you by your mortgage broker or lender, if your application is to purchase residential real property and the Lender will take a first lien on the property.

Footnotes

\1\The name of the lender shall be placed at the top of the form. Additional information identifying the loan application and property may appear at the bottom of the form or on a separate page. Exception: If the disclosure is being made by a mortgage broker who is not an exclusive agent of the lender, the lender's name will not appear at the top of the form, but the following legend must appear:

This Good Faith Estimate is being provided by XXXXXXXX, a mortgage broker, and no lender has yet been obtained.

\2\Items for which there is estimated to be no charge to the borrower are not required to be listed. Any additional items for which there is estimated to be a charge to the borrower shall be listed if required on the HUD - 1.

[58 FR 17165, Apr. 1, 1993, as amended at 59 FR 6521, Feb. 10, 1994]

Date Modified 1/14/98

Figure 7-9   *Continued.*

A. Settlement Statement

U.S. Department of Housing and Urban Development

OMB Approval No. 2502-0265

B. Type of Loan

1. ☐ FHA	2. ☐ FmHA	3. ☐ Conv. Unins.	6. File Number:
4. ☐ VA	5. ☐ Conv. Ins.		7. Loan Number:

8. Mortgage Insurance Case Number:

C. Note: This form is furnished to give you a statement of actual settlement costs. Amounts paid to and by the settlement agent are shown. Items marked "(p.o.c.)" were paid outside the closing; they are shown here for informational purposes and are not included in the totals.

D. Name & Address of Borrower:	E. Name & Address of Seller:	F. Name & Address of Lender:

G. Property Location:	H. Settlement Agent:
	Place of Settlement:	I. Settlement Date:

J. Summary of Borrower's Transaction		K. Summary of Seller's Transaction	
100. Gross Amount Due From Borrower		**400. Gross Amount Due To Seller**	
101. Contract sales price		401. Contract sales price	
102. Personal property		402. Personal property	
103. Settlement charges to borrower (line 1400)		403.	
104.		404.	
105.		405.	
Adjustments for items paid by seller in advance		**Adjustments for items paid by seller in advance**	
106. City/town taxes to		406. City/town taxes to	
107. County taxes to		407. County taxes to	
108. Assessments to		408. Assessments to	
109.		409.	
110.		410.	
111.		411.	
112.		412.	
120. Gross Amount Due From Borrower		**420. Gross Amount Due To Seller**	
200. Amounts Paid By Or In Behalf Of Borrower		**500. Reductions In Amount Due To Seller**	
201. Deposit or earnest money		501. Excess deposit (see instructions)	
202. Principal amount of new loan(s) 502.		Settlement charges to seller (line 1400)	
203. Existing loan(s) taken subject to 503.		Existing loan(s) taken subject to	
204.		504. Payoff of first mortgage loan	
205.		505. Payoff of second mortgage loan	
206.		506.	
207.		507.	
208.		508.	
209.		509.	
Adjustments for items unpaid by seller		**Adjustments for items unpaid by seller**	
210. City/town taxes to		510. City/town taxes to	
211. County taxes to		511. County taxes to	
212. Assessments to		512. Assessments to	
213.		513.	
214.		514.	
215.		515.	
216.		516.	
217.		517.	
218.		518.	
219.		519.	
220. Total Paid By/For Borrower		**520. Total Reduction Amount Due Seller**	
300. Cash At Settlement From/To Borrower		**600. Cash At Settlement To/From Seller**	
301. Gross Amount due from borrower (line 120)		601. Gross amount due to seller (line 420)	
302. Less amounts paid by/for borrower (line 220)	( )	602. Less reductions in amt. due seller (line 520)	( )
303. Cash ☐ From ☐ To Borrower		603. Cash ☐ To ☐ From Seller	

Section 5 of the Real Estate Settlement Procedures Act (RESPA) requires the following: • HUD must develop a Special Information Booklet to help persons borrowing money to finance the purchase of residential real estate to better understand the nature and costs of real estate settlement services; • Each lender must provide the booklet to all applicants from whom it receives or for whom it prepares a written application to borrow money to finance the purchase of residential real estate; • Lenders must prepare and distribute with the Booklet a Good Faith Estimate of the settlement costs that the borrower is likely to incur in connection with the settlement. These disclosures are manadatory.

Section 4(a) of RESPA mandates that HUD develop and prescribe this standard form to be used at the time of loan settlement to provide full disclosure of all charges imposed upon the borrower and seller. These are third party disclosures that are designed to provide the borrower with pertinent information during the settlement process in order to be a better shopper.

The Public Reporting Burden for this collection of information is estimated to average one hour per response, including the time for reviewing instructions, searching existing data sources, gathering and maintaining the data needed, and completing and reviewing the collection of information.

This agency may not collect this information, and you are not required to complete this form, unless it displays a currently valid OMB control number. The information requested does not lend itself to confidentiality.

Previous editions are obsolete

form HUD-1 (3/86)
ref Handbook 4305.2

(continues)

Figure 7-9 *Continued.*

L. Settlement Charges

		Paid From Borrowers Funds at Settlement	Paid From Seller's Funds at Settlement
700. Total Sales/Broker's Commission based on price $ @ % =			
Division of Commission (line 700) as follows:			
701. $ to			
702. $ to			
703. Commission paid at Settlement			
704.			
800. Items Payable In Connection With Loan			
801. Loan Origination Fee %			
802. Loan Discount %			
803. Appraisal Fee to			
804. Credit Report to			
805. Lender's Inspection Fee			
806. Mortgage Insurance Application Fee to			
807. Assumption Fee			
808.			
809.			
810.			
811.			
900. Items Required By Lender To Be Paid In Advance			
901. Interest from to @$ /day			
902. Mortgage insurance Premium for months to			
903. Hazard Insurance Premium for years to			
904. years to			
905.			
1000. Reserves Deposited With Lender			
1001. Hazard insurance months@$ per month			
1002. Mortgage insurance months@$ per month			
1003. City property taxes months@$ per month			
1004. County property taxes months@$ per month			
1005. Annual assessments months@$ per month			
1006. months@$ per month			
1007. months@$ per month			
1008. months@$ per month			
1100. Title Charges			
1101. Settlement or closing fee to			
1102. Abstract or title search to			
1103. Title examination to			
1104. Title insurance binder to			
1105. Document preparation to			
1106. Notary fees to			
1107. Attorney's fees to			
(includes above items numbers:)			
1108. Title insurance to			
(includes above items numbers:)			
1109. Lender's coverage $			
1110. Owner's coverage $			
1111.			
1112.			
1113.			
1200. Government Recording and Transfer Charges			
1201. Recording fees: Deed $; Mortgage $; Releases $			
1202. City/county tax/stamps: Deed $; Mortgage $			
1203. State tax/stamps: Deed $; Mortgage $			
1204.			
1205.			
1300. Additional Settlement Charges			
1301. Survey to			
1302. Pest inspection to			
1303.			
1304.			
1305.			
1400. Total Settlement Charges (enter on lines 103, Section J and 502, Section K)			

Figure 7-9 *Continued.*

```
              ESTIMATED CLOSING CHARGES        DATE: _____ 19____

                                          BUYER              SELLER

Sale Price:                          $_____    $_____
    Less Mortgage                     _____     _____
    Less Deposit Paid on Amt.         _____     _____
    Other Credits                     _____     _____
    Balance Due                      $_____(1)$ $_____(1)
                                      _____     _____


Settlement Costs:
    Title Company Charges:

        Title Insurance              $_____    $_____
        Mechanics Leins Ins.          _____     _____
        Recording Deed, Mtg.          _____     _____
        Notary Fees                   _____     _____
        Title Search                  _____     _____
        Title Co. Dist. Fee           _____     _____
    Taxes:
        Transfer                      _____     _____
        Adjustment                    _____     _____
        Tax Certification             _____     _____
    Mortgage Company Charges:
        Appraisal & Credit Fees       _____     _____
        Escrow Taxes                  _____     _____
        Escrow Fire Insurance         _____     _____
        Solicitor's Fee               _____     _____
        Mortgage Int. in Advance      _____     _____
        VA-FHA Charges                _____     _____
        MGIC Premium                  _____     _____
        Mtg. Prepayment Penalty       _____     _____
        Mtg. Processing Fee           _____     _____
        Other Charges                 _____     _____
    Conveyancing:
        Mtg./Bond & Warrant           _____     _____
        Deed                          _____     _____
    Miscellaneous:
        Water & Sewer Adj.            _____     _____
        Fire Ins. Binder & Premium    _____     _____
        Sale Commission               _____     _____
        Certification Fees            _____     _____
        Survey                        _____     _____
        Others                        _____     _____

TOTAL SETTLEMENT CHARGES             $_____(2)      _____(2)


Additional cash to complete sale based    Estimated proceeds of
on settlement date of: _____        sale (1) less (2)
        (1) plus (2) $_____          $_____

Approximate monthly payments:              Mortgage Terms
    Principal & Interest  $_____     Amount $_____
    Estimated Taxes        _____     Years  _____
    Fire Insurance         _____     Interest_____%____
    M. I. P.               _____
Total                     $_____

Settlement will be held _____

BUYER bring $_____ to settlement in CASH, CERTIFIED CHECK or
CASHIER'S CHECK payable to order of _____

BUYERS:_____        SELLERS:_____
```

(continues)

Figure 7-10 Non-RESPA forms.

Figure 7-10 *Continued.*

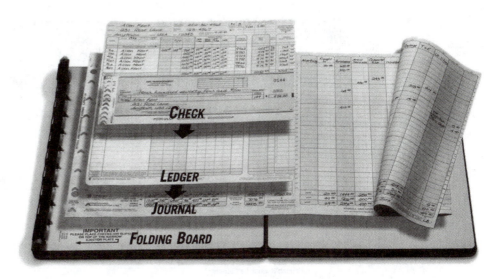

Figure 7-11   Safeguard one-write system.

One-Write Systems

ONE-WRITE SYSTEMS   A series of special journals characterized by multicarbon sets, which permit a single entry to record a general journal entry and a ledger entry

One-write systems, or pegboard systems, are a series of special journals. A special journal is one set up to save time in making repetitive entries. For example, each time cash is received from a client to be held in escrow, a recurring entry is made to cash and to a liability account in favor of the client. With a special journal sheet, the single amount can be entered. With a one-write system, a separate card can be maintained for each client that is placed over the special journal. With a carbon or specially coated paper, the entry can be made once on the client card and the journal sheet. The total of the journal sheet is the total cash in escrow for all clients and this same amount is the total liability to clients, while the individual amounts are shown on the individual client cards. Disbursements are recorded in the same manner with a cash disbursement journal sheet (Fig. 7-11).

Computerized Accounting Systems

Up to this point, we have been discussing manual accounting systems. With an understanding of the flow of information in the manual accounting system, some of the mystery of what occurs in the computer system is eliminated. There are a number of computer accounting packages available. Some, like Quicken (Fig. 7-12), are little more than electronic checkbooks. Others, including Quickbooks and Peachtree, are integrated accounting programs with many parts, called modules, for the different parts of the accounting recording process (e.g., accounts payable, accounts receivable, and payroll). Additional modules have been developed for specialized applications, such as the time records for service businesses, such as a law office, and escrow account maintenance for client funds.

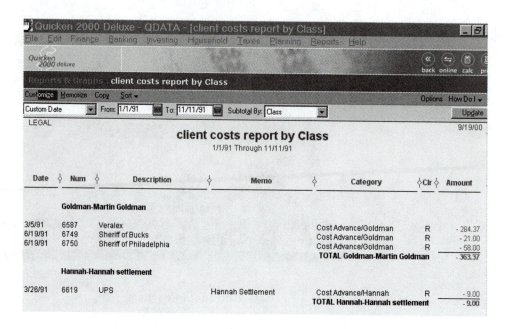

Figure 7-12   Quicken cost report screen.

The advantage of these types of systems is the ability to sort the information and provide useful reports for the specialized needs of the business. For the law office, this may include preparation of bills for clients, including chargeable time, and costs advanced and received. At the years' end, it allows for individual reports on revenue sorted by areas of practice, fee generation by lawyer, and expenses for use in preparing the firm tax return.

Service Bureaus

In larger firms, it is not unusual for the payroll function to be handled by an outside payroll processing company such as ADP. These firms maintain computer systems dedicated to the preparation of payroll checks, deposits of withholding taxes, and preparation of quarterly and annual filings, such as the W-2 form for employees. One of the advantages of the outside payroll firm is the ability to limit information on the earnings of partners, associates, and support staff from internal dissemination. The hours and rates are usually handled by a limited number of individuals, usually the senior or managing partner or a trusted member of the human resources department.

While not as prevalent today as in the past, some firms use outside service bureaus for the preparation of tax returns. With the increased power of the personal computer and the availability of quality tax preparation software at reasonable cost, more of this is handled in house. Among the most popular software systems is Turbotax. This program is updated annually for all of the federal income tax forms and is available with state tax return modules for most state income and fiduciary returns. An advantage to the use of these programs is the ability to carry over information from year to year, thereby avoiding repetitious reentry of basic information. With federal and state modules linked together, even the need to reenter information on state returns is eliminated. With the increased use of electronic filing, these programs also offer the ability to electronically file returns, without the need to generate paper copies.

Billing and Escrow Accounts

Billing is the most important function for a law firm. Without billings there is no revenue to pay expenses and provide the salaries. As important as it is, in many offices, billing is not treated with enough importance. Time records are the basis for most lawyers' billings. Without accurate time records billings cannot be made. The expense records are usually well maintained since a check will usually be written, which provides a record for billing purposes. But the time record must come from the recording of the time spent by the attorney or the paralegal. This information is usually maintained manually on time slips or time records (Fig. 7-13).

ACCOUNT NUMBER	NAME OF CLIENT	MON.	TUE.	WED.	THUR.	FRI.	SAT.	SUN.	TOTAL	AMOUNT
013582	Ethan Marshall	.3	5.0		2.1				7.4	
		HOURS WORKED								

DO NOT WRITE IN SHADED AREA BELOW

DATE	TIME START	TIME STOP	TIME ELAPSED	CODE	DESCRIPTION OF SERVICES PERFORMED
2/1/00	9:00	9:18	.3	V	Telephone call with client
2/2/00	9:00	12:00			
	1:00	3:00	5.0	R	Research in library
2/3/00	10:00	12:06	2.1	D	Dictate Memo of Law and opinion letter

CODE		NAME CLIENT → ← STAFF MEMB.	
	D. Thomas		Ethan Marshall

Figure 7-13 Time slip.

Client bills can be manually prepared from these records. More frequently, the client billing is prepared using a computer program (a popular example is Timeslip; Fig. 7-14). As with most of these programs, it allows the input of individual time records in a random order that can be automatically sorted by client and project. In addition to the time billing, it allows for the entry and inclusion in the final billing of the costs expended and costs and payments received from previous billing periods and retainers (Fig. 7-15).

Escrow accounting is documented in Figure 7-16. An individual card is maintained for each client and a master summary sheet of receipts and disbursements is kept as a combined record of all clients.

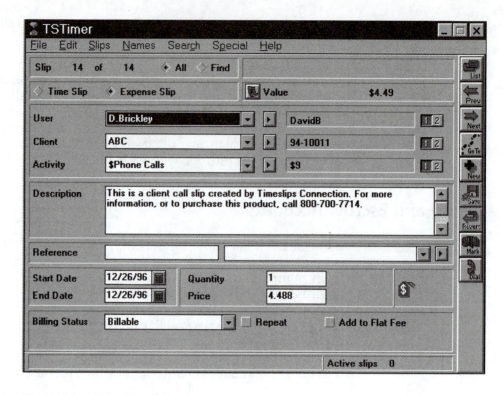

Figure 7-14 Timeslip entry screen.

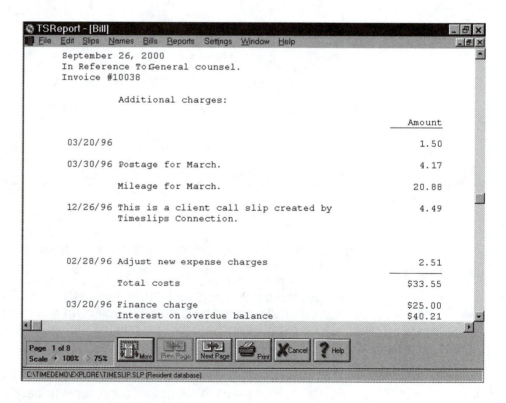

Figure 7-15 Output billing record.

Figure 7-16 Escrow disbursement sheet and client's card.

TRUST ACCOUNT DISBURSEMENTS JOURNAL

ALL ENTRIES IN COLUMN 1 SHOULD APPEAR IN BLUE.

	DATE	PAID TO	CHECK NO.	AMOUNT	2 (MEMO) BANK BALANCE	3 AMOUNT	DATE	CASE	DESCRIPTION
		BALANCE FORWARD →			26,052.10				
1	4/3	COUNTY COURT CLERK	3004	25.00		1		#1309 PAUL BRENT	TITLE SEARCH
2	4/3	COUNTY COURT CLERK	3005	8.50		2		#1621 ALANN ADAMS	FILING FEE
3	4/3	LAWYER'S SERVICE CO.	3006	12.00		3		#1618 LEE WEST	SERVICE PAPERS
4	4/3	CREST PHOTO SERVICE	3007 INV. NO. 2102	35.00		4		#1321 CHARLES SOLO	CAR PHOTOS
5	4/3	DAILY NEWSPAPER	3008 INV. NO. 18921	8.00		5		#1532 ADAM WISE	THIRD NOTICE
6	4/3	MR. + MRS. J. KLINE	3009	500.00		6		#1656 ROBERT LAKE	DOWN PAYMENT
7	4/3	SMITH, COLPITTS + KLINE	3010	100.00		7		#1624 WM. BARR	BROKER'S FEE
8	4/3	J.W. ADOCK (COUNTY CLERK)	3011	35.00	25308.60	8 8,075.00	4/3	#1836 FRANK HILL	SETTLEMENT FEE
								DEXTER BEAN	DONATION
								CARL WADE	PROPERTY DAMAGE PHOTOS
								MARTIN JONES	HOMEOWNERS POLICY
								RAYMOND BROWN	GOVERNMENT SAVINGS BOND
								LEO ANDREWS	PROPERTY TAX
								RONALD CLARK	RECALL OF DEBTS
								DAVID CARSON	TAX ON STOCKS (PERSONAL)
								JOHN ADAMS	FEE
								JOHN ADAMS	FINAL SETTLEMENT
								LEWIS AIKEN	COST / FEE
								LEWIS AIKEN	FINAL SETTLEMENT
								VINCENT MATTHEWS	COST / FEE
								VINCENT MATTHEWS	FINAL SETTLEMENT

MONTH OF _____ 19___ PAGE NO. ___ BY ___

Copyright Safeguard Business Systems, Inc. 1977

CLIENTS LEDGER

VINCENT MATTHEWS VS.
ALL COVERAGE INS. CO.
J. HENSEL #1901

DATE	NAME	CK.-REC. OR CASE NO.	COSTS ADVANCED	COSTS RECEIVED	TRUST FUNDS RECEIVED	TRUST FUNDS DISBURSED	FEES CHARGED	FEES RECEIVED	BAL. COSTS	BAL. TRUST	BAL. FEES
2/4	VINCENT MATTHEWS	#1901			50.00						
2/5	COUNTY COURT CLERK	#2410				8.50					
2/18	CREST PHOTO SERVICE	#2501				40.00				1.50	-0-
4/3	CITY BANK + TRUST CO.	#2099	785.00								
4/3	CITY HOSPITAL	#3000	35.00								
4/4	ALL COVERAGE INS. CO.	#1701			10,000.00		2500.00		20.00	0,001.50	2500.00
4/4	HENSEL, BERRY + MOORE	#3023				3320.00			-0-	6,681.50	
4/4	VINCENT MATTHEWS - TRANSFER	#1701		820.00				2500.00	-0-		
4/4	VINCENT MATTHEWS - SETTLEMENT					250.00				-0-	-0-

SAFEGUARD BUSINESS SYSTEMS
FORM NO. CL-3S WP

Ethical Issue

> **ABA Model Code:**
>
> DR2-106 Fees for Legal Services
>
> (A) A lawyer shall not enter into an agreement for, charge, or collect an illegal or clearly excessive fee.

> In the absence of time records, how can the attorney defend a fee as not being clearly excessive?

CHAPTER SUMMARY

Many of the basic accounting functions can be used to complete other tasks within the law office. The organized, systematic methods for gathering necessary information and preparing worksheets can be used in preparing client bills, real estate settlement sheets, client disbursement sheets, and escrow reconciliation. The most common calculation used is the proration calculation. With a basic understanding of how to prorate amounts, allocations can be made between buyers and sellers and between amounts charged to clients, and adjustments and charges can be made for interest.

GLOSSARY

Checking account reconciliation   Comparing the bank records with the business records and identifying the differences caused by unrecorded checks and deposits and mechanical errors

Contingent fee   A fee system based on a percentage of the amount collected on behalf of a client, usually as a result of litigation

Hourly rate   A fee system based upon a charge for each hour of service performed

One-write systems   A series of special journals characterized by multicarbon sets, which permit a single entry to record a general journal entry and a ledger entry

Proration   The process of allocating amounts between different entities or accounting cycles

REVIEW QUESTIONS

1. What is the basic formula for determining interest?
2. Why should checking accounts be reconciled promptly upon receipt of the bank statement?
3. On whom is the burden for verification of a forged signature?
4. How is a personal financial statement like a business's balance sheet?
5. What is a typical proration in a real estate settlement?
6. What is the purpose of a special journal?
7. How is the real estate settlement sheet like a trial balance?
8. What is the purpose of the checking account reconciliation?
9. What are the most common errors leading to a difference between the bank balance and the company balance?
10. Which takes precedence on a check, words or figures?

Chapter 8

Payroll Accounting

In This Chapter

Why Study Payroll Accounting?

Even in the smallest law office with only a part-time employee, the payroll must be calculated. Compensation must be calculated based on the rate of pay, withholding taxes computed, and payroll taxes reported and paid to the appropriate federal, state, and local government tax agencies. In the larger offices, this may require the calculation of payrolls for full-time employees, including salaried and hourly employees and part-time and seasonal labor brought in for special projects, such as during tax season or during a major trial.

In addition to the traditional payroll tax obligations are the requirements for pre-employment verification of immigration status and the continuing obligations imposed under the Fair Labor Standards Act and state and local minimum age regulations.

An understanding of how payroll information is assembled, processed, and presented to the employee and the tax agencies is also invaluable in a family law practice. One of the major issues in a family law practice is determining appropriate support payments and sources of income and support. Since these payments are based on income, it is helpful to know how to re-create the information from missing or sketchy documentation.

Federal, State, and Local Laws Affecting Employment

Federal and state laws and regulations must be complied with in the hiring process and during the period of employment. These laws determine who may be hired, rates of pay, total hours worked, deductions withheld, and reports that must be filed. Legislation and administrative regulations limit the hiring of foreign workers, either because of illegal entry status or limitations imposed at the time the U.S. entry visa was granted.

Workers' protection legislation sets minimum ages for employment and limits the nature of the employment, particularly for under-age workers in what are determined to be hazardous occupations. In some cases, employment requires the minor to obtain working papers from the state before commencing employment. An additional protection for the covered employee is the obligation of the employer to pay overtime rates for hours worked beyond a maximum number of hours per day or pay period.

Initial Hiring Issues

Under the Immigration Reform and Control Act, a federal law designed to prevent the hiring of aliens unauthorized to work, all employees at the time of hiring must complete the U.S. Department of Justice, Immigration, and Naturalization Service, Employment Eligibility Verification form I-9. The employer is also required to review copies of documentation provided by the prospective employee to verify identity and employment eligibility. The employer must retain copies of the I-9 (Fig. 8-1) form after hiring or for one year after termination.

Fair Labor Standards Act

FLSA: The Federal Labor Standards Act legislation that mandates minimum standards for hours and working conditions

The **Fair Labor Standards Act** (FLSA), also known as the Wage and Hour Law, and state law equivalents, establish minimum hourly rates of pay and set maximum numbers of hours that may be worked before overtime rates must be paid. Typically, employees must be paid time and a half the normal hourly wages for hours worked in excess of 40 hours per week. Some states impose higher minimum rates of pay than the federal mandate. In these cases, the employee is paid the higher of the two minimums.

Employers must maintain adequate records for government inspection to verify the actual hours worked by both hourly and salaried employees. These records are subject to audit and review by the wage and hour administrators in cases of employee complaint or routine audit.

Frequency of Payment

The frequency of payment is also a matter of federal and state law. Generally, hourly employees must be paid at least twice a month and salaried employees at least once a month. The most common pay schedule is the weekly schedule of 52 pay days. Many employers use a twice-a-month pays period. Payroll is made with payment on the first and the fifteenth of

U.S. Department of Justice
Immigration and Naturalization Service

OMB No. 1115-0136

Employment Eligibility Verification

Please read instructions carefully before completing this form. The instructions must be available during completion of this form. ANTI-DISCRIMINATION NOTICE: It is illegal to discriminate against work eligible individuals. Employers CANNOT specify which document(s) they will accept from an employee. The refusal to hire an individual because of a future expiration date may also constitute illegal discrimination.

Section 1. Employee Information and Verification To be completed and signed by employee at the time employment begins.

Print Name: Last	First	Middle Initial	Maiden Name

Address (Street Name and Number)	Apt. #	Date of Birth (month/day/year)

City	State	Zip Code	Social Security #

I am aware that federal law provides for imprisonment and/or fines for false statements or use of false documents in connection with the completion of this form.

I attest, under penalty of perjury, that I am (check one of the following):
☐ A citizen or national of the United States
☐ A Lawful Permanent Resident (Alien # A _____)
☐ An alien authorized to work until ___/___/___
(Alien # or Admission #) _____

Employee's Signature   Date (month/day/year)

Preparer and/or Translator Certification. (To be completed and signed if Section 1 is prepared by a person other than the employee.) I attest, under penalty of perjury, that I have assisted in the completion of this form and that to the best of my knowledge the information is true and correct.

Preparer's/Translator's Signature   Print Name

Address (Street Name and Number, City, State, Zip Code)   Date (month/day/year)

Section 2. Employer Review and Verification. To be completed and signed by employer. Examine one document from List A OR examine one document from List B and one from List C, as listed on the reverse of this form, and record the title, number and expiration date, if any, of the document(s)

List A	OR	List B	AND	List C
Document title: _____		_____		_____
Issuing authority: _____		_____		_____
Document #: _____		_____		_____
Expiration Date (if any): ___/___/___	___/___/___		___/___/___	
Document #: _____				
Expiration Date (if any): ___/___/___				

CERTIFICATION - I attest, under penalty of perjury, that I have examined the document(s) presented by the above-named employee, that the above-listed document(s) appear to be genuine and to relate to the employee named, that the employee began employment on (month/day/year) ___/___/___ and that to the best of my knowledge the employee is eligible to work in the United States. (State employment agencies may omit the date the employee began employment.)

Signature of Employer or Authorized Representative	Print Name	Title

Business or Organization Name	Address (Street Name and Number, City, State, Zip Code)	Date (month/day/year)

Section 3. Updating and Reverification To be completed and signed by employer.

A. New Name (if applicable)	B. Date of rehire (month/day/year) (if applicable)

C. If employee's previous grant of work authorization has expired, provide the information below for the document that establishes current employment eligibility.

Document Title: _____   Document #: _____   Expiration Date (if any): ___/___/___

I attest, under penalty of perjury, that to the best of my knowledge, this employee is eligible to work in the United States, and if the employee presented document(s), the document(s) I have examined appear to be genuine and to relate to the individual.

Signature of Employer or Authorized Representative	Date (month/day/year)

Form I-9 (Rev. 11-21-91)N Page 2

Figure 8-1   Immigration and Naturalization Service (INS) form I-9, page 2.

the month for a total of 24 pay periods. Some employers pay every two weeks but on the same day of the week, such as Friday, for a total of 26 pay days. The annual salary remains the same in all cases.

Payroll Taxes

WITHHOLDING: The amount required by law or voluntary agreement with the employer to be withheld from an employee's wages

Federal, state, and local laws require the withholding and payment of taxes based on employment. Employers are required to act as the agent of the government in **withholding** from the employees' pay income taxes for the federal, state, city, and local governments. These may be income taxes that are based on a flat rate, such as a flat percentage of gross; a graduated scale, such as the federal system; or an annual amount, such as a head or privilege tax. The employer is required to withhold these amounts from the employee's earnings. These withheld funds do not and should never be treated as belonging to the employer; they are held in trust for the government. The employer is merely acting as a collection agent. The amounts withheld must be deposited with the appropriate agencies in a timely fashion to avoid imposition of penalties and interest. The rules for frequency of deposit vary depending upon the amounts collected and the agencies to which they are paid. As a general rule, all amounts must be paid at least quarterly with the filing of the quarterly employment tax returns, such as the federal form 941, or in the case of some local taxes, with an annual accounting. Employers are also required to submit an annual record to the employee with a W-2 form.

Taxes on Employees

PAY AS YOU GO: A tax system that provides for the periodic payments of taxes by employer withholding or periodic payments, usually quarterly

EXEMPTION: An amount permitted to be deducted for the taxpayer, his or her spouse, and other dependents in calculating taxable income

The concept of employee withholding is based on a **pay-as-you-go** method. Estimated taxes based on the level of income are withheld in amounts that approximate the amount the employee will owe at the end of the year. For the federal government, as well as some states, the amount of tax withheld depends on the amount of total earnings and the number of **exemptions** claimed.

For example, in the federal system, employees are entitled to one exemption for themselves plus one exemption for each dependent claimed on the tax return. The employer authorization for the number of exemptions to be used in calculating the withholding is the Internal Revenue Service form W-4, Employee's Withholding Allowance Certificate (Fig. 8-2).

The federal withholding amounts are calculated using the tables and rates in the **Circular E**, Employer's Tax Guide (Fig. 8-3), income tax withholding tables (Fig. 8-4), and Social Security and Medicare tax rate information (Fig. 8-5).

CIRCULAR E: An Internal Revenue Service publication providing the necessary withholding tables and information required by employers in preparing payroll

While many states and local governments impose flat percentage rates on employee wages, a number of states use a set of withholding tables similar to the federal withholding table and these should be consulted in preparing the payroll.

Form W-4 (2000)

Purpose. Complete Form W-4 so your employer can withhold the correct Federal income tax from your pay. Because your tax situation may change, you may want to refigure your withholding each year.

Exemption from withholding. If you are exempt, complete only lines 1, 2, 3, 4, and 7, and sign the form to validate it. Your exemption for 2000 expires February 16, 2001.

Note: *You cannot claim exemption from withholding if (1) your income exceeds $700 and includes more than $250 of unearned income (e.g., interest and dividends) and (2) another person can claim you as a dependent on their tax return.*

Basic instructions. If you are not exempt, complete the **Personal Allowances Worksheet** below. The worksheets on page 2 adjust your withholding allowances based on itemized deductions, adjustments to income, or two-earner/two-job situations. Complete all worksheets that apply. They will help you figure the number of withholding allowances you are entitled to claim. **However, you may claim fewer (or zero) allowances.**

Child tax and higher education credits. For details on adjusting withholding for these and other credits, see **Pub. 919,** How Do I Adjust My Tax Withholding?

Head of household. Generally, you may claim head of household filing status on your tax return only if you are unmarried and pay more than 50% of the costs of keeping up a home for yourself and your dependent(s) or other qualifying individuals. See line **E** below.

Nonwage income. If you have a large amount of nonwage income, such as interest or dividends, you should consider making estimated tax payments using **Form 1040-ES,** Estimated Tax for Individuals. Otherwise, you may owe additional tax.

Two earners/two jobs. If you have a working spouse or more than one job, figure the total number of allowances you are entitled to claim on all jobs using worksheets from only one Form W-4. Your withholding usually will be most accurate when all allowances are claimed on the Form W-4 prepared for the highest paying job and zero allowances are claimed for the others.

Check your withholding. After your Form W-4 takes effect, use Pub. 919 to see how the dollar amount you are having withheld compares to your projected total tax for 2000. Get Pub. 919 especially if you used the **Two-Earner/Two-Job Worksheet** on page 2 and your earnings exceed $150,000 (Single) or $200,000 (Married).

Recent name change? If your name on line 1 differs from that shown on your social security card, call 1-800-772-1213 for a new social security card.

Personal Allowances Worksheet (Keep for your records.)

A Enter "1" for **yourself** if no one else can claim you as a dependent . . . . **A** ____

B Enter "1" if:
- You are single and have only one job; or
- You are married, have only one job, and your spouse does not work; or
- Your wages from a second job or your spouse's wages (or the total of both) are $1,000 or less.

. . **B** ____

C Enter "1" for your **spouse.** But, you may choose to enter -0- if you are married and have either a working spouse or more than one job. (Entering -0- may help you avoid having too little tax withheld.) . . . . **C** ____

D Enter number of **dependents** (other than your spouse or yourself) you will claim on your tax return . . . . **D** ____

E Enter "1" if you will file as **head of household** on your tax return (see conditions under **Head of household** above) **E** ____

F Enter "1" if you have at least $1,500 of **child or dependent care expenses** for which you plan to claim a credit . . **F** ____

G **Child Tax Credit:**
- If your total income will be between $18,000 and $50,000 ($23,000 and $63,000 if married), enter "1" for each eligible child.
- If your total income will be between $50,000 and $80,000 ($63,000 and $115,000 if married), enter "1" if you have two eligible children, enter "2" if you have three or four eligible children, or enter "3" if you have five or more eligible children **G** ____

H Add lines A through G and enter total here. **Note:** *This may be different from the number of exemptions you claim on your tax return.* ► **H** ____

For accuracy, complete all worksheets that apply.
- If you plan to **itemize or claim adjustments to income** and want to reduce your withholding, see the **Deductions and Adjustments Worksheet** on page 2.
- If you are **single,** have **more than one job** and your combined earnings from all jobs exceed $34,000, OR if you are **married** and have a **working spouse or more than one job** and the combined earnings from all jobs exceed $60,000, see the **Two-Earner/Two-Job Worksheet** on page 2 to avoid having too little tax withheld.
- If **neither** of the above situations applies, **stop here** and enter the number from line H on line 5 of Form W-4 below.

Cut here and give Form W-4 to your employer. Keep the top part for your records.

Form W-4
Department of the Treasury
Internal Revenue Service

Employee's Withholding Allowance Certificate
► For Privacy Act and Paperwork Reduction Act Notice, see page 2.

OMB No. 1545-0010

2000

1 Type or print your first name and middle initial   Last name

2 Your social security number

Home address (number and street or rural route)

3 ☐ Single ☐ Married ☐ Married, but withhold at higher Single rate.
Note: If married, but legally separated, or spouse is a nonresident alien, check the Single box.

City or town, state, and ZIP code

4 If your last name differs from that on your social security card, check here. **You must call 1-800-772-1213 for a new card** . . . ► ☐

5 Total number of allowances you are claiming (from line **H** above **OR** from the applicable worksheet on page 2) **5** ____

6 Additional amount, if any, you want withheld from each paycheck . . . . **6** $ ____

7 I claim exemption from withholding for 2000, and I certify that I meet **BOTH** of the following conditions for exemption:
- Last year I had a right to a refund of **ALL** Federal income tax withheld because I had **NO** tax liability **AND**
- This year I expect a refund of **ALL** Federal income tax withheld because I expect to have **NO** tax liability.

If you meet both conditions, write "EXEMPT" here . . . . ► **7** ____

Under penalties of perjury, I certify that I am entitled to the number of withholding allowances claimed on this certificate, or I am entitled to claim exempt status.

Employee's signature
(Form is not valid unless you sign it) ►

Date ►

8 Employer's name and address (Employer: Complete lines 8 and 10 only if sending to the IRS.)

9 Office code (optional)

10 Employer identification number

Cat. No. 10220Q

Figure 8-2 Form W-4, Employee's Withholding Allowance Certificate.

2000 Tax Table

Use if your taxable income is less than $100,000.
If $100,000 or more, use the Tax Rate Schedules.

Example. Mr. and Mrs. Brown are filing a joint return. Their taxable income on line 39 of Form 1040 is $25,300. First, they find the $25,300–25,350 income line. Next, they find the column for married filing jointly and read down the column. The amount shown where the income line and filing status column meet is $3,799. This is the tax amount they should enter on line 40 of their Form 1040.

Sample Table

At least	But less than	Single	Married filing jointly *	Married filing separately	Head of a household
			Your tax is—		
25,200	25,250	3,784	3,784	4,213	3,784
25,250	25,300	3,791	3,791	4,227	3,791
25,300	25,350	3,799	3,799	4,241	3,799
25,350	25,400	3,806	3,806	4,255	3,806

If line 39 (taxable income) is— At least	But less than	Single	Married filing jointly *	Married filing separately	Head of a household
			Your tax is—		
0	5	0	0	0	0
5	15	2	2	2	2
15	25	3	3	3	3
25	50	6	6	6	6
50	75	9	9	9	9
75	100	13	13	13	13
100	125	17	17	17	17
125	150	21	21	21	21
150	175	24	24	24	24
175	200	28	28	28	28
200	225	32	32	32	32
225	250	36	36	36	36
250	275	39	39	39	39
275	300	43	43	43	43
300	325	47	47	47	47
325	350	51	51	51	51
350	375	54	54	54	54
375	400	58	58	58	58
400	425	62	62	62	62
425	450	66	66	66	66
450	475	69	69	69	69
475	500	73	73	73	73
500	525	77	77	77	77
525	550	81	81	81	81
550	575	84	84	84	84
575	600	88	88	88	88
600	625	92	92	92	92
625	650	96	96	96	96
650	675	99	99	99	99
675	700	103	103	103	103
700	725	107	107	107	107
725	750	111	111	111	111
750	775	114	114	114	114
775	800	118	118	118	118
800	825	122	122	122	122
825	850	126	126	126	126
850	875	129	129	129	129
875	900	133	133	133	133
900	925	137	137	137	137
925	950	141	141	141	141
950	975	144	144	144	144
975	1,000	148	148	148	148

1,000

At least	But less than	Single	Married filing jointly *	Married filing separately	Head of a household
1,000	1,025	152	152	152	152
1,025	1,050	156	156	156	156
1,050	1,075	159	159	159	159
1,075	1,100	163	163	163	163
1,100	1,125	167	167	167	167
1,125	1,150	171	171	171	171
1,150	1,175	174	174	174	174
1,175	1,200	178	178	178	178
1,200	1,225	182	182	182	182
1,225	1,250	186	186	186	186
1,250	1,275	189	189	189	189
1,275	1,300	193	193	193	193

At least	But less than	Single	Married filing jointly *	Married filing separately	Head of a household
1,300	1,325	197	197	197	197
1,325	1,350	201	201	201	201
1,350	1,375	204	204	204	204
1,375	1,400	208	208	208	208
1,400	1,425	212	212	212	212
1,425	1,450	216	216	216	216
1,450	1,475	219	219	219	219
1,475	1,500	223	223	223	223
1,500	1,525	227	227	227	227
1,525	1,550	231	231	231	231
1,550	1,575	234	234	234	234
1,575	1,600	238	238	238	238
1,600	1,625	242	242	242	242
1,625	1,650	246	246	246	246
1,650	1,675	249	249	249	249
1,675	1,700	253	253	253	253
1,700	1,725	257	257	257	257
1,725	1,750	261	261	261	261
1,750	1,775	264	264	264	264
1,775	1,800	268	268	268	268
1,800	1,825	272	272	272	272
1,825	1,850	276	276	276	276
1,850	1,875	279	279	279	279
1,875	1,900	283	283	283	283
1,900	1,925	287	287	287	287
1,925	1,950	291	291	291	291
1,950	1,975	294	294	294	294
1,975	2,000	298	298	298	298

2,000

At least	But less than	Single	Married filing jointly *	Married filing separately	Head of a household
2,000	2,025	302	302	302	302
2,025	2,050	306	306	306	306
2,050	2,075	309	309	309	309
2,075	2,100	313	313	313	313
2,100	2,125	317	317	317	317
2,125	2,150	321	321	321	321
2,150	2,175	324	324	324	324
2,175	2,200	328	328	328	328
2,200	2,225	332	332	332	332
2,225	2,250	336	336	336	336
2,250	2,275	339	339	339	339
2,275	2,300	343	343	343	343
2,300	2,325	347	347	347	347
2,325	2,350	351	351	351	351
2,350	2,375	354	354	354	354
2,375	2,400	358	358	358	358
2,400	2,425	362	362	362	362
2,425	2,450	366	366	366	366
2,450	2,475	369	369	369	369
2,475	2,500	373	373	373	373
2,500	2,525	377	377	377	377
2,525	2,550	381	381	381	381
2,550	2,575	384	384	384	384
2,575	2,600	388	388	388	388
2,600	2,625	392	392	392	392
2,625	2,650	396	396	396	396
2,650	2,675	399	399	399	399
2,675	2,700	403	403	403	403

At least	But less than	Single	Married filing jointly *	Married filing separately	Head of a household
2,700	2,725	407	407	407	407
2,725	2,750	411	411	411	411
2,750	2,775	414	414	414	414
2,775	2,800	418	418	418	418
2,800	2,825	422	422	422	422
2,825	2,850	426	426	426	426
2,850	2,875	429	429	429	429
2,875	2,900	433	433	433	433
2,900	2,925	437	437	437	437
2,925	2,950	441	441	441	441
2,950	2,975	444	444	444	444
2,975	3,000	448	448	448	448

3,000

At least	But less than	Single	Married filing jointly *	Married filing separately	Head of a household
3,000	3,050	454	454	454	454
3,050	3,100	461	461	461	461
3,100	3,150	469	469	469	469
3,150	3,200	476	476	476	476
3,200	3,250	484	484	484	484
3,250	3,300	491	491	491	491
3,300	3,350	499	499	499	499
3,350	3,400	506	506	506	506
3,400	3,450	514	514	514	514
3,450	3,500	521	521	521	521
3,500	3,550	529	529	529	529
3,550	3,600	536	536	536	536
3,600	3,650	544	544	544	544
3,650	3,700	551	551	551	551
3,700	3,750	559	559	559	559
3,750	3,800	566	566	566	566
3,800	3,850	574	574	574	574
3,850	3,900	581	581	581	581
3,900	3,950	589	589	589	589
3,950	4,000	596	596	596	596

4,000

At least	But less than	Single	Married filing jointly *	Married filing separately	Head of a household
4,000	4,050	604	604	604	604
4,050	4,100	611	611	611	611
4,100	4,150	619	619	619	619
4,150	4,200	626	626	626	626
4,200	4,250	634	634	634	634
4,250	4,300	641	641	641	641
4,300	4,350	649	649	649	649
4,350	4,400	656	656	656	656
4,400	4,450	664	664	664	664
4,450	4,500	671	671	671	671
4,500	4,550	679	679	679	679
4,550	4,600	686	686	686	686
4,600	4,650	694	694	694	694
4,650	4,700	701	701	701	701
4,700	4,750	709	709	709	709
4,750	4,800	716	716	716	716
4,800	4,850	724	724	724	724
4,850	4,900	731	731	731	731
4,900	4,950	739	739	739	739
4,950	5,000	746	746	746	746

(Continued on page 60)

* This column must also be used by a qualifying widow(er).

-59-

Figure 8-3   Withholding tax table.

2000 Tax Rate Schedules

 CAUTION

Use **only** if your taxable income (Form 1040, line 39) is $100,000 or more. If less, use the **Tax Table.** Even though you cannot use the Tax Rate Schedules below if your taxable income is less than $100,000, all levels of taxable income are shown so taxpayers can see the tax rate that applies to each level.

Schedule X—Use if your filing status is **Single**

If the amount on Form 1040, line 39, is: Over---	But not over---	Enter on Form 1040, line 40	of the amount over---
$0	$26,250	.... 15%	$0
26,250	63,550	$3,937.50 + 28%	26,250
63,550	132,600	14,381.50 + 31%	63,550
132,600	288,350	35,787.00 + 36%	132,600
288,350	....	91,857.00 + 39.6%	288,350

Schedule Y-1—Use if your filing status is **Married filing jointly** or **Qualifying widow(er)**

If the amount on Form 1040, line 39, is: Over—	But not over—	Enter on Form 1040, line 40	of the amount over—
$0	$43,850	.... 15%	$0
43,850	105,950	$6,577.50 + 28%	43,850
105,950	161,450	23,965.50 + 31%	105,950
161,450	288,350	41,170.50 + 36%	161,450
288,350	....	86,854.50 + 39.6%	288,350

Schedule Y-2—Use if your filing status is **Married filing separately**

If the amount on Form 1040, line 39, is: Over---	But not over---	Enter on Form 1040, line 40	of the amount over---
$0	$21,925	.... 15%	$0
21,925	52,975	$3,288.75 + 28%	21,925
52,975	80,725	11,982.75 + 31%	52,975
80,725	144,175	20,585.25 + 36%	80,725
144,175	....	43,427.25 + 39.6%	144,175

Schedule Z—Use if your filing status is **Head of household**

If the amount on Form 1040, line 39, is: Over---	But not over—	Enter on Form 1040, line 40	of the amount over---
$0	$35,150	.... 15%	$0
35,150	90,800	$5,272.50 + 28%	35,150
90,800	147,050	20,854.50 + 31%	90,800
147,050	288,350	38,292.00 + 36%	147,050
288,350	....	89,160.00 + 39.6%	288,350

-71-

Figure 8-4   Withholding tax schedule.

Important Reminders

Employment Tax Rates and Wage Bases for 2001

1. Social Security Tax:
   a. Tax Rate—6.2% each for employers and employees
   b. Wage Base—$80,400

2. Medicare Tax:
   a. Tax Rate—1.45% each for employers and employees
   b. All wages subject to Medicare tax

3. Federal Unemployment (FUTA) Tax:
   a. Tax Rate—6.2% before state credits (employers only)
   b. Wage base—$7,000

Figure 8-5   Social Security and Medicare rates.

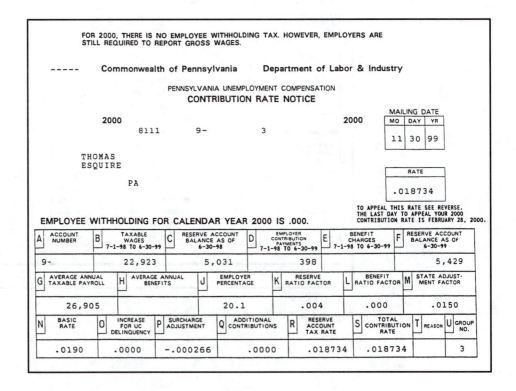

Figure 8-6   Experience rating form for unemployment tax (FUTA).

Taxes on Employers

FICA: The Federal Insurance Contribution Act, which establishes the contributions required for Social Security

EXPERIENCE RATING: The rate of tax assessed against a business for unemployment compensation purposes, based on the number of claims of former employees

Employers are required to make contributions towards Social Security, Medicare, and unemployment taxes based on their employees' earnings. Social Security, Medicare, and federal and state unemployment taxes are based on employees' wages subject to limits on gross wages within one year. Like the employee withholdings, these contributions are also required to be deposited periodically and reported quarterly and annually.

The employer's portion of the Social Security tax **(FICA)** and Medicare tax is equal to the employee's share. Unemployment taxes vary according to state law and are generally based on a sliding scale that makes allowance for low turnover or claims by employees for unemployment insurance benefits by reducing the percentage based on this **experience rating**. The percentage to be paid can be found on the report submitted by the state to the employer on the experience-rating report form (Fig. 8-6). The actual amount of the federal unemployment tax (FUTA) is calculated annually with a credit for state taxes paid (Fig. 8-7).

Figure 8-8 is typical of the forms used to prepare payroll. Step-by-step instructions are keyed to the individual items in the form.

Other Withholding Amounts

Employees may require or request that additional amounts be deducted from their salary or wages and be paid to third parties. These deductions include voluntary savings in the form of tax-deferred retirement accounts or payroll purchase of savings bonds. Employers may also be required to withhold amounts for employees under court-ordered withholding for child support.

One of the most common tax-deferred plans is the retirement plan contribution known as the 401(k) plan. The federal government allows a pretax contribution to an employee's tax-deferred retirement plan. An individual's tax obligation is calculated after deducting the amount of the 401(k) contribution. The 401(k) plan must be initiated by the employer and approved by the Internal Revenue Service. Generally, for the year 2001, the maximum contribution is $10,500. The employer may contribute to the plan on behalf of the employee, but such contribution is not required. The funds deducted from the employee's salary and any funds added by the employer are paid to a plan administrator or trustee.

Employers are being required more and more frequently to withhold and pay directly to the court amounts for child support. In most cases, the employer receives a court order specifying the amount to be withheld and paid to the domestic relations office of the court. Employees may also voluntarily request that the employer withhold and pay the amount to the court as a convenience. These amounts do not affect the normal tax calculation; they are after-tax deductions—unlike the tax-deferred savings plan—that are deducted just before the tax calculation.

Form **940**

Department of the Treasury
Internal Revenue Service (99)

Employer's Annual Federal Unemployment (FUTA) Tax Return

▶ **See separate Instructions for Form 940 for information on completing this form.**

OMB No. 1545-0028

2000

T
FF
FD
FP
I
T

Name (as distinguished from trade name) — Calendar year

Trade name, if any

Address and ZIP code — Employer identification number

A	Are you required to pay unemployment contributions to only one state? (If No, skip questions B and C.)	☐ **Yes** ☐ **No**
B	Did you pay all state unemployment contributions by January 31, 2001? ((1) If you deposited your total FUTA tax when due, check Yes if you paid all state unemployment contributions by February 12, 2001. (2) If a 0% experience rate is granted, check Yes. (3) If No, skip question C.)	☐ **Yes** ☐ **No**
C	Were all wages that were taxable for FUTA tax also taxable for your state s unemployment tax?	☐ **Yes** ☐ **No**

If you answered No to any of these questions, you must file Form 940. If you answered Yes to all the questions, you may file Form 940-EZ, which is a simplified version of Form 940. (Successor employers see **Special credit for successor employers** on page 3 of the instructions.) You can get Form 940-EZ by calling 1-800-TAX-FORM (1-800-829-3676) or from the IRS Web Site at **www.irs.gov.**

If you will not have to file returns in the future, check here (see **Who Must File** in separate instructions), **and complete and sign the return** . . . ▶ ☐

If this is an Amended Return, check here. . . . ▶ ☐

Part I Computation of Taxable Wages

1	Total payments (including payments shown on lines 2 and 3) during the calendar year for services of employees		1
2	Exempt payments. (Explain all exempt payments, attaching additional sheets if necessary.) ▶	2	
3	Payments of more than $7,000 for services. Enter only amounts over the first $7,000 paid to each employee. (See separate instructions.) Do not include any exempt payments from line 2. The $7,000 amount is the Federal wage base. Your state wage base may be different. **Do not use your state wage limitation.**	3	
4	Total exempt payments (add lines 2 and 3)		4
5	**Total taxable wages** (subtract line 4 from line 1) ▶		5

Be sure to complete both sides of this form, and sign in the space provided on the back.

For Privacy Act and Paperwork Reduction Act Notice, see separate instructions. Cat. No. 11234O Form **940** (2000)

DETACH HERE

Form **940-V**

Department of the Treasury
Internal Revenue Service

Form 940 Payment Voucher

Use this voucher only when making a payment with your return.

OMB No. 1545-0028

2000

Complete boxes 1, 2, 3, and 4. Do not send cash, and do not staple your payment to this voucher. Make your check or money order payable to the **"United States Treasury"**. Be sure to enter your employer identification number, Form 940, and 2000 on your payment.

1 Enter the first four letters of your last name (business name if partnership or corporation).	**2** Enter your employer identification number.	**3** Enter the amount of your payment. $
Instructions for Box 1	**4** Enter your business name (individual name for sole proprietors)	
Individuals (sole proprietors, trusts, and estates) Enter the first four letters of your last name.	Enter your address	
Corporations and partnerships Enter the first four characters of your business name (omit The if followed by more than one word).	Enter your city, state, and ZIP code	

Figure 8-7 Federal form 940, used for calculating federal unemployment tax (FUTA).

Employee: _____									Regular Hourly Rate: $____								
Social Security Number: _____									Exemptions claimed: ____								
Month	Week									Regular	Overtime	Gross	Employee Withholdings						Net	Employer	Employer
	Ending	M	T	W	T	F	S	S	Reg.	OT	Wages	Wages	Wages	FWT	FICA	Mcare	SWT	LWT	Other	Wages	FICA	Mcare
									1a	1b	1c	1d	1e	2	3	4	5	6	7	8	9	10
Totals																						

Figure 8-8   Payroll sheet.

Step-by-Step Payroll Calculation (Fig. 8-8)

1. Calculate gross earnings
   a. Add total regular hours worked
   b. Add total overtime hours worked
   c. Multiply total hours at regular hourly rate times hourly wage
   d. Multiply total hours at overtime hourly rate times 1.5 times hourly wage
   e. Combine regular wages and overtime wages
2. Federal income tax withholding amount
   Use federal withholding tables
3. Social Security tax on gross income up to current year's maximum
   Use federal Social Security tax table
4. Medicare tax on gross income up to current year's maximum
   Use federal Medicare tax table
5. State income tax withholding amount
   Use state tax tables or percentage amount
6. Local income tax withholding amount
   Use local tax table or percentage amount
7. Other withholding amounts
8. Net wages payable
   Total gross wages less total of all employee withholdings
9. Calculate employer's share of FICA
   Use federal tax table
10. Calculate employer's share of Medicare
    Use federal Medicare tax table

Form **941** (Rev. January 2000)
Department of the Treasury
Internal Revenue Service

Employer's Quarterly Federal Tax Return

▶ **See separate instructions for information on completing this return.**

Please type or print.

Enter state code for state in which deposits were made ONLY if different from state in address to the right ▶ (see page 2 of instructions).

Name (as distinguished from trade name) | Date quarter ended

Trade name, if any | Employer identification number

Address (number and street) | City, state, and ZIP code

OMB No. 1545-0029

T
FF
FD
FP
I
T

If address is different from prior return, check here ▶

IRS Use

1 1 1 1 1 1 1 1 1 1 2 3 3 3 3 3 3 3 3 4 4 4 5 5 5

6 7 8 8 8 8 8 8 8 8 9 9 9 9 9 10 10 10 10 10 10 10 10 10 10

If you do not have to file returns in the future, check here ▶ ☐ and enter date final wages paid ▶

If you are a seasonal employer, see **Seasonal employers** on page 1 of the instructions and check here ▶ ☐

1	Number of employees in the pay period that includes March 12th . ▶	1
2	Total wages and tips, plus other compensation	2
3	Total income tax withheld from wages, tips, and sick pay	3
4	Adjustment of withheld income tax for preceding quarters of calendar year	4
5	Adjusted total of income tax withheld (line 3 as adjusted by line 4—see instructions)	5
6	Taxable social security wages . . . . . 6a ______ × 12.4% (.124) =	6b
	Taxable social security tips . . . . . 6c ______ × 12.4% (.124) =	6d
7	Taxable Medicare wages and tips . . . 7a ______ × 2.9% (.029) =	7b
8	Total social security and Medicare taxes (add lines 6b, 6d, and 7b). Check here if wages are not subject to social security and/or Medicare tax . . . ▶ ☐	8
9	Adjustment of social security and Medicare taxes (see instructions for required explanation) Sick Pay $ ______ ± Fractions of Cents $ ______ ± Other $ ______ =	9
10	Adjusted total of social security and Medicare taxes (line 8 as adjusted by line 9—see instructions)	10
11	**Total taxes** (add lines 5 and 10)	11
12	Advance earned income credit (EIC) payments made to employees	12
13	Net taxes (subtract line 12 from line 11). **If $1,000 or more, this must equal line 17, column (d) below (or line D of Schedule B (Form 941))**	13
14	Total deposits for quarter, including overpayment applied from a prior quarter	14
15	**Balance due** (subtract line 14 from line 13). See instructions	15
16	**Overpayment.** If line 14 is more than line 13, enter excess here ▶ $ ______ and check if to be: ☐ Applied to next return **OR** ☐ Refunded.	

- **All filers:** If line 13 is less than $1,000, you need not complete line 17 or Schedule B (Form 941).
- **Semiweekly schedule depositors:** Complete Schedule B (Form 941) and check here . . . ▶ ☐
- **Monthly schedule depositors:** Complete line 17, columns (a) through (d), and check here. . . ▶ ☐

17 Monthly Summary of Federal Tax Liability. Do not complete if you were a semiweekly schedule depositor.

(a) First month liability	(b) Second month liability	(c) Third month liability	(d) Total liability for quarter

Sign Here Under penalties of perjury, I declare that I have examined this return, including accompanying schedules and statements, and to the best of my knowledge and belief, it is true, correct, and complete.

Signature ▶ Print Your Name and Title ▶ Date ▶

For Privacy Act and Paperwork Reduction Act Notice, see back of Payment Voucher. Cat. No. 17001Z Form **941** (Rev. 1-2000)

Figure 8-9 Federal form 941.

Preparing the Quarterly Returns

At the end of each calendar quarter (March, June, September, and December), a summary of the earnings, withholdings, and deposits of withheld amounts must be filed. For federal withholding, Social Security, and Medicare accounting, this is accomplished by the completion and filing of federal form 941 (Fig. 8-9). Any balance not previously deposited must be paid with the return or deposited with the approved depositary bank or agency.

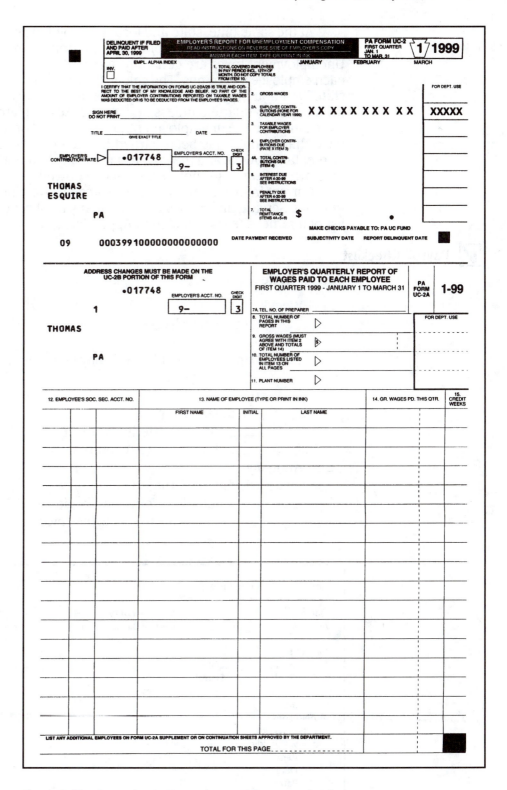

Figure 8-10   Pennsylvania Unemployment Compensation form.

At the same time, state and local withholding amounts may also have to be filed (Fig. 8-10). Unemployment tax returns may also be required. Unemployment taxes are generally assessed only on a limited amount of each employee's earnings. The calculation requires a determination of the state limit and may result in no additional tax being owed in the second, third or fourth quarters unless new employees are hired later in the year. For example, if the unemployment tax is assessed only on the first $7,500, once that amount has been earned in each year by each employee, no further tax is owed, and the return is filed only to report the information of employment earnings, not to calculate tax owed.

Current information and tax forms can be obtained from the Internal Revenue Service, and most states and many local government agencies. A list of Internet sites is included in Appendix A.

✓ Payroll Checklist

Payroll Cycle

____ Weekly
____ Prepare paychecks
____ Monthly
____ Deposit withheld taxes (may be required weekly depending on amount due)
____ Quarterly
____ File federal form 940
____ State quarterly returns
____ Local quarterly returns
____ Annually
____ File federal form 941
____ File federal W-3 form with copies of W-2 forms
____ Issue W-2 forms to employees by end of January

Employee Personnel File

Name: Social Security number: Marital Status:
Address: Date of Birth: Exemptions:

Rate of pay:
Form INS I-9   Date:
      IRS W-4   Date:
                     Exemptions claimed:
      IRS W-2
Time record:
Vacation record:
Other withholdings: State   Local   Other
     Item:
     Date:
     Rate:

Figure 8-11   Sample employee personnel form.

Sample Employer Records Forms

Employer					
Employer ID number — Federal:					
Employer ID number — State:					
Employer ID number — Local:					
	Year				
	2000	2001	2002	2003	2004
Current rate					
Social Security					
Medicare					
State UC					
Local					
FUTA					

Figure 8-12 Employer checklist of rates and identification numbers.

Form	1st Quarter		2nd Quarter		3rd Quarter		4th Quarter		
	Date	Amount	Date	Amount	Date	Amount	Date	Amount	Total

Figure 8-13 Quarterly payroll payment checklist.

Employee	Address	Social Sec. #	Form	Date Delivered

Figure 8-14 Record of distribution of forms to employees.

Employee versus Independent Contractor

A continuing problem in employment law is the classification of workers. If they are employees, all of the rules for wage and hour laws apply, as well as the obligation to withhold and pay employer-imposed taxes. If a worker is not an employee, but rather an independent contractor, the employer is relieved of paying contributions towards Social Security, Medicare, and unemployment taxes. For the independent contractor, this may be a mixed blessing. There is a continuing obligation to pay at least the Social Security

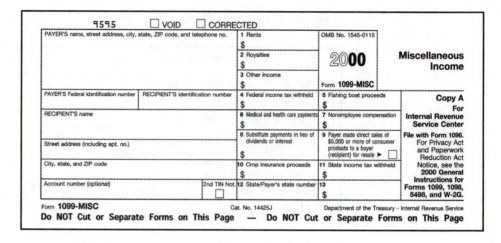

Figure 8-15   Federal form 1099.

and Medicare taxes, but at a higher rate than those imposed as an employee. For many employers, there is an additional savings, the cost of benefits for insurance, retirement, and sickness and maternity leave.

By classifying a worker as an independent contractor, the government loses out on the employer's withholding tax payments. The total revenue is reduced for the Social Security and Medicare system and for the unemployment system. An additional concern is that the amount paid will not be reported at all by the independent contractor. All of which results in substantial revenue loss for the government. The Internal Revenue Service (IRS) has taken a strong stand against the independent contractor status.

Payment to employees is reported on the quarterly reports, annual report, and the Wage Statement W-2 form. Payments to noncorporate independent contractors are reported on the form 1099. Some independent contractors also set themselves up as corporations. Again, the payments should be reported by the issuance of a form 1099 (Fig. 8-15).

Accounting for Payroll

The Journal Entries

	Debit	Credit
Payroll expense	$12,125	
Federal withholding tax payable		$4,250
FICA payable		752
Medicare payable		176
State withholding tax payable		340
Local withholding tax payable		121
Cash		$6,486

(to record the payment of wages and the increase in employees withholding taxes payable)

	Debit	Credit
Payroll tax expense	$1,152	
FICA tax payable		$752
Medicare tax payable		176
State unemployment tax payable		224

(to record the employer's payroll tax expense and increase the payroll tax payable)

	Debit	Credit
Federal withholding tax payable	$4,250	
FICA payable	1504	
Medicare payable	352	
Cash		$6,106

(to record the payment of the federal employment tax payable to the federal depository agency)

Withholding Tax Deposits and Payments

Federal regulations require periodic payment of the taxes withheld from employees and from the employer's federal payroll tax liability. The frequency of payment is dependent on the amounts owed. The greater the amounts owed, the more frequent the required payment. Since this amount changes, it is important to determine the current deposit obligations. The following list is offered for reference only.

Less than $1,000 per quarter	Deposit or pay quarterly
Less than $50,000 in the four quarters, ending on the previous June 30	Monthly deposits by the 15th of the next month
More than $50,000 in the four quarters, ending on the previous June 30	Semiweekly deposits
$100,000 or more on one day	Deposit by the close of next business day

The deposits may be made using deposit coupons (Federal Tax Deposit Coupons; Fig. 8-16), form 8109, or by electronic deposit using the Electronic Federal Tax Payment System (EFTPS). As a general rule, any employer with an employment tax liability—employee and employers combined—of over $50,000 is required to make electronic deposits. For those able to make deposits using the federal deposit coupons, these deposits must be made to an authorized financial institution or to the Federal Reserve Bank.

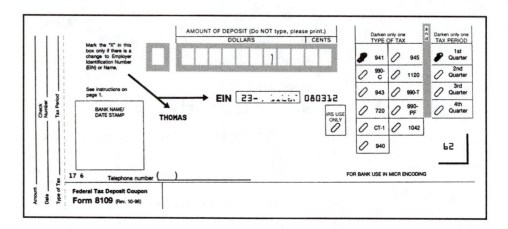

Figure 8-16   Depository coupon.

Quarterly Filings

Employers must file a quarterly report of wages paid and taxes withheld from employees and payroll taxes owed by the employer. For the federal obligations, this is on the federal form 941: Employer's Quarterly Federal Tax Return. Most states and local governments assessing a wage or payroll tax have adopted a similar quarterly filing requirement.

The failure to file the required forms and make the required payments can result in civil penalties of five percent, plus five percent per month in which failure continues, not to exceed 25 percent, plus a penalty of up to 75 percent for fraudulent failure to file. Criminal penalties and imprisonment may also be imposed with fines of $25,000 for individuals and $100,000 for corporations.

Unemployment Taxes

Employers who pay wages in excess of $1,500 during any calendar quarter or employ one or more persons for some portion of a day in each or 20 or more calendar weeks are subject to the federal unemployment tax act or FUTA. While the individual state laws vary, anyone covered under the FUTA will have a state obligation. Federal form 940 is used to calculate and report the FUTA tax. The completion of this form requires reference to the state experience rating assigned to the employer. Each employer is assigned a tax rate upon registering as an employer. Based on the number of claims made against the employer's account, a state experience rating is assigned. The fewer the claims, the lower the experience rating and, hence, the lower the state tax. The federal calculation takes the experience rating into account in determining the amount due for federal purposes, after allowing a credit for taxes paid to the state up to a maximum percentage. Figure 8-17 is a graphic representation of the annual process of preparing the employment-related tax forms.

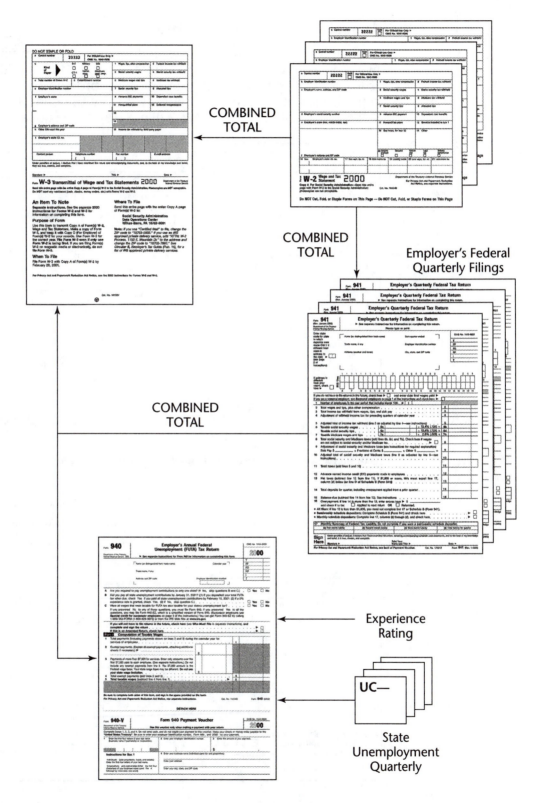

COMBINED
TOTAL

COMBINED
TOTAL

Employer's Federal
Quarterly Filings

COMBINED
TOTAL

Experience
Rating

UC—

State
Unemployment
Quarterly

Figure 8-17   Annual process of preparing the employment-related tax forms.

Annual Filings and Reconciliation

In addition to the quarterly filings and annual tax return filing, each employer is required to file a summary of wages and withholdings with the federal state and local governments and provide the employee with copies. Each employee must be provided by the end of January with a wage and tax statement, the W-2 (Fig. 8-18). Copies of all the W-2 forms

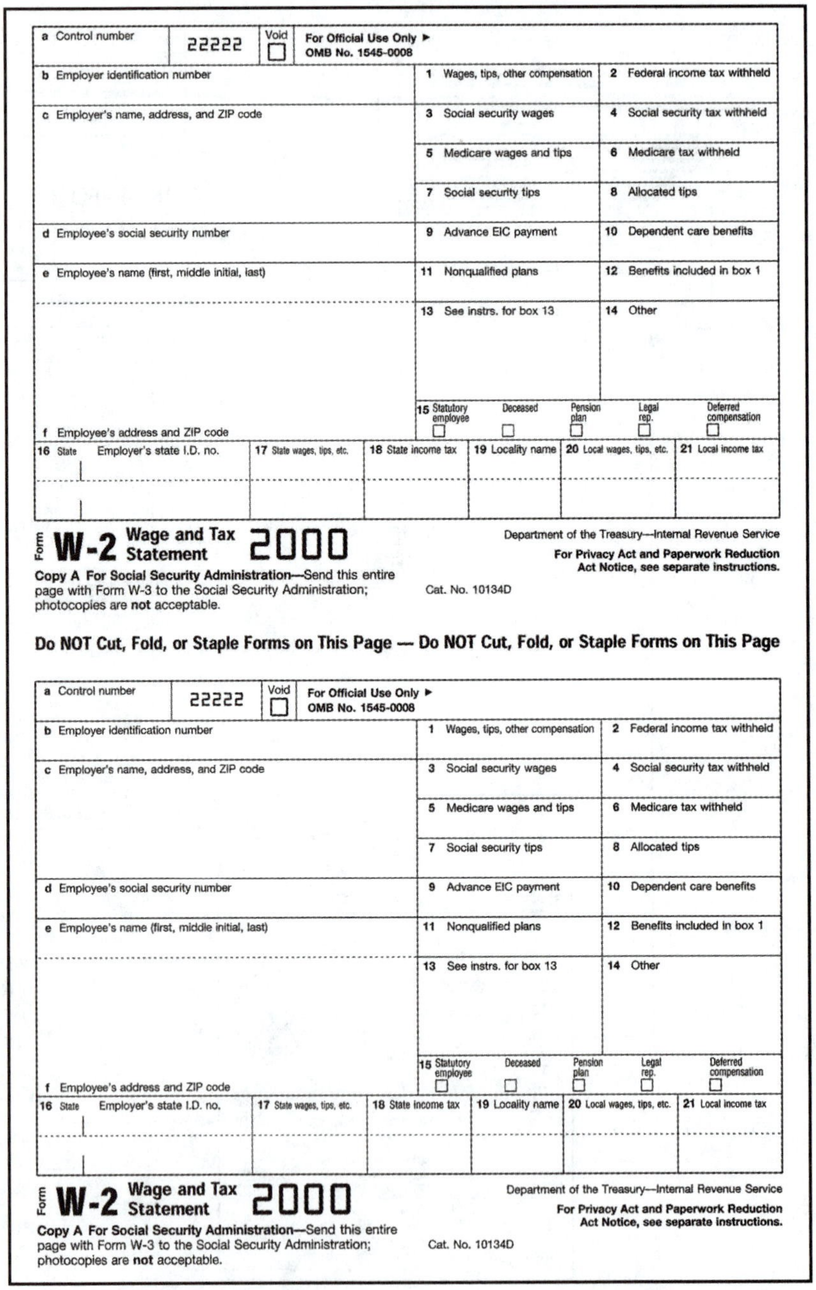
a Control number 22222 Void For Official Use Only ► OMB No. 1545-0008
b Employer identification number
1 Wages, tips, other compensation
2 Federal income tax withheld
c Employer's name, address, and ZIP code
3 Social security wages
4 Social security tax withheld
5 Medicare wages and tips
6 Medicare tax withheld
7 Social security tips
8 Allocated tips
d Employee's social security number
9 Advance EIC payment
10 Dependent care benefits
e Employee's name (first, middle initial, last)
11 Nonqualified plans
12 Benefits included in box 1
13 See instrs. for box 13
14 Other
15 Statutory employee Deceased Pension plan Legal rep. Deferred compensation
f Employee's address and ZIP code
16 State Employer's state I.D. no. 17 State wages, tips, etc. 18 State income tax 19 Locality name 20 Local wages, tips, etc. 21 Local income tax

Form **W-2** Wage and Tax Statement 2000
Department of the Treasury—Internal Revenue Service
For Privacy Act and Paperwork Reduction Act Notice, see separate instructions.
Copy A For Social Security Administration—Send this entire page with Form W-3 to the Social Security Administration; photocopies are **not** acceptable.
Cat. No. 10134D

Do NOT Cut, Fold, or Staple Forms on This Page — Do NOT Cut, Fold, or Staple Forms on This Page

a Control number 22222 Void For Official Use Only ► OMB No. 1545-0008
b Employer identification number
1 Wages, tips, other compensation
2 Federal income tax withheld
c Employer's name, address, and ZIP code
3 Social security wages
4 Social security tax withheld
5 Medicare wages and tips
6 Medicare tax withheld
7 Social security tips
8 Allocated tips
d Employee's social security number
9 Advance EIC payment
10 Dependent care benefits
e Employee's name (first, middle initial, last)
11 Nonqualified plans
12 Benefits included in box 1
13 See instrs. for box 13
14 Other
15 Statutory employee Deceased Pension plan Legal rep. Deferred compensation
f Employee's address and ZIP code
16 State Employer's state I.D. no. 17 State wages, tips, etc. 18 State income tax 19 Locality name 20 Local wages, tips, etc. 21 Local income tax
Form W-2 Wage and Tax Statement 2000
Department of the Treasury—Internal Revenue Service
For Privacy Act and Paperwork Reduction Act Notice, see separate instructions.
Copy A For Social Security Administration—Send this entire page with Form W-3 to the Social Security Administration; photocopies are not acceptable.
Cat. No. 10134D

Figure 8-18 Federal form W-2.

issued by the employer, together with a reconciliation form, the form W-3 (Fig. 8-19), must also be filed with the federal government. Since many state and local governments use the same system, copies of the W-2 form or a similar document that shows the state and local wages and taxes withheld must be filed as well.

DO NOT STAPLE OR FOLD

a Control number	33333	**For Official Use Only ►** **OMB No. 1545-0008**

b **Kind of Payer** — 941 ☐ Military ☐ 943 ☐ CT-1 ☐ Hshld. emp. ☐ Medicare govt. emp. ☐	1 Wages, tips, other compensation / 2 Federal income tax withheld / 3 Social security wages / 4 Social security tax withheld
c Total number of Forms W-2 / d Establishment number	5 Medicare wages and tips / 6 Medicare tax withheld
e Employer identification number	7 Social security tips / 8 Allocated tips
f Employer's name	9 Advance EIC payments / 10 Dependent care benefits
	11 Nonqualified plans / 12 Deferred compensation
	13
g Employer's address and ZIP code	14
h Other EIN used this year	15 Income tax withheld by third-party payer
i Employer's state I.D. no.	

Contact person	Telephone number	Fax number	E-mail address
	( )	( )	

Under penalties of perjury, I declare that I have examined this return and accompanying documents, and, to the best of my knowledge and belief, they are true, correct, and complete.

Signature ► Title ► Date ►

Form **W-3 Transmittal of Wage and Tax Statements 2000** Department of the Treasury Internal Revenue Service

Send this entire page with the entire Copy A page of Form(s) W-2 to the Social Security Administration. Photocopies are NOT acceptable.
Do NOT send any remittance (cash, checks, money orders, etc.) with Forms W-2 and W-3.

An Item To Note

Separate Instructions. See the separate **2000 Instructions for Forms W-2 and W-3** for information on completing this form.

Purpose of Form

Use this form to transmit Copy A of **Form(s) W-2,** Wage and Tax Statement. Make a copy of Form W-3, and keep it with Copy D (For Employer) of Form(s) W-2 for your records. Use Form W-3 for the correct year. **File Form W-3 even if only one Form W-2 is being filed.** If you are filing Form(s) W-2 on magnetic media or electronically, **do not** file Form W-3.

When To File

File Form W-3 with Copy A of Form(s) W-2 by February 28, 2001.

Where To File

Send this entire page with the entire Copy A page of Form(s) W-2 to:

Social Security Administration
Data Operations Center
Wilkes-Barre, PA 18769-0001

Note: *If you use "Certified Mail" to file, change the ZIP code to "18769-0002." If you use an IRS approved private delivery service, add "ATTN: W-2 Process, 1150 E. Mountain Dr." to the address and change the ZIP code to "18702-7997." See* ***Circular E,*** *Employer's Tax Guide (Pub. 15), for a list of IRS approved private delivery services.*

For Privacy Act and Paperwork Reduction Act Notice, see the 2000 Instructions for Forms W-2 and W-3.

Cat. No. 10159Y

Figure 8-19 Federal form W-3.

Ethical Issue

> Every attorney working in a firm must be authorized to practice law. This is frequently thought of as a license to practice. With the license to practice come many responsibilities, not the least of that is the primary obligation to the client to act independently in the client's best interest. Internal Revenue Code (IRC) regulation 31.3401 provides in part that one of the tests of employee status is the right to control and direct the individual who provides the service. If the attorney is required to act for the client exercising independent judgement, should the attorney be classified as an independent contractor or as an employee? What about the paralegal in those states where the paralegal profession is regulated by the state?

CHAPTER SUMMARY

Every business with one or more employees must prepare a payroll. The payroll calculation includes determining the proper gross amount due the employee and the required withholdings to determine net pay. Federal law, in part, determines the relationship between employee and employer. The Immigration Reform and Control Act imposes certain obligations upon the employer in the hiring process. These rules are used to minimize the hiring of the illegal immigrants.

The Fair Labor Standards Act, also known as the Wage and Hour Law, establishes a maximum numbers of hours that may be worked without the payment of overtime pay. Federal, state and local laws also obligate the employer to withhold certain taxes and make matching contributions for other taxes. These same laws also impose obligations for periodic payments of the amounts withheld to the government tax authorities on behalf of the employee and the employer.

GLOSSARY

Circular E: An Internal Revenue Service publication providing the necessary withholding tables and information required by employers in preparing payroll

Exemption: An amount permitted to be deducted for the taxpayer, his or her spouse, and other dependents in calculating taxable income

Experience rating: The rate of tax assessed against a business for unemployment compensation purposes, based on the number of claims of former employees

FICA: The Federal Insurance Contribution Act, which establishes the contributions required for Social Security

FLSA: The Federal Labor Standards Act legislation that mandates minimum standards for hours and working conditions

Pay as you go: A tax system that provides for the periodic payments of taxes by employer withholding or periodic payments, usually quarterly

Withholding: The amount required by law or voluntary agreement with the employer to be withheld from an employee's wages

REVIEW QUESTIONS

1. Is it legal to save taxes by classifying a paralegal or an attorney who works in a firm as an independent contractor?
2. Can the firm use the money withheld for taxes from employees' pay for operating expenses?
3. Can all banks be used to make the required withheld tax deposits?
4. What is the purpose of the Employment Eligibility Verification form I-9?
5. Which federal law establishes the minimum rates of pay?
6. What annual report must be supplied to employees?
7. What is the purpose of the federal 941 form?
8. Which employers are subject to the federal unemployment tax?
9. Why is the state experience rating important in calculating FUTA?
10. What is a function of the federal form W-3?

Chapter 9

Attorney–Client Accounting

In This Chapter

Why Study Attorney–Client Accounting?

FIDUCIARY One holding property belonging to another in a situation of trust and confidence

Lawyers are frequently called upon to hold funds for or on behalf of clients. These are monies that belong to the client or are being held as security to ensure payment for a client. It is not uncommon for the lawyer to act as the intermediary in a dispute. As the neutral party, or intermediary, the lawyer holds the funds pending resolution of the dispute, be it a commercial dispute, family law issue or tort case settlement. In these cases, the lawyer is acting as a **fiduciary**. As a fiduciary, the lawyer must maintain a separate set of books and be able to prepare a proper accounting for the initial deposit, any income earned on the funds, and the ultimate disbursement.

Client Retainers and Costs

RETAINER An advance payment by a client to a law firm to be used to offset the fee for services to be rendered or for costs advanced by the firm on behalf of the client

Law firms will frequently request a **retainer**, a payment at the beginning of the handling of a new matter for a client. This amount may be used to offset the fee for services rendered or costs advanced on behalf of the client. Unless there is some other arrangement agreed upon in conformity with applicable court rules and ABA guidelines, these funds only belong to the law firm when they have been earned by the rendering of the service or the actual expenditure of the cost. Unused amounts may have to be returned to the client, and therefore accounted for.

CONTINGENT FEE The fee is based on a percentage of the recovery for the client; typically used in tort actions

Increasingly, under the rules of professional conduct, many states also require a written fee agreement in **contingent fee** cases, while in other types of cases it is preferred but not required (Fig. 9-1).

A lawyer may request a *nonrefundable retainer*. This is a common practice when the client does not want the law firm to be able to represent the opposing party in a pending legal action. This is most commonly seen

August 12, 2000

Mr. & Mrs. E. Morris

Re: Martin versus Morris

Dear Mr. and Mrs. Morris:

This will confirm your hiring us as lawyers to defend you with regard to the lawsuit filed by Mr. Martin for damage to his begonia bush.

We have agreed to bill you on a time basis for our services, plus any costs of litigation. I will be billing at the rate of $120.00 per hour. For your information, we keep our time records broken down into 1/10 of one hour increments and will include descriptions of the work. We will use our best efforts to minimize the expenditure of time consistent with getting you a result with which you will be satisfied.

We will bill you on a monthly basis so that you may be kept advised as to the extent of the expenditures being made on your behalf so that you may take whatever action you deem appropriate at that time.

Please sign and return the enclosed copy of this letter, indicating your agreement.
Thank you for retaining our services. We look forward to working with you.

Very truly yours,

D. Thomas & Associates

D. Thomas, Esquire

DT:eq
Enclosure

I acknowledge my acceptance of this fee agreement as outlined above.

Date: _____   _____

Figure 9-1   (a) Sample fee letter.

in family law in divorce actions. Legal ethics prohibit taking on a client where there is a conflict of interest. In cases of nonrefundable retainers, a statement of the application of the funds may or should also be made as a matter of good financial accounting practice.

CONTINGENT FEE AGREEMENT

I, (we) hereby constitute and appoint _____

of the law firm of _____

as my (our) attorney to prosecute a claim for _____

against _____. The claimant (deceased) is _____

and the cause of action arose on _____.

I (we) hereby agree that the compensation of my (our) attorney for services shall be determined as follows:

One third (1/3) of any settlement, plus out-of-pocket expenses prior to

the institution of suit; Forty (40%) of any settlement, plus out-of-pocket

expenses after the institution of suit, but prior to the commencement of

trial; Fifty (50%) of any settlement or verdict, plus out-of-pocket

expenses after the commencement of trial.

I (we) was (were) recommended to my (our) attorney by:

Name: _____

Address: _____

Relationship: _____

I (we) hereby acknowledge receipt of a duplicate copy of this Contingent Fee Agreement.

Date: _____   _____

Date: _____   _____

Figure 9-1   (b) contingent fee agreement.

Costs Advanced

It is common for law firms to pay directly to the court any fees for the filing of documents for the client. In some cases, the costs of stenographers, expert witnesses, the making of copies, travel, phone, and copying will also be advanced. Proper accounting for these items must be kept to be able to properly bill the client or charge the amounts expended against prepaid costs or retainers. Good practice is to include the nature and amounts of costs that will be charged for these various items in the initial client fee letter.

Timely Disbursements. A lawyer is not required to make disbursements until a draft or check has cleared. A draft or check is deemed cleared when the funds are available for disbursement. However, lawyers cannot retain the amount for an unreasonable amount of time. The client is entitled to earn the potential interests on the amount to be disbursed. The lawyer is not entitled to keep the amount, earning interest in his account.

Trust Accounts

A trust account or fiduciary account should be considered as a separate legal entity. A clear record of all trust transactions must be maintained. When a checking account has been established, the check register is a prime source for creating any required or desired reports. With some larger accounts, checking accounts may not have been set up. Many trust and estate accounts may be invested in money-market funds, stocks, bonds, and mutual funds. Keeping a clear record is made more difficult by the potential for periodic increases and decreases in value that are not actually realized. These are referred to as **paper gains and losses**. They exist on paper but have not been realized by an actual sale or transfer of the asset. For the attorney, the client or state law must authorize any investment of assets held in trust.

PAPER GAINS AND LOSSES The difference between the value at the time of acquisition and a time in the future, but before the asset has been disposed of or sold

For purposes of this chapter, we will consider the investments made only in banks or financial institutions paying interest and withhold any change in the principal amounts, except for interest earned or bank fees charged.

A separate ledger sheet should be set up showing the activity in the account (Fig. 9-2). This would include all deposits, interest earned, and disbursements, including bank charges.

		Check Number	Trust Funds		Trust Balance		
			Received	Disbursed			
Date	Description						

Figure 9-2 Ledger sheet trust account.

IOLATA Accounts

IOLATA ACCOUNT
An escrow account for holding client funds that would otherwise not earn interest

Many states, by court rule, impose an obligation to deposit client funds too small to earn interest into a special interest-bearing account, the **IOLATA account**. Interest generated from these small accounts is paid to the court-designated agency, usually the local legal aid agency, to fund their activities. Since the cost of setting up individual small accounts is greater than the interest earned, or the amount deposited is so small that no interest would accrue to the client, everyone wins by having these funds generate some income for the public good. The reconciliation of this account is simpler since no accounting for interest to the client needs to be made.

Interest-Bearing Escrow Accounts

ESCROW AGENT
One who holds funds or property for the benefit of another in a fiduciary capacity

Lawyers are frequently called on to act as **escrow agents** or to retain client funds for future disbursements. In some cases, the amounts may be significant. Prudent handling of these clients' monies dictates that the fiduciary treat them in the same manner as would any prudent investor. If the amount is sufficient to earn interest, the amount earned belongs to the client, not to the attorney, and must be accounted for to the client.

It is good practice, if earning interest can be expected, to open up separate accounts for each client. In opening these accounts, the client's Social Security number, or other employer identification number, should be used. If the law firm maintains the account under its tax identification number, it will have to report interest to the client and to the federal and state government annually.

MONEY LAUNDERING A scheme for taking money obtained from illegal activities and giving it the appearance of legitimacy

A significant body of law has emerged to avoid **money laundering**. In a law firm, this may require the reporting of the receipt of significant amounts of cash (Fig. 9-3). The problem is balancing between the money-laundering rules and the attorney–client privilege. Where amounts in excess of $10,000 are received in cash from a client, current legislation and regulations must be consulted.

FEDERAL IDENTIFICATION NUMBER For an individual, this is the individual's Social Security number. For other legal entities, it is the federal employer identification number.

To open an account with a financial institution requires a **federal identification number**. This identification number may be that of the client, the trust, estate, or other legal entity having a current identification number. In some cases, the financial institution may require copies of any documentation that created the client's entity, such as the trust documents, the death certificate, and the will. The concern of the financial institution is that it properly complies with existing regulations on federal withholding and money-laundering or large-deposit reporting obligations. A standard requirement is the completion of the federal form W-9 (Fig. 9-4).

(U.S. Customs Use Only)

Control No.

31 U.S.C. 5316; 31 CFR 103.23 and 103.25

▶ Please type or print.

DEPARTMENT OF THE TREASURY
UNITED STATES CUSTOMS SERVICE

REPORT OF INTERNATIONAL TRANSPORTATION OF CURRENCY OR MONETARY INSTRUMENTS

Form Approved
OMB No. 1515-0079

▶ This form is to be filed with the United States Customs Service

▶ For Paperwork Reduction Act Notice and Privacy Act Notice, see back of form.

Part I FOR INDIVIDUAL DEPARTING FROM OR ENTERING THE UNITED STATES

1. NAME *(Last or family, first, and middle)*	2. IDENTIFYING NO. *(See instructions)*	3. DATE OF BIRTH *(Mo./Day/Yr.)*
4. PERMANENT ADDRESS IN UNITED STATES OR ABROAD		5. OF WHAT COUNTRY ARE YOU A CITIZEN/SUBJECT?
6. ADDRESS WHILE IN THE UNITED STATES		7. PASSPORT NO. & COUNTRY
8. U.S. VISA DATE	9. PLACE UNITED STATES VISA WAS ISSUED	10. IMMIGRATION ALIEN NO. *(If any)*

11. CURRENCY OR MONETARY INSTRUMENT WAS: *(Complete 11A or 11B)*

A. EXPORTED		B. IMPORTED	
Departed From: *(City in U.S.)*	Arrived At: *(Foreign City/Country)*	From: *(Foreign City/Country)*	At: *(City in U.S.)*

Part II FOR PERSON SHIPPING, MAILING, OR RECEIVING CURRENCY OR MONETARY INSTRUMENTS

12. NAME *(Last or family, first, and middle)*	13. IDENTIFYING NO. *(See instructions)*	14. DATE OF BIRTH *(Mo./Day/Yr.)*
15. PERMANENT ADDRESS IN UNITED STATES OR ABROAD		16. OF WHAT COUNTRY ARE YOU A CITIZEN/SUBJECT?
17. ADDRESS WHILE IN THE UNITED STATES		18. PASSPORT NO. & COUNTRY
19. U.S. VISA DATE	20. PLACE UNITED STATES VISA WAS ISSUED	21. IMMIGRATION ALIEN NO. *(If any)*

22. CURRENCY OR MONETARY INSTRUMENTS DATE SHIPPED	23. CURRENCY OR MONETARY INSTRUMENTS ☐ Shipped To ▶	NAME AND ADDRESS	24. IF THE CURRENCY OR MONETARY INSTRUMENT WAS MAILED, SHIPPED, OR TRANSPORTED COMPLETE BLOCKS A AND B. A. Method of Shipment *(Auto, U.S. Mail, Public Carrier, etc.)*
DATE RECEIVED	☐ Received From ▶		B. Name of Transporter/Carrier

Part III CURRENCY AND MONETARY INSTRUMENT INFORMATION (SEE INSTRUCTIONS ON REVERSE)(To be completed by everyone)

25. TYPE AND AMOUNT OF CURRENCY/MONETARY INSTRUMENTS		Value in U.S. Dollars	26. IF OTHER THAN U.S. CURRENCY IS INVOLVED, PLEASE COMPLETE BLOCKS A AND B. *(SEE SPECIAL INSTRUCTIONS)*
Coins	☐ A. ▶	$	A. Currency Name
Currency	☐ B. ▶		
Other Instruments *(Specify Type)*	☐ C. ▶		B. Country
(Add lines A, B and C)	TOTAL AMOUNT ▶	$	

Part IV GENERAL - TO BE COMPLETED BY ALL TRAVELERS, SHIPPERS, AND RECIPIENTS

27. WERE YOU ACTING AS AN AGENT, ATTORNEY OR IN CAPACITY FOR ANYONE IN THIS CURRENCY OR MONETARY INSTRUMENT ACTIVITY? *(If "Yes" complete A, B and C)* ☐ Yes ☐ No

PERSON IN WHOSE BEHALF YOU ARE ACTING ▶	A. Name	B. Address	C. Business activity, occupation, or profession

Under penalties of perjury, I declare that I have examined this report, and to the best of my knowledge and belief it is true, correct and complete.

28. NAME AND TITLE	29. SIGNATURE	30. DATE

(Replaces IRS Form 4790 which is obsolete.)

Customs Form 4790 (031695)

Figure 9-3 U.S. Customs form 4790.

Depending on the nature of the account, the interest earned may be reported directly to the client for inclusion on his or her tax return. Where a trust or estate is involved, the interest will need to be included on the fiduciary's tax return, which may be prepared by the law firm or accounting firm. Interest that may be earned in an account not bearing the client's own federal identification number must be reported to the client on federal form 1099 (Fig. 9-5).

Form **W-9**
(Rev. November 1999)
Department of the Treasury
Internal Revenue Service

**Request for Taxpayer
Identification Number and Certification**

Give form to the
requester. Do NOT
send to the IRS.

Please print or type

Name (If a joint account or you changed your name, see **Specific Instructions** on page 2.)

Business name, if different from above. (See **Specific Instructions** on page 2.)

Check appropriate box: ☐ Individual/Sole proprietor ☐ Corporation ☐ Partnership ☐ Other ▶ ....

Address (number, street, and apt. or suite no.)

Requester's name and address (optional)

City, state, and ZIP code

Part I   Taxpayer Identification Number (TIN)

List account number(s) here (optional)

Enter your TIN in the appropriate box. For individuals, this is your social security number (SSN). However, if you are a resident alien OR a sole proprietor, see the instructions on page 2. For other entities, it is your employer identification number (EIN). If you do not have a number, see **How to get a TIN** on page 2.

Note: *If the account is in more than one name, see the chart on page 2 for guidelines on whose number to enter.*

Social security number

OR

Employer identification number

Part II   For Payees Exempt From Backup Withholding (See the instructions on page 2.)

▶

Part III   Certification

Under penalties of perjury, I certify that:

1. The number shown on this form is my correct taxpayer identification number (or I am waiting for a number to be issued to me), **and**

2. I am not subject to backup withholding because: (a) I am exempt from backup withholding, or (b) I have not been notified by the Internal Revenue Service (IRS) that I am subject to backup withholding as a result of a failure to report all interest or dividends, or (c) the IRS has notified me that I am no longer subject to backup withholding.

Certification instructions. You must cross out item **2** above if you have been notified by the IRS that you are currently subject to backup withholding because you have failed to report all interest and dividends on your tax return. For real estate transactions, item 2 does not apply. For mortgage interest paid, acquisition or abandonment of secured property, cancellation of debt, contributions to an individual retirement arrangement (IRA), and generally, payments other than interest and dividends, you are not required to sign the Certification, but you must provide your correct TIN. (See the instructions on page 2.)

Sign Here Signature ▶   Date ▶

Purpose of form. A person who is required to file an information return with the IRS must get your correct taxpayer identification number (TIN) to report, for example, income paid to you, real estate transactions, mortgage interest you paid, acquisition or abandonment of secured property, cancellation of debt, or contributions you made to an IRA.

Use Form W-9, if you are a U.S. person (including a resident alien), to give your correct TIN to the person requesting it (the requester) and, when applicable, to:

1. Certify the TIN you are giving is correct (or you are waiting for a number to be issued),

2. Certify you are not subject to backup withholding, or

3. Claim exemption from backup withholding if you are an exempt payee.

If you are a foreign person, IRS **prefers** you use a Form W-8 (certificate of foreign status). After December 31, 2000, foreign persons **must** use an appropriate Form W-8.

Note: *If a requester gives you a form other than Form W-9 to request your TIN, you must use the requester's form if it is substantially similar to this Form W-9.*

What is backup withholding? Persons making certain payments to you must withhold and pay to the IRS 31% of such payments under certain conditions. This is called "backup withholding." Payments that may be subject to backup withholding include interest, dividends, broker and barter exchange transactions, rents, royalties, nonemployee pay, and certain payments from fishing boat operators. Real estate transactions are not subject to backup withholding.

If you give the requester your correct TIN, make the proper certifications, and report all your taxable interest and dividends on your tax return, payments you receive will not be subject to backup withholding. Payments you receive **will be** subject to backup withholding if:

1. You do not furnish your TIN to the requester, or

2. You do not certify your TIN when required (see the Part III instructions on page 2 for details), or

3. The IRS tells the requester that you furnished an incorrect TIN, or

4. The IRS tells you that you are subject to backup withholding because you did not report all your interest and dividends on your tax return (for reportable interest and dividends only), or

5. You do not certify to the requester that you are not subject to backup withholding under 3 above (for reportable interest and dividend accounts opened after 1983 only).

Certain payees and payments are exempt from backup withholding. See the Part II instructions and the separate **Instructions for the Requester of Form W-9.**

Penalties

Failure to furnish TIN. If you fail to furnish your correct TIN to a requester, you are subject to a penalty of $50 for each such failure unless your failure is due to reasonable cause and not to willful neglect.

Civil penalty for false information with respect to withholding. If you make a false statement with no reasonable basis that results in no backup withholding, you are subject to a $500 penalty.

Criminal penalty for falsifying information. Willfully falsifying certifications or affirmations may subject you to criminal penalties including fines and/or imprisonment.

Misuse of TINs. If the requester discloses or uses TINs in violation of Federal law, the requester may be subject to civil and criminal penalties.

Cat. No. 10231X

Form **W-9** (Rev. 11-99)

Figure 9-4   Federal form W-9, Request for Taxpayer Identification Number and Certification.

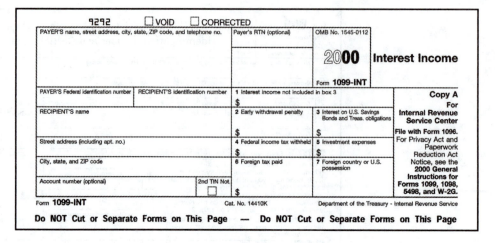

Figure 9-5 (a) Federal form 1099, Interest Income

(b) federal form 1099-B, Proceeds from Broker and Barter Exchange Transactions

(c) federal form 1099-S, Proceeds from Real Estate Transactions.

 **Ethical Issue**

> **ABA**
>
> Rule 1.15 of the ABA rules of professional conduct provides, in part, that:
>
> (a) A lawyer shall hold property of clients or third persons and that is in a lawyer's possession in connection with a representation separate from a lawyer's own property. Funds shall be kept in a separate account maintained in the state where the lawyer's office is situated or elsewhere with the consent of the client or third person. . . .
>
> Complete records of such account funds and other property shall be kept by the lawyer and shall be preserved for a period of five years after termination of the representation.
>
> (b). . . upon request . . . shall promptly render a full accounting regarding such property.
>
> (c). . . property in which both the lawyer and another person claim interests, the property shall be kept separate by the lawyer until there is an accounting and severance of other interests.

CHAPTER SUMMARY

Attorneys are frequently called upon to hold funds for clients. These may be amounts held pending settlement of litigation or of business transactions. The attorney acts as a fiduciary in the handling of these funds. As a fiduciary, proper records must be kept to account for the investment and disbursements of the monies. Federal and state regulations may also require the reporting of the receipt or disbursement of large sums of cash. Where income is generated, there may also be the obligation to file reports with tax authorities and to the client. This may include the amounts distributed from a real-estate settlement or from interest earned on an escrow account.

GLOSSARY

Contingent fee   The fee is based on a percentage of the recovery for the client; typically used in tort actions

Escrow agent   One who holds funds or property for the benefit of another in a fiduciary capacity

Federal identification number   For an individual, this is the individual's Social Security number. For other legal entities, it is the federal employer identification number.

Fiduciary   One holding property belonging to another in a situation of trust and confidence

IOLATA account   An escrow account for holding client funds that would otherwise not earn interest

Money laundering   A scheme for taking money obtained from illegal activities and giving it the appearance of legitimacy

Paper gains and losses The difference between the value at the time of acquisition and a time in the future, but before the asset has been disposed of or sold

Retainer An advance payment by a client to a law firm to be used to offset the fee for services to be rendered or for costs advanced by the firm on behalf of the client

REVIEW QUESTIONS

1. May an attorney borrow funds being held in an escrow account for internal law office operations?
2. Instead of borrowing from the bank, may an attorney borrow from a client's escrow account paying the same rate of interest as demanded by a bank?
3. When may amounts received as a retainer be used to pay personal expenses?
4. What is the difference between a refundable and a nonrefundable retainer?
5. Why is it important do keep a careful record of costs advanced?
6. Why should the trust account be treated as a separate economic entity?
7. What is meant by paper gains?
8. What is an IOLATA account?
9. For how long should trust account records be maintained after termination of representation?
10. Why should a client fee letter be issued even when not required by local rule or regulations?

Chapter 10

Court Accounting

In This Chapter
Why Study Court Accounting?
Uniform System of Accounts
Estate Accounting
Presentation of Information
Accounting to the Court in Minors' Settlements
Ethical Issue

Why Study Court Accounting?

ACCOUNTING A report of the handling of the funds belonging to another, usually by a fiduciary to the beneficiary or the court

In addition to the preparation and filing of federal and state estate tax returns, it is frequently necessary to file an **accounting** with the local court that administers or supervises trust and estate matters. These reports are designed to show that the fiduciary has properly administered the estate or trust.

Reports to the court are also required in many jurisdictions in civil cases involving minors. Approval of tort actions involving a minor may be negotiated between the counsel and the minor's parent or guardian, subject to the approval of the court. This usually requires the submission of a brief accounting of the expenses, including counsel fees, and the proposed disbursements to compensate for out-of-pocket expenses and proposed investment of the proceeds until the minor reaches a set age or by other order of the court. All of the parties are considered as acting as fiduciaries in the best interest of the minor.

Uniform System of Accounts

UNIFORM SYSTEM OF ACCOUNTS A proposed method of fiduciary accounting providing for a consistent presentation to the courts and interested parties.

Local practice and court rules will normally dictate the form and methods of fiduciary accounting. The **Uniform System of Accounts** has been accepted by some jurisdictions without formal court rule and others by inclusion in the local court rules.

The basic objective of the Uniform System of Accounts is to present the financial information in a consistent manner that is understandable to the court and all the interested parties. The parties are entitled to full disclosure, clarity, and, when appropriate, supplemental information.

Basic disclosure includes a listing of the assets with their value at the time the fiduciary acquired the asset and their value at the time of the

FIDUCIARY A person in a position of trust and confidence, acting for or on behalf of another, the management of assets

accounting. For tax purposes, the difference may be reportable by the **fiduciary** or by the beneficiary. Sufficient information to allow proper preparation of tax returns should be provided. It should be remembered that the acquisition value by the fiduciary might not be the tax basis for the estate or beneficiaries. Preparation of this information as part of the process of preparing the accounting will save time.

The introductory comments to the American Law Institute's model accounts provide, in part, as follows.

1. Accounts should be stated in the manner that is understandable by persons who are not familiar with practices and terminology peculiar to the administration of estates and trusts.

2. A fiduciary account shall begin with a concise summary of its purpose and content.

3. A fiduciary account shall contain sufficient information to put the interested parties on notice as to all significant transactions affecting administration during the accounting period.

4. A fiduciary account shall include both carrying values representing the value of assets at acquisition by the fiduciary and current values at the beginning and end of the accounting period.

5. Gains and losses incurred during the accounting period shall be shown separately in the same schedule.

6. The account shall show significant transactions that do not affect the amount for which the fiduciary is accountable.

The basic form of the executor's account and the trustee's account, is the same (see Appendix C). It is helpful to remember that the executor's account is for the administration of a decedent's estate, most of which is settled within a reasonably short time. Although the estate may remain open (unsettled) for more than one year, in most cases, the intent is to close the estate as quickly as possible. Trusts, unlike estates, will frequently continue on for a number of years until all the funds have been disbursed or the purposes of the trust completed. A trust accounting may also be prepared by the fiduciary—the trustee—upon replacement by a successor trustee.

REALIZED GAIN OR LOSS The amount of gain or loss upon the actual sale or transfer of an asset

The information required to prepare the accounting may also be used to prepare the fiduciary's tax returns (Fig. 10-1). The fiduciary's tax returns must be prepared annually to report income earned, losses sustained, and distributions to the beneficiaries. Any taxes paid with the filing of the fiduciary's tax returns will appear on the accounting as an expense. The difference between the accounting and the tax returns is that only **realized gains and losses** are reported on the tax return. In the accounting, unrealized gains and losses will appear on the form as current value next to the fiduciary's acquisition value in the principal-on-hand report.

Form **1041** Department of the Treasury—Internal Revenue Service **U.S. Income Tax Return for Estates and Trusts**	19**99**	

For calendar year 1999 or fiscal year beginning , 1999, and ending , | OMB No. 1545-0092

A Type of entity:	Name of estate or trust (If a grantor type trust, see page 8 of the instructions.)	**C** Employer identification number
☐ Decedent s estate		
☐ Simple trust		**D** Date entity created
☐ Complex trust		
☐ Grantor type trust	Name and title of fiduciary	**E** Nonexempt charitable and split-interest trusts, check applicable boxes (see page 10 of the instructions):
☐ Bankruptcy estate–Ch. 7		
☐ Bankruptcy estate–Ch. 11	Number, street, and room or suite no. (If a P.O. box, see page 8 of the instructions.)	
☐ Pooled income fund		☐ Described in section 4947(a)(1)
B Number of Schedules K-1 attached (see instructions) ▶	City or town, state, and ZIP code	☐ Not a private foundation ☐ Described in section 4947(a)(2)

F Check applicable boxes:	☐ Initial return ☐ Final return ☐ Amended return ☐ Change in fiduciary s name ☐ Change in fiduciary s address	**G** Pooled mortgage account (see page 10 of the instructions): ☐ Bought ☐ Sold Date:

Income
1	Interest income .	1
2	Ordinary dividends.	2
3	Business income or (loss) (attach Schedule C or C-EZ (Form 1040))	3
4	Capital gain or (loss) (attach Schedule D (Form 1041)).	4
5	Rents, royalties, partnerships, other estates and trusts, etc. (attach Schedule E (Form 1040))	5
6	Farm income or (loss) (attach Schedule F (Form 1040))	6
7	Ordinary gain or (loss) (attach Form 4797)	7
8	Other income. List type and amount	8
9	**Total income.** Combine lines 1 through 8 . ▶	9

Deductions
10	Interest. Check if Form 4952 is attached ▶ ☐	10
11	Taxes .	11
12	Fiduciary fees .	12
13	Charitable deduction (from Schedule A, line 7)	13
14	Attorney, accountant, and return preparer fees	14
15a	Other deductions NOT subject to the 2% floor (attach schedule)	15a
b	Allowable miscellaneous itemized deductions subject to the 2% floor.	15b
16	**Total.** Add lines 10 through 15b	16
17	Adjusted total income or (loss). Subtract line 16 from line 9. Enter here and on Schedule B, line 1 ▶	17
18	Income distribution deduction (from Schedule B, line 15) (attach Schedules K-1 (Form 1041))	18
19	Estate tax deduction (including certain generation-skipping taxes) (attach computation)	19
20	Exemption	20
21	**Total deductions.** Add lines 18 through 20 ▶	21

Tax and Payments
22	Taxable income. Subtract line 21 from line 17. If a loss, see page 14 of the instructions	22
23	**Total tax** (from Schedule G, line 8)	23
24	**Payments: a** 1999 estimated tax payments and amount applied from 1998 return	24a
b	Estimated tax payments allocated to beneficiaries (from Form 1041-T)	24b
c	Subtract line 24b from line 24a	24c
d	Tax paid with extension of time to file: ☐ Form 2758 ☐ Form 8736 ☐ Form 8800	24d
e	Federal income tax withheld. If any is from Form(s) 1099, check ▶ ☐	24e
	Other payments: **f** Form 2439 ; **g** Form 4136 ; Total ▶	24h
25	**Total payments.** Add lines 24c through 24e, and 24h ▶	25
26	Estimated tax penalty (see page 15 of the instructions)	26
27	**Tax due.** If line 25 is smaller than the total of lines 23 and 26, enter amount owed	27
28	**Overpayment.** If line 25 is larger than the total of lines 23 and 26, enter amount overpaid	28
29	Amount of line 28 to be: **a Credited to 2000 estimated tax** ▶ ; **b Refunded** ▶	29

Please Sign Here Under penalties of perjury, I declare that I have examined this return, including accompanying schedules and statements, and to the best of my knowledge and belief, it is true, correct, and complete. Declaration of preparer (other than fiduciary) is based on all information of which preparer has any knowledge.

▶ Signature of fiduciary or officer representing fiduciary	Date	▶ EIN of fiduciary if a financial institution (see page 5 of the instructions)

Paid Preparer's Use Only	Preparer s signature ▶	Date	Check if self-employed ▶ ☐	Preparer's SSN or PTIN
	Firm s name (or yours if self-employed) and address		EIN ▶ ZIP code ▶	

For Paperwork Reduction Act Notice, see the separate instructions.   Cat. No. 11370H   Form **1041** (1999)

Figure 10-1   Federal form 1041, U.S. Income Tax Return for Estates and Trusts.

Estate Accounting

FORMAL ACCOUNTING The preparation of a formal statement of the handling of funds on behalf of another, including receipt, management, and disbursement, usually presented to the supervising court

INFORMAL ACCOUNTING A statement of the receipt, disbursement, and handling of funds by a fiduciary to the interested parties not requiring a presentation to the supervising court

FAMILY SETTLEMENT AGREEMENT An agreement, usually by members of a decedent's family, beneficiaries, and heirs, acknowledging the receipt and approval of an informal accounting by the fiduciary, generally the executor or administrator of the estate

In actual practice, most estates in most jurisdictions are settled without the need for a **formal court accounting**. The usual procedure is to prepare an **informal written accounting** listing all of the receipts and disbursements; in some jurisdictions, this is referred to as a **family settlement agreement** (Fig. 10-2). This is provided to all of the beneficiaries for their approval and consent. Good practice dictates that the executor or administrator of the estate obtain the written approval and consent before making the final distributions. Failing this, a formal court accounting and release can be obtained as protection against the claims of the beneficiaries for improper handling of the estate.

Preparing the Accounting

The estate of a decedent, for accounting purposes, is a separate legal entity. It will have property, and, generally, income during the time the estate remains open, and will need a tax return filed to report the income during the period of administration. If the period of administration extends over multiple tax years, tax returns will have to be filed in each tax year. These returns may include the federal fiduciary return, state fiduciary returns, and, in some jurisdictions, a local fiduciary return. The same financial information will be needed to prepare the tax returns and, ultimately, the accounting for the administration of the estate.

The law firm representing the executor or the administrator of the estate usually prepares the actual returns and the accounting. The preparer signs and certifies the accuracy of the returns and the accounting based on all the information they know. From a legal and ethical position, this means that a reasonable effort has been made to determine all of the information. With a standard procedure to follow, the efforts to determine all the information can be documented, if necessary.

A reasonable starting point to determine this information is the preparation of a balance sheet as of the date of death. This will include all the assets and liabilities of the estate at the moment of death and the balances available for the administration of the estate, which, ultimately, will be distributed to the beneficiaries of the estate.

Although the normal rules of income and losses that apply to business do not apply to the estate, there is a similarity. During the administration of the estate, there will usually be income in the form of interest, rents, and royalties, and expenses will be incurred in the administration of the estate. All of these items will be reported on the tax returns and on the final accounting.

In assembling the information, it is useful to break the items down into the traditional accounting categories of assets, liabilities, income, expenses, with the net equity being the claims of the beneficiaries.

To prepare the balance sheet for the decedent at the date of death and the income statement for the last lifetime return and the estate fiduciary returns, you will need to assemble specific information. In many cases, the heirs, including the surviving spouse, may not know about all of the financial activity of the decedent. Obtaining the information frequently

IN THE COURT OF COMMON PLEAS OF BUCKS COUNTY, PENNSYLVANIA
ORPHANS' COURT DIVISION

ESTATE OF WENDELL, DECEASED

WAIVER OF ACCOUNT, RECEIPT, RELEASE
REFUNDING AND INDEMNIFICATION AGREEMENT

This Agreement by and between Paul, David, and Thomas, (hereinafter referred to as "Executors") and Martha, Paul, and David (hereinafter referred to as "Beneficiaries") and Thomas (hereinafter referred to as "Trustee").

WITNESSETH:

Whereas, Wendell died on June 10, 2001, having first made and published his Last Will and Testament dated December 22, 1997, in which he named Paul, David and Thomas as Executors; and

Whereas, on June 22, 2001, said Will was duly probated by the Register of Wills of Bucks County, Pennsylvania, and Letters Testamentary granted thereon to Paul, David, and Thomas, as Executors; and

Whereas, the decedent's tangible personal property has been distributed to his children pursuant to item II of said Will;

Whereas, the Executors have proceeded with the administration of said estate and are now ready to close the estate and to make distribution of the entire residue pursuant to item III of said Will to Thomas, Esquire, Trustee under Trust dated December 22, 1997; and

Whereas, the parties hereto desire that the Executors shall not be required to file an Account with the Orphans' Court of Bucks County, and that the net estate of the decedent shall be distributed without the necessity of filing a formal accounting, hereto intending to be legally bound hereby, mutually agree as follows:

1. The parties hereto, and each of them, agree and acknowledge that they have fully and carefully examined the Last Will and Testament of the decedent, the Trust Agreement dated

(continues)

Figure 10-2   Sample family settlement agreement.

December 22, 1997, and have been personally involved with the estate administration, having access to all documents, financial records and the estate check book.

2. The parties hereto do hereby release, remise and forever discharge the Estate of Wendell L. Minor and the Executors, of and from all manner of acts, suits, claims, accounts, accountings, debts, dues and demands whatsoever which they or any of them or their legal representatives or assigns may at any time hereafter have, against the Executors, the said Estate or the assets thereof, from, for, touching or concerning any of the assets and property of the said Estate and/or any claim or interest thereto or therein, and the administration, management, collection, sale or distribution of any of the said assets and for or on account of any money, interest, income, assets or proceeds out of the same, from the time of the death of the said decedent to and including the date of this Agreement and release.

3. The estate assets shall be transferred to the Trustee to be administered under and pursuant to a written Trust Agreement dated December 22, 1997 between Wendell Settlor, and Thomas, Trustee, the terms and provisions of which are acknowledge by the parties.

4. This instrument is a full and final Family Settlement Agreement by and among the parties hereto, both fiduciary and individual, all of the same having been arrived at, concluded and executed after a full and complete disclosure of the assets and liabilities of the said estate and the rights of the parties therein and thereto and all of the parties thereto, and each of them, agrees to abide by the terms hereof.

5. The parties hereto, and each of them, agree that they will at all times in the future and whenever necessary, appropriate or convenient make, execute and deliver to the said Executor, Trustee, and/or to any other party or persons, any and all instruments, documents, conveyances, deeds, releases or other instruments of any kind necessary or convenient to carry out the intention of this Agreement and/or to permit, assist and enable the Executor and Trustee to fulfill their duties with reference to the said estate and Trust and all of the assets thereof.

(continues)

Figure 10-2   *Continued.*

6. The Trustee hereto further agrees to refund to the Executors from the trust assets to be delivered to him any amount or amounts that may at any time hereafter be determined to have been an erroneous distribution to him regardless of the cause of such erroneous distribution, even if attributable to negligence, and agrees that any period for the limitation of actions for the collection of any erroneous distribution to him shall commence only at such time as the Executors shall have obtained actual knowledge of such erroneous distribution, and that in no event shall the period for collection of any erroneous distribution be less than two years after the actual discovery thereof by the Executors.

7. This Agreement constitutes the entire understanding of the parties hereto, and each of them acknowledges that no representations or statements of any kind, written or oral, have been made to them or any of them prior hereto by the Executors, Trustee, or by any other person or party upon their or his behalf.

8. This Agreement shall inure to the benefit of and shall be binding upon, the parties hereto, and each of them, their heirs, executors, administrators, successors and assigns.

IN WITNESS WHEREOF, the parties hereto have hereunto set their respective hands and seals.

In the presence of:

Figure 10-2   *Continued.*

requires making specific requests for information and background items that may lead to the necessary information. In some cases, heirs may try to avoid disclosure of assets in an attempt to avoid taxation. A diligent effort must be made to gather *all* the information.

From certain basic documents, financial information can be reconstructed. The decedent's last three years' tax returns are a good source of information on income and possible assets. Banks, stock brokerages, and other payers of income-type items are required to submit annual statements that must be reported on the personal lifetime income tax return. The appearance on the return of rents and similar income may indicate property that should be included in the estate. From the itemized deductions, a realty tax deduction may appear, alerting the preparer to the existence of a second home. Contributions to charities may indicate memberships in organizations. Pension information will appear as an income source. These organizations and the payers of pensions and unions should all be contacted to learn of the possible existence of life insurance policies or other death benefits. From the decedent's personal effects, credit card information should be obtained. Many credit card companies provide credit life on unpaid balances or even small life insurance benefits.

In some jurisdictions, state agencies may have advanced monies for various purposes, including nursing home care. In many of these cases, a lien may exist as a priority claim against the assets of the estate of the decedent. This is another liability that can be verified by contacting the appropriate state agency.

☑ Checklist for Estate Accounting

Assemble the basic information and sources of potential assets.

_____ Names

　　_____ Legal name as shown on birth records

　　_____ Legal name change

　　_____ Alias or name variation used

_____ Social Security number

_____ Date of birth

_____ Place of birth

_____ Date of death

_____ Place of death

_____ Residence at time of death

_____ Length of last illness

_____ Bank records

　　_____ Safety box information

　　　　_____ Locations

　　　　_____ Titles

　　　　_____ Any required notifications

　　_____ Checking account statements

　　_____ Savings books

　　_____ Christmas clubs

　　_____ Vacation clubs

　　_____ Credit union shares

_____ Stock information

　　_____ Brokerage accounts

　　_____ Certificates

_____ Insurance policies
    _____ Life
    _____ Fraternal organizations
    _____ Unions
    _____ From banks
    _____ Credit life insurance
_____ Military service
    _____ Life insurance or burial benefits
_____ Social Security
    _____ Death benefits
    _____ Obligation to return prepaid benefit
_____ Bills and invoices
    _____ Final balances due
    _____ Last lifetime bills
    _____ Deposits returnable
        _____ Utilities
        _____ Rent
        _____ Leases
        _____ Telephone
        _____ Cable
_____ Previous year's tax returns
    _____ Federal
    _____ State
    _____ Local
    _____ Other state and local, if second property in different state
_____ Beneficiaries
    _____ Identify all beneficiaries
        _____ Address
        _____ Social Security number
    _____ Determine degree of relationship-spouse
        _____ Children
        _____ Degree of consanguinity
    _____ Identify property passing at time of death to others
        _____ Surviving spouse
        _____ Joint tenant with right of survivorship
        _____ Partnership interests under agreement
    _____ Identify specific property bequests
        _____ Tangible personal property
_____ Real property
    _____ Primary residence

____ Second or vacation Home
____ Time share property
____ Rental property

☑ Steps in Estate Accounting

____ Assets
    ____ Determine date-of-death Value
    ____ Determine alternate date valuation, if appropriate
____ Income
    ____ Beginning of the tax year to the date of death
    ____ Income after date of death to end of tax year
____ Prepare
    ____ Decedent's last lifetime returns
        ____ Federal
        ____ State
        ____ Local
    ____ Estate inheritance tax return
        ____ State
        ____ Federal
    ____ Fiduciary return
        ____ Federal form 1041
        ____ State
        ____ Local
____ Accounting
    ____ Family settlement
    ____ Formal accounting

Presentation of Information

The format for the accounting varies from jurisdiction to jurisdiction. Common to all accounting formats is the requirement to make essential information available to the concerned parties, heirs, beneficiaries, creditors, and the supervising court. The same financial information may be listed in different ways, but it will always show what came into the hands of the fiduciary, what increases or decreases in value occurred, what income was generated, what expenses were incurred, and what was left for distribution to the beneficiaries.

In the language of fiduciary accounting, **principal** refers to the assets of the estate. For a decedent's estate, these are the assets in the deceased's ownership at the time of death. For a trust, these assets are trans-

PRINCIPAL The amount or value of the asset coming into the hands of the fiduciary, or the base amount invested or available for investment

ferred to the trustee for management. Gains refer to the increase in value and loss refers to a decrease in value. Publicly traded stocks and bonds have a market value. This market value may change from day to day, but until the asset is sold, exchanged, or disposed of, the changes are only on paper, hence the use of the term **paper gains and losses**. Once the transfer is finalized, a realized gain or loss occurs that needs to be reported. Income refers to the amount of revenue generated as a result of the ownership or holding of the assets. This includes the interest on bank accounts, notes receivable, dividends on stocks, and rents on real estate holdings. A summary might look like the following:

PAPER GAINS AND LOSSES   The amount of gain or loss that would have been realized if the asset had been sold

Principal	$
Plus: Gains on disposition of principal assets	
Less: Losses on disposition of principal assets	_____
Net Principal Available	$
Income from Principal Assets	_____
Total Principal and Income Available	$
Less Expenses and Disbursements	_____
Total Available for Distribution	$
Distribution to Beneficiaries	_____
Combined Balance of Income and Principal on Hand	$

This basic format can also be used as a cover page or summary for a more detailed accounting. Schedules of principal assets can be attached showing details, including appraisals and other methods used to determine the values. When specific principal assets are promptly distributed to the intended beneficiary, changes in valuation may not be important. However, any diminution in value caused by a delay in distribution is an issue that should be addressed. When the administration of the estate is extended over time, the fiduciary's asset values should be listed with the current value by the addition of another column.

	Current Value	Fiduciary's Acquisition Value
Principal	$123,456	$ 90,876

Accounting to the Court in Minors' Settlements

It is common practice for the attorney for a plaintiff who is a minor to negotiate the settlement of a personal injury case with the attorney for the defendant (Fig. 10-3). Usually, this is with the advice and consent of the minor's parent or other guardian. In many jurisdictions, the settlements are subject to the approval of the supervising court. These may be called petitions or motions for settlement, or a minor's compromise. Attached

THOMAS F. GOLDMAN & ASSOCIATES
BY: Thomas F. Goldman, Esquire
Attorney I.D. #12345
138 N. State Street
Newtown, PA 18940
(215) 860-1100

IN RE: KATHRYN KELSEY, a minor by her parent and guardian, JOHN KELSEY and JOHN KELSEY individually	: IN THE COURT OF COMMON PLEAS BUCKS COUNTY, PENNSYLVANIA : ORPHAN'S COURT DIVISION : NO.

PETITION FOR APPROVAL OF
MINOR'S COMPROMISE

COME NOW, the Petitioner, Casualty Insurance Company, insurer for John Runner, and move this Honorable Court to enter the proposed Order granting the instant Petition and in support thereof are the following:

1. This civil action arises out of personal injuries sustained by the minor Plaintiff, Kathryn Kelsey, date of birth April 11, 1997, in connection with an accident that took place on August 13, 2001.

2. Said accident involved an automobile accident in which the minor was a passenger in a vehicle which was struck by a vehicle being driven by John Runner, at the intersection of Heacock and Stony Hill Roads, Lower Makefield, Bucks County, Pennsylvania.

3. The vehicle in which the minor, Kathryn Kelsey, was riding was violently struck, when John Runner illegally made a left turn into the path of the vehicle in which the minor, Kathryn Kelsey was a passenger.

4. As a result of the said accident, the said minor, Kathryn Kelsey, sustained a Laceration of the right eyebrow and a chest contusion.

Figure 10-3   Sample minor's compromise.

5. The said minor, Kathryn Kelsey, has fully recovered from her injuries, and has no permanent effects from the accident as evidenced by the medical report of her family physician, Joseeph Cast, M.D., attached hereto and marked as Exhibit "A".

6. An offer of $12,500.00 has been tendered by the Petitioner, Casualty Insurance Company, and accepted by the minor Plaintiff's father and natural guardian, John Kelsey, pending approval of the Court.

7. The proposed settlement distribution is as follows:

Gross Recovery: $12,500.00

1. To: All funds should be deposited in the name
   of the minor, Kathryn Kelsey, to be placed in
   a federally insured, interest bearing certificate
   or savings account on behalf of the minor plaintiff
   and to be marked "not to be withdrawn until
   Kathryn Kelsey reaches the age of eighteen (18)
   or by Order of the Court. $12,500.00

WHEREFORE, Petitioner hereby prays this Honorable Court approve the Petition for Approval of Minor's Compromise and the within Order.

THOMAS F. GOLDMAN & ASSOCIATES

BY: _____
       Thomas F. Goldman, Esquire
       Attorney for Petitioner

Figure 10-3   *Continued.*

to the motion or petition is usually a statement showing the financial issues, the amount of the proposed settlement, the costs incurred, and the proposed distribution, including reimbursement to the parents and attorney for costs and the attorney's fee for handling the case. In a number of jurisdictions, by rule, statute, or practice, these amounts may be limited. Depending on local custom and practice, the fee, if a contingent fee, may be based on the *gross* recovery or on the *net* recovery.

Ethical Issue

> **NFPA model code**
> EC-1.2(d): A paralegal shall not knowingly engage in fraudulent billing practices. . . .

> Based on the model code ethical consideration, does a paralegal have any ethical obligation after learning that a client has been charged a clearly excessive fee based upon those charged other clients for similar services?

CHAPTER SUMMARY

A necessary part of the responsibility of a fiduciary is to properly account for all funds coming into their possession or control, including the disbursement, distribution, and investment of the funds. The responsibility for reporting this information typically falls on the law firm representing the fiduciary. For the person preparing the accounting, it is important to have a form and procedure for preparing the documentation for the court and interested parties. With an understanding of the need for the information in tax return and accounting report preparation, duplication of effort can be avoided. With an understanding of the documentation needed, steps can be taken from the start of the fiduciary's representation to gather the necessary information in an orderly form.

GLOSSARY

Accounting   A report of the handling of the funds belonging to another, usually by a fiduciary to the beneficiary or the court

Family settlement agreement   An agreement, usually by members of a decedent's family, beneficiaries, and heirs, acknowledging the receipt and approval of an informal accounting by the fiduciary, generally the executor or administrator of the estate

Fiduciary   A person in a position of trust and confidence, acting for or on behalf of another, the management of assets

Formal accounting   The preparation of a formal statement of the handling of funds on behalf of another, including receipt, management, and disbursement, usually presented to the supervising court

Informal accounting   A statement of the receipt, disbursement, and handling of funds by a fiduciary to the interested parties not requiring a presentation to the supervising court

Paper gains and losses   The amount of gain or loss that would have been realized if the asset had been sold

Principal   The amount or value of the asset coming into the hands of the fiduciary, or the base amount invested or available for investment

Realized gain or loss   The amount of gain or loss upon the actual sale or transfer of an asset

Uniform system of accounts   A proposed method of fiduciary accounting providing for a consistent presentation to the courts and interested parties

REVIEW QUESTIONS

1. Why do courts request an accounting by the executor or trustee?
2. What is the purpose of the Uniform System of Accounts?
3. What is a family settlement agreement?
4. In fiduciary accounting, what does the term *principal* mean?
5. What is meant by *paper gains and losses*?
6. Are the fees in a contingent-fee case based upon net or gross recovery?
7. How is an accounting different from a tax return?
8. Is the acquisition value by the fiduciary the same as the tax basis?
9. What is the usual accounting procedure in the settling of estates in most jurisdictions?
10. What is a common requirement for all accounting formats?

Chapter 11

Federal Income Tax

In This Chapter
Why Study Federal Income Tax?
Types of Taxes
History and Sources of Federal Income Tax Law
Federal Tax Laws
Who Must File?
Information Returns
Tax Year
Getting the Information Together
Preparing Form 1040
IRS-Imposed Obligation on Preparers
Ethical Issue

Why Study Federal Income Tax?

Virtually every client who comes into the law office will have to file a tax return—individuals, corporations, trusts, estates, and unincorporated business entities. Some of these clients may need to file more than one return. The client may be the executor of an estate, which must file a fiduciary return, or an individual required to report the fee received as the executor or administrator of the estate. With the increased complexity of the tax code, law firms are more involved in assuring client compliance by directly preparing returns and by working with other tax professionals, such as accountants and financial planners.

It is important to know when returns must be filed, who must file them, and what must be reported. With this understanding, it becomes easier to assemble the information in a usable form in a time-conscious manner and ensure the necessary compliance to avoid inadvertent malpractice and possible tax evasion issues.

Types of Taxes

SALES AND USE TAX
A tax levied on the sale and/or use of a product or service, generally collected by the seller or service provider

We all are faced with paying taxes. These taxes take many forms and are assessed on many different activities and sources of revenue. In most states, and in many local areas, there are taxes assessed on the sale and use of goods and services; these are generally referred to, collectively, as **sales and use taxes**. These are the most noticeable taxes in daily life.

MERCANTILE TAX
A tax generally levied on the amount of sales as a tax on the privilege of doing business in a jurisdiction

BUSINESS PRIVILEGE TAX A tax levied for the privilege of being allowed to do business; this may be a flat tax or a tax on the gross or net receipts

SOCIAL ENGINEERING A use of tax policy to encourage certain types of behavior

Some taxes are less noticeable and are assessed on specific activities and products. Included within the price of some goods and services are less noticeable assessments, such as the federal and state tax included in the price of gasoline at the pump and the retail sale of cigarettes. Other less obvious taxes are those assessed on the right to perform certain activities, such as local **mercantile and business privilege taxes**. Some of these taxes are imposed primarily to raise the necessary revenue for the operation of government.

Other taxes are more for the purpose of **social engineering** less for the purpose of revenue generation, are frequently used to discourage the use of certain products (e.g., cigarettes). Within the social engineering scheme is a concept of encouraging activity, such as saving for retirement, home purchases, or payments for higher education, by the granting of tax breaks, credits, and deductions in determining the final tax to be paid. To encourage retirement savings, deductions are allowed for some of the retirement savings we make on federal and some state income tax returns. In some cases, certain classes of income are exempt from taxation, such as retirement income from certain sources (e.g., government pensions).

It is important to be aware of these types of tax adjustments and the concept of social engineering. The specifics will change from year to year and among the different government agencies, but the concept will probably continue, barring a major tax overhaul. We will discuss some of these tax adjustments in reviewing the preparation of certain tax returns.

The computation and assessment of the many specialized local, state, and federal taxes is beyond the scope of this book. We will concentrate on three major forms of tax: the income, estate, and gift taxes. These taxes generally fit into two categories; those assessed on income and those assessed on the transfer of wealth. The federal government imposes a tax on the income of individuals, businesses, fiduciaries, and other income-generating entities. The majority of states also impose a broad-based income tax. Seven states have not as yet imposed this form of tax, and two impose a limited tax on income from stocks, bonds, and interest.

INTERNAL REVENUE CODE The federal tax enactment

This chapter is designed to introduce you to the general concepts of the **Internal Revenue Code**. Detailed analysis and planning issues are left to advanced courses, accountants, and tax attorneys. The paralegal and legal assistant are called upon to organize the raw information for preparation of tax returns. These returns may involve individuals, business entities, estates, or trusts. It is necessary to have an understanding of what returns are used, to whom they apply, and their general organization. The list of federal tax return forms and schedules is very large and growing. We will concentrate on the basic forms and some of the more commonly used schedules that are used to support specific entries on these tax forms.

History and Sources of Federal Income Tax Law

In the law office, it is frequently necessary to locate a particular tax law or regulation. Finding the applicable law is easier when you have an understanding of the source of the law.

Article I of the U.S. Constitution gives the power to levy and collect taxes to Congress. The 16th amendment gives Congress the authority to levy the tax on income from whatever sources derived. In 1913, a broad-based income tax was imposed called the Tariff Act of 1913. Some of the Act's concepts are still utilized today, such as itemized deduction and personal exemption. Although the concepts have undergone change, they remain and are frequently discussed, if not from the revenue-generating standpoint, then from the political implication of any change.

INTERNAL REVENUE CODE   The federal tax enactment

The tax-levying authority of the Congress can be found in Title 26 of the United States Code (USC), titled and referred to as the **Internal Revenue Code**, and frequently referred to as the Code or cited as IRC. In 1986, the Congress recodified the tax law into the current version, known as the Internal Revenue Code of 1986.

Title 26 is broken down in an outline fashion with subtitles:

Subtitle

A   Income Taxes
B   Estate and Gift Taxes
C   Employment Taxes
D   Miscellaneous Excise Taxes
E   Alcohol, Tobacco, and Certain Other Excise Taxes
F   Procedure and Administration
G   The Joint Committee on Taxation
H   Financing of Presidential Election Campaigns
I   Trust Fund Code
J   Coal Industry Health Benefits
K   Group Health Plan Portability, Access, and Renewability Requirements

These subtitles are then further broken down as follows:

Chapters (1–100)
    Subchapters (A, B, C, etc.)
        Parts (I, II, III, etc.)
            Subparts (A . . . B . . . C, etc.)
                Sections (1, 2, 3, etc.)
                    Subsections [(a), (b), (c), etc.)].

For example, the listing of items included in Gross Income is found in

Title 26—Internal Revenue Code
    Subtitle A—Income Taxes
        Chapter 1—Normal Taxes and Surtaxes
            Subchapter B—Computation of Taxable Income
                Part I—Definition of Gross Income, Adjusted Gross Income, Taxable Income, etc.
                Section 61—Gross Income Defined
                Subsection (a) General Definition
                    (1) Compensation for services, including. . . .

Note that in this particular chapter there are no subparts.

Federal Tax Laws

Federal tax laws are administered by the Department of the Treasury, a Presidential cabinet department, through the **Internal Revenue Service** (IRS), an agency whose mission statement says, " the purposes of the Internal Revenue Service is to collect the proper amount of tax revenue."

---

26 USC Sec. 61

TITLE 26 - INTERNAL REVENUE CODE

Subtitle A - Income Taxes

CHAPTER 1 - NORMAL TAXES AND SURTAXES

Subchapter B - Computation of Taxable income

PART I - DEFINITION OF GROSS INCOME, ADJUSTED GROSS INCOME, TAXABLE INCOME, ETC.

Sec. 61. Gross income defined

(a) General definition

Except as otherwise provided in this subtitle, gross income means all income from whatever source derived, including (but not limited to) the following items:

(1) Compensation for services, including fees, commissions, fringe benefits, and similar items;

(2) Gross income derived from business;

(3) Gains derived from dealings in property;

(4) Interest;

(5) Rents;

(6) Royalties;

(7) Dividends;

(8) Alimony and separate maintenance payments;

(9) Annuities;

(10) Income from life insurance and endowment contracts;

(11) Pensions;

(12) Income from discharge of indebtedness;

(13) Distributive share of partnership gross income;

(14) Income in respect of a decedent; and

(15) Income from an interest in an estate or trust.

Figure 11-1   U.S. Internal Revenue Code Section 61.

COMPUTATION OF TAXABLE INCOME

Sec. 1.61-1 Gross income.

(a) General definition. Gross income means all income from whatever source derived, unless excluded by law. Gross income includes income realized in any form, whether in money, property, or services. Income may be realized, therefore, in the form of services, meals, accommodations, stock, or other property, as well as in cash. Section 61 lists the more common items of gross income for purposes of illustration. For purposes of further illustration, Sec. 1.61-14 mentions several miscellaneous items of gross income not listed specifically in section 61. Gross income, however, is not limited to the items so enumerated.

(b) Cross references. Cross references to other provisions of the Code are to be found throughout the regulations under section 61. The purpose of these cross references is to direct attention to the more common items which are included in or excluded from gross income entirely, or treated in some special manner. To the extent that another section of the Code or of the regulations thereunder, provides specific treatment for any item of income, such other provision shall apply notwithstanding section 61 and the regulations thereunder. The cross references do not cover all possible items.

Figure 11-2   U.S. Internal Revenue Code Regulation 1.61.

The IRS, in its function of administering the Internal Revenue Code, carries out this mission.

INTERNAL REVENUE REGULATIONS The rules issued for the implementation of the Internal Revenue Code

As part of the administration of the Code, the Treasury Department and the IRS issue various guidelines. Most significant are the **Internal Revenue Regulations** (Figs. 11-1 and 11-2). These are broad-based explanations of the individual Code sections. Since each of the regulations refers to a specific Code section, subsection, part, or subpart, the same numbering method is used, but with the addition of a numeral 1 and a period before the Code section. For example, the regulation for section 61 on gross income would be 1.61.

Additional guidelines on more specific matters or on case-by-case matters are issued by the IRS in the form of Revenue Rulings, Private Letter Rulings, and a Technical Advice Memorandum.

Who Must File?

In chapter 2, we learned about the economic entity concept. Every person, organization, or legal entity can be viewed as an individual economic entity. For tax-filing purposes, the same concept applies. If an economic entity receives income, as defined in Code section 61, unless otherwise exempted from the filing requirement, it will probably have to file a return of some type. This does not mean that taxes will necessarily have to be paid by the taxable entity, but only that some form of return probably will be required.

It is beyond the scope of this chapter to discuss all the possibilities, such as when returns must be filed when gifts are made. We will discuss the returns most often encountered in the small law office: the personal return, the partnership return, the corporation return, and the fiduciary return, shown in Figure 11-3. Selected major return forms are listed below.

Form	Used By
1040	Individuals
1041	Fiduciaries—estates and trusts
1065	Partnerships
1120	Corporations
1120S	Small business corporations
706	Estates

Information Returns

Many types of tax returns must be filed with the federal government. Most people are familiar with the tax returns used to determine the amount of tax on income. There is also a group of returns that are informational in nature. They give information that is used to determine the amounts of income and deductions to be included on other income tax returns; for example, the federal partnership form 1065 (Fig. 11-4) is an information return. There is no direct federal tax assessment that is paid by the partnership. The individual partners include on their personal returns their respective share of income and deductions.

As part of the system to encourage compliance and prevent tax fraud, a separate group of information returns has gained new importance for filers. These include the forms advising of nonemployee compensation, gambling winnings, and deposits and transfers of funds in excess of set amounts. Most of the forms that the law firm will be required to file are related to the payment to other professionals, such as court reporters, investigators, witnesses, and title abstractors. Occasionally, forms must also be filed to document the payment of interest on escrow accounts. Some of these information forms are listed below. Forms 1099-MISC and 1098 are shown in Figures 11-5 and 11-6.

Form	Purpose
W-2	Wage and tax statement
W-2 G	Certain gambling winnings
W-8	Certificate of Foreign status
W-9	Request for Taxpayer Identification Number and Certification
1098	Interest paid
1099-DIV	Dividends and distributions
1099-INT	Interest income
1099-MISC	Miscellaneous income
1099-B	Proceeds from broker or barter exchange transactions
1065	Partnership
1065 K-1	Partner's share of income and loss

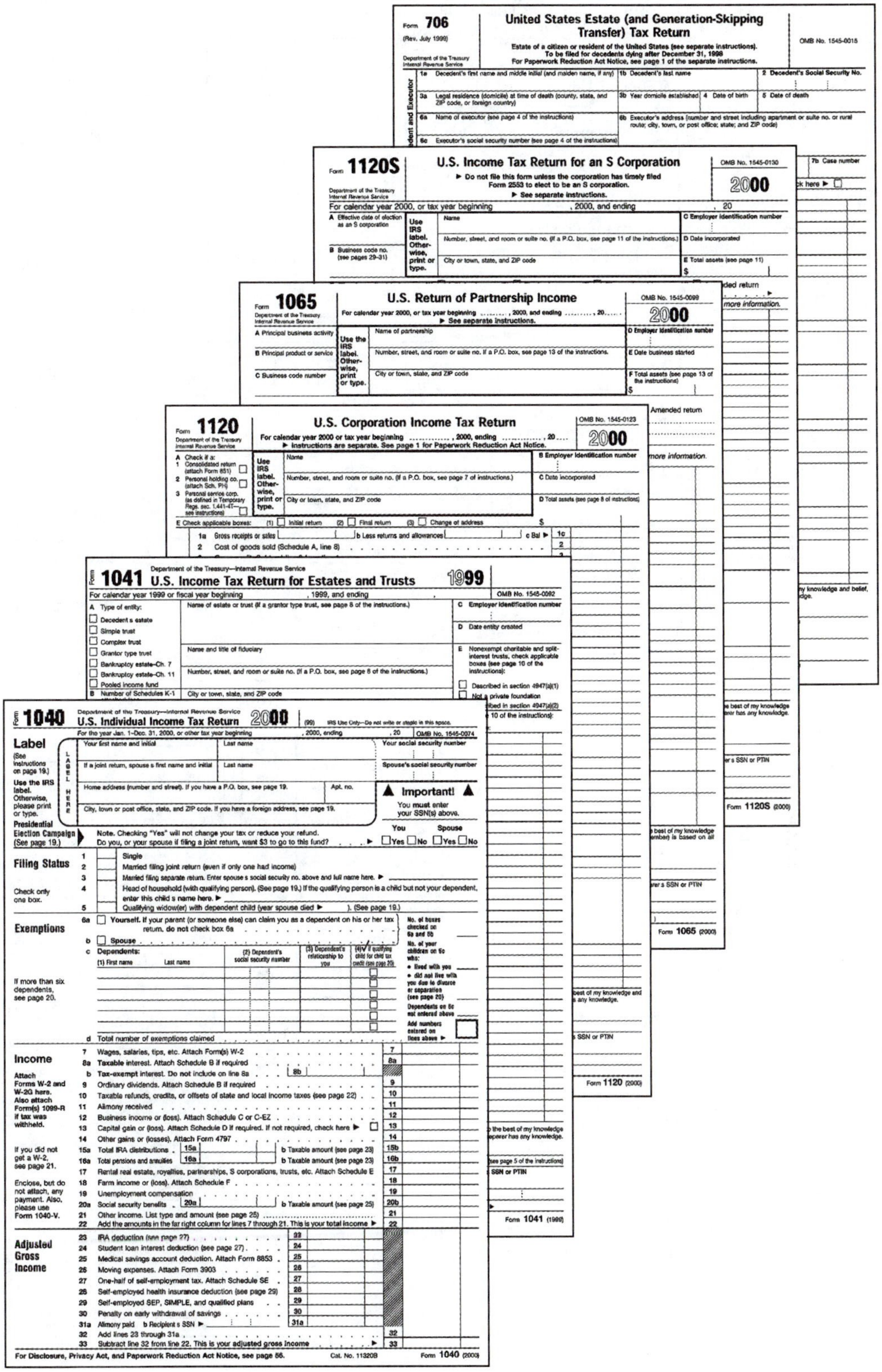

Figure 11-3 Selected major tax return forms.

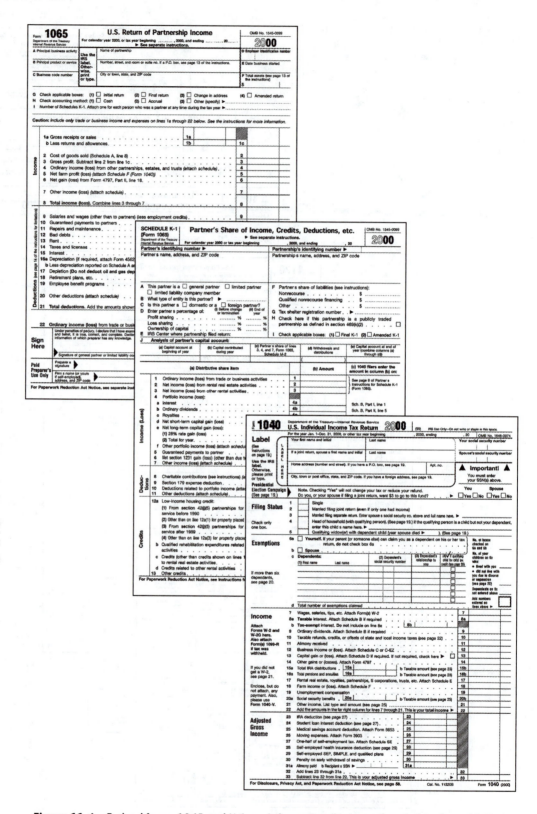

Figure 11-4   Federal forms 1065 and K-1 are informational returns that tie into form 1040.

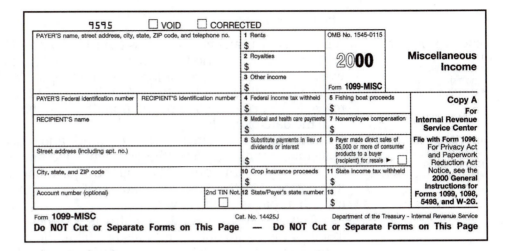

Figure 11-5   Federal form 1099 MISC, Miscellaneous Income.

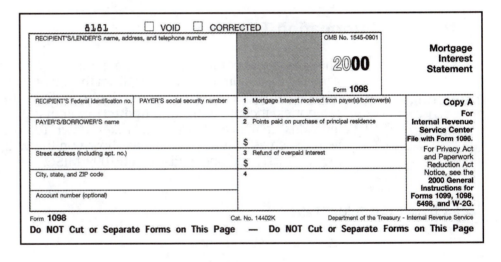

Figure 11-6   Federal form 1098, Mortgage Interest Statement.

Tax Year

CALENDAR YEAR
The period from January 1 to December 31

TAX YEAR   A period of generally 12 months used for the computation of taxes

Calendar Year versus Fiscal Year

Normally, tax returns are filed on a **calendar-year** basis, January 1 to December 31. This is generally true for most taxpayers. Some entities, however, such as corporations, may elect to file on a fiscal-year basis. A fiscal year **(tax year)** is any reporting period that is consistent from year to year and covers the full year of 12 months.

Short Tax Years

A **short year** is any period of less than 12 months. Normally, tax returns are prepared for a period covering 12 months. There are some situations when a tax return is filed for less than a full year. The last lifetime tax return will usually be for less than the full year of 12 months. In this case, a return is filed covering the period from the beginning of the year, January 1, to the date of death.

Income from interest, dividends, rents, and other continuing sources of income not directly from the decedent's lifetime activity is included in the fiduciary return, form 1041, and the equivalent state and/or local return prepared by the executor or administrator of the decedent's estate in his or her role as a fiduciary.

The settlement of estates and trusts and the distribution of all of the assets or the estate of trust may also result in the filing of a short-year return covering the period from the beginning of the fiduciary return to the date of the final distribution.

Getting the Information Together

The individual tax forms represent a good checklist for requesting and organizing the required information from the client (Fig. 11-7). A logical way of organizing the required information is to divide the raw data into two categories, income items and **deduction** items. Within these categories, individual items can be further broken down to conform to the types of items, such as ordinary income as shown on the W-2, interest income on the 1099-INT, and dividends on the 1099-MISC.

✓ Checklist of Folder Tabs

_____ Bank statements
   _____ 1099- INT
_____ Securities accounts
   _____ 1099-DIV
   _____ 1099-B
_____ Mortgage statements and amortization statement
   _____ 1098
   _____ 1099-MISC, rents
_____ Business interests
   _____ 1120S, small business corporations
   _____ 1065, partnerships

Income	7	Wages, salaries, tips, etc. Attach Form(s) W-2	7	
	8a	**Taxable** interest. Attach Schedule B if required	8a	
Attach Forms W-2 and W-2G here. Also attach Form(s) 1099-R if tax was withheld.	b	**Tax-exempt** interest. **Do not** include on line 8a . . . [8b]		
	9	Ordinary dividends. Attach Schedule B if required	9	
	10	Taxable refunds, credits, or offsets of state and local income taxes (see page 22) . .	10	
	11	Alimony received	11	
	12	Business income or (loss). Attach Schedule C or C-EZ	12	
	13	Capital gain or (loss). Attach Schedule D if required. If not required, check here ▶ ☐	13	
	14	Other gains or (losses). Attach Form 4797	14	
If you did not get a W-2, see page 21.	15a	Total IRA distributions . [15a] b Taxable amount (see page 23)	15b	
	16a	Total pensions and annuities [16a] b Taxable amount (see page 23)	16b	
	17	Rental real estate, royalties, partnerships, S corporations, trusts, etc. Attach Schedule E	17	
Enclose, but do not attach, any payment. Also, please use Form 1040-V.	18	Farm income or (loss). Attach Schedule F	18	
	19	Unemployment compensation	19	
	20a	Social security benefits . [20a] b Taxable amount (see page 25)	20b	
	21	Other income. List type and amount (see page 25)	21	
	22	Add the amounts in the far right column for lines 7 through 21. This is your **total income** ▶	22	

Figure 11-7   Income portion of federal form 1040, page 1.

Web Sites

The Internal Revenue Service maintains an excellent web site, http://www.ustreas.irs.gov, providing current information and copies of tax forms in downloadable form (Fig. 11-8).

Figure 11-8   IRS home page.

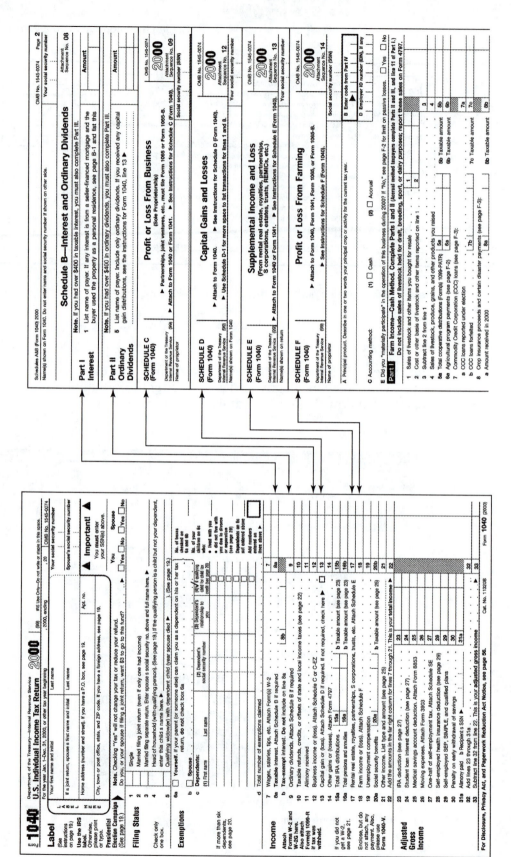

Figure 11-9 Federal form 1040 with supporting schedules.

Preparing Form 1040

Preparing the Supporting Schedules

Most of the federal tax return forms are a summary of items from supporting schedules. Pages 1 and 2 of form 1040 are typical of these forms and are similar to the Fiduciary 1041, the Partnership 1065, the Corporate 1120, and the Small Business Corporation 1120S (Fig. 11-9).

Income Items

The IRC lists items included under Gross Income. For most of these items, there is a supporting schedule and a form that is provided to the recipient containing the information.

Section 61(a) Items	Information Source	Supporting Schedule
(1) Compensation for Services	1099, W-2	1040 page 1
(2) Gross Income from Business	1099, K-1	Schedule C
(3) Gains from Dealing in Property	1099-B	Schedule D
(4) Interest	1099	Schedule B
(5) Rents	1099	Schedule E
(6) Royalties	1099	Schedule E
(7) Dividends—Ordinary	1099	Schedule B
—Capital Gains		Schedule D
(8) Alimony	1099	1040 page 1
(9) Annuities	1099-R	1040 page 1
(10) Income from Life Insurance—Interest and Endowments—Interest	1099-R	Schedule B
(11) Pensions	1099-R	1040 page 1
(12) Discharge of Indebtedness	1099C	varies
(13) Partnership Income	K-1 Form 1065	Schedule E
(14) Income in Respect of Decedent	K-1 Form 1041	Schedule E
(15) Income from Estate or Trust	K-1 Form 1041	Schedule E

Exclusions from Income

EXCLUSIONS
Amounts not required to be reported for tax purposes

Although it sometimes seems that every item one receives is taxable, the IRC excludes certain items from being included in the recipient's income for federal tax purposes. Subject to limitations and some restrictions, generally excluded under the IRC Code sections are the following:

Section

101   Life insurance proceeds payable by reason of death
       (note: interest earned on the proceeds is included)
102   The value of property acquired by gift, bequest, devise,
       or inheritance
103   Interest on state and local bonds
104   Amounts received under workmen's compensation or
       for personal physical injuries or sickness

105	Amounts received under accident and health plans
106	Contributions by employers to accident and health plans
107	Rental value of a parsonage
108	Income from discharge of indebtedness
109	Improvements by the lessee on the lessor's property
110	Qualified lessee construction allowances for short-term leases
137	Adoption assistance programs

Personal Exemptions

PERSONAL EXEMPTIONS
Amounts permitted to be deducted from gross income for the taxpayer and each dependent in determining taxable income

A **personal exemption** is an amount allowed as a deduction from Adjusted Gross Income in calculating the Taxable Income. As a general rule, a person may claim one exemption for themselves, his or her spouse, and each dependent. Under current regulations, the Social Security number of each person claimed as a dependent must be listed. The actual amount of the deduction will depend on the amount allowed in a particular tax year.

Itemized Deductions

ITEMIZED DEDUCTIONS
Amounts permitted to be deducted for specific expenditures under the code, generally in place of a permitted standard deduction

The amounts paid for selected items of a personal nature, such as home mortgage interest and real estate taxes, are deductible in computing taxable income (Fig. 11-10). The items and limitations for deductibility change frequently. In this area, both the federal and state governments respond to the political issues and social engineering issues of the times by permitting or not permitting deductions. In past years, deductions were allowed for sales and use taxes, which, at present, are not permitted. Some clients may question the tax preparer about these deduction changes. Under the current law, there is a set of limits imposed. Medical expenses must exceed 7.5 percent of adjusted gross income to be deductible, casualty losses must exceed 10 percent of adjusted gross income, and items lumped as miscellaneous itemized deductions must exceed 2 percent of adjusted gross income. A limit on the amount of total itemized deductions is imposed on high-income tax payers, and a minimum standard deduction is provided for lower income taxpayers or those without substantial itemized deductions. Because these amounts can change from year to year, it is wise to review the official instructions for the year or years of the returns being prepared.

Tax Calculation

Calculating the actual owed tax requires a multistep computation (Fig. 11-11). The first step is the calculation of adjusted gross income or AGI. AGI is reduced initially by amounts for personal exemptions, and itemized or standard deductions. The actual amounts of the reductions depend, in part, on the level of the AGI, the filing status of the taxpayer, and the amounts determined by inflation indexing and current actions of Congress. The actual amounts should be checked for each year for which a return is being prepared.

The tax will then be based on the taxable income (AGI after reductions for exemptions and deductions). The tax may then be deducted by certain allowable credits and increased by other taxes (Fig. 11-12).

SCHEDULES A&B (Form 1040) Department of the Treasury Internal Revenue Service (99)	Schedule A—Itemized Deductions (Schedule B is on back) ▶ Attach to Form 1040. ▶ See Instructions for Schedules A and B (Form 1040).	OMB No. 1545-0074 **20**00 Attachment Sequence No. **07**
Name(s) shown on Form 1040		Your social security number

Medical and Dental Expenses		**Caution.** Do not include expenses reimbursed or paid by others.		
	1	Medical and dental expenses (see page A-2) . . .	1	
	2	Enter amount from Form 1040, line 34 . ⌊ **2** ⌋		
	3	Multiply line 2 above by 7.5% (.075)	3	
	4	Subtract line 3 from line 1. If line 3 is more than line 1, enter -0-		4
Taxes You Paid (See page A-2.)	5	State and local income taxes	5	
	6	Real estate taxes (see page A-2)	6	
	7	Personal property taxes	7	
	8	Other taxes. List type and amount ▶	8	
	9	Add lines 5 through 8		9
Interest You Paid (See page A-3.)	10	Home mortgage interest and points reported to you on Form 1098	10	
	11	Home mortgage interest not reported to you on Form 1098. If paid to the person from whom you bought the home, see page A-3 and show that person s name, identifying no., and address ▶		
Note. Personal interest is not deductible.		------------------------------- -------------------------------	11	
	12	Points not reported to you on Form 1098. See page A-3 for special rules	12	
	13	Investment interest. Attach Form 4952 if required. (See page A-3.)	13	
	14	Add lines 10 through 13		14
Gifts to Charity If you made a gift and got a benefit for it, see page A-4.	15	Gifts by cash or check. If you made any gift of $250 or more, see page A-4	15	
	16	Other than by cash or check. If any gift of $250 or more, see page A-4. You **must** attach Form 8283 if over $500	16	
	17	Carryover from prior year	17	
	18	Add lines 15 through 17		18
Casualty and Theft Losses	19	Casualty or theft loss(es). Attach Form 4684. (See page A-5.)		19
Job Expenses and Most Other Miscellaneous Deductions (See page A-5 for expenses to deduct here.)	20	Unreimbursed employee expenses—job travel, union dues, job education, etc. You **must** attach Form 2106 or 2106-EZ if required. (See page A-5.) ▶ .... -------------------------------	20	
	21	Tax preparation fees	21	
	22	Other expenses—investment, safe deposit box, etc. List type and amount ▶	22	
	23	Add lines 20 through 22	23	
	24	Enter amount from Form 1040, line 34 . ⌊ **24** ⌋		
	25	Multiply line 24 above by 2% (.02)	25	
	26	Subtract line 25 from line 23. If line 25 is more than line 23, enter -0- . . .		26
Other Miscellaneous Deductions	27	Other—from list on page A-6. List type and amount ▶ .... -------------------------------		27
Total Itemized Deductions	28	Is Form 1040, line 34, over $128,950 (over $64,475 if married filing separately)? ☐ **No.** Your deduction is not limited. Add the amounts in the far right column for lines 4 through 27. Also, enter this amount on Form 1040, line 36. ☐ **Yes.** Your deduction may be limited. See page A-6 for the amount to enter.	▶	28

For Paperwork Reduction Act Notice, see Form 1040 instructions.	Cat. No. 11330X	Schedule A (Form 1040) 2000

Figure 11-10   Schedule A.

Tax Payments

The income tax regulations require taxpayers, whether individuals, fiduciaries, or businesses, to make periodic payments of the estimated tax owed. These payments are generally made on a quarterly basis when

	23	IRA deduction (see page 27)	23		
Adjusted Gross Income	24	Student loan interest deduction (see page 27) . . .	24		
	25	Medical savings account deduction. Attach Form 8853 .	25		
	26	Moving expenses. Attach Form 3903	26		
	27	One-half of self-employment tax. Attach Schedule SE	27		
	28	Self-employed health insurance deduction (see page 29)	28		
	29	Self-employed SEP, SIMPLE, and qualified plans . .	29		
	30	Penalty on early withdrawal of savings	30		

Figure 11-11   Tax calculation portion of Form 1040.

Figure 11-12   Form 1040, credits and other taxes section.

there is no other federal income tax withheld at the payment's source (e.g., the employer). Failure to make the required payments will result in the imposition of interest on the unpaid balances not timely paid and may also result in the imposition of a penalty. Under some circumstances, the amount of interest and penalty can be reduced or eliminated by the preparation and filing of form 2210.

IRS-Imposed Obligation on Preparers

In addition to the ethical rules imposed on lawyers and CPAs engaged in tax practices, the IRC imposes an additional set of obligations on income tax return preparers. Excluded from the IRC definition are those who prepare gift and estate tax returns. The IRC defines a preparer for the purpose of imposing its rules as "a person who prepares for compensation, or employees [. . .] person to prepare for compensation, any return of tax imposed by subtitle A or any claim for refund of tax imposed by subtitle A in the Income Tax section of the code."

Penalties of $50 per incident may be imposed for failure to

1. furnish the taxpayer with a copy of the return;
2. failure to sign the return or claim;
3. failure to provide the preparer's identification number;
4. failure to keep a copy of the return or claim or to keep a list of taxpayers for whom returns or claims were prepared;
5. failure to identify employed tax preparers.

A $500 per-check penalty will be imposed for endorsing or negotiating a taxpayer's refund check. In addition to the penalties for these procedural-type offenses, a penalty of $1,000 may be imposed for knowingly assisting the taxpayer in understating their income tax liability.

In addition to all of the other obligations and penalties is the possible imposition of a penalty of $500 for the preparation of a frivolous tax return.

 **Ethical Issue**

ABA Model Code

Canon 4

A lawyer should be fully informed of all the facts of the matter he is handling in order for the client to take full advantage of our legal system . . . the ethical obligation of a lawyer to hold inviolate the confidences and secrets of his clients. . . .

Disciplinary Rule 4-101 states, in part, that:

a lawyer shall not knowingly reveal a confidence or secret of his client, and a lawyer may reveal the intention of his client to commit a crime and the information necessary to prevent the crime.

It is not uncommon for a client to tell the tax preparer about unde-clared income items. In certain occupations, it is a normal occur-rence to receive cash payments, either as a tip or other gratuity. In other situations, it may be known from general observation that the information presented is not accurate. For example, clients have been known to list medical expenses for their pets as dependent medical care and seek to take a medical deduction.

CHAPTER SUMMARY

The payment of federal taxes is governed by the Internal Revenue Code (IRC). The obligation for the collection of these taxes has been delegated to the Internal Revenue Service (IRS). The IRS issues as part of its assess-ment activities its interpretation of the IRC code in the form of the Internal Revenue Regulations. Gross income, for purposes of the Code, is defined in section 61 as all income from whatever sources derived, including the listed items of income. However, not all income is taxable. The U.S. Con-gress has specifically exempted certain types of income for political or social-engineering purposes. In determining the actual tax due, gross income may be adjusted for certain exclusions, exemptions, deductions, and credits.

GLOSSARY

Business privilege tax   A tax levied for the privilege of being allowed to do business; this may be a flat tax or a tax on the gross or net receipts

Calendar year   The period from January 1 to December 31

Deductions   Amounts permitted by tax law to be deducted from gross income in determining taxable income

Exclusions   Amounts not required to be reported for tax purposes

Income   Income from the sale of merchandise or rendering of services

Internal Revenue Code   The federal tax enactment

Internal Revenue Regulations   The rules issued for the implementation of the Internal Revenue Code

Internal Revenue Service   The agency of the U.S. Treasury Department charged with the responsibility of enforcing the tax code

Itemized deductions   Amounts permitted to be deducted for specific expendi-tures under the code, generally in place of a permitted standard deduction

Mercantile tax   A tax generally levied on the amount of sales as a tax on the privilege of doing business in a jurisdiction

Personal exemptions   Amounts permitted to be deducted from gross income for the taxpayer and each dependent in determining taxable income

Sales and use tax   A tax levied on the sale and/or use of a product or service, generally collected by the seller or service provider

Short year   A period of less than 12 months used for financial or tax-reporting purposes

Social engineering   A use of tax policy to encourage certain types of behavior

Tax year   A period of generally 12 months used for the computation of taxes

REVIEW QUESTIONS

1. What is the tax obligation on the executor of an estate?
2. How is tax policy used for social engineering?
3. Under what authority is the income tax imposed?
4. Where is gross income defined for income tax purposes?
5. What is an information tax return?
6. What is the difference between a calendar year and a fiscal year for tax purposes?
7. What is a short tax year?
8. What is a personal exemption?
9. What are estimated tax payments?
10. Is it proper to ignore information on cash receipts when preparing a client's tax return?

Chapter 12

State and Local Income Tax

In This Chapter
Why Study State and Local Tax?
Types of State and Local Taxes
Determining the Returns to Be Filed
A Starting Point
Assembling the Information

Why Study State and Local Tax?

Paying taxes is a fact of life. Keeping track of all the taxes that apply to any individual, estate, trust, or business client can be very difficult. For purposes of this chapter, we will eliminate any discussion of federal taxes. The problem is to determine what state and local governments or agencies impose a tax, how the tax is computed, and how it is reported. A starting point is with recognizing the possible taxing authorities. With a few exceptions, each state has a broad-based tax on income or wealth transfer; many cities, counties, parishes, towns, and boroughs also impose some tax on income. In many states, school districts also have independent taxation schemes.

Types of State and Local Taxes

Many state and local governments assess taxes based on income. These commonly are income taxes similar to that imposed by the federal government (Fig. 12-1). In fact, some of these taxes are based on the same formulas used by the federal government. Amounts are frequently transferred directly from the federal personal income tax return, form 1040, to the state income tax form. Adjustments may be made to delete deductions included on the federal return for such things as estate and local taxes based on income.

FLAT-RATE TAX
Generally, a tax computed without regard to deductions

Other states and localities assess a **flat-rate tax**, either on gross income or some other amounts, allowing for the exclusion of income from certain sources, such as retirement income (Fig. 12-2).

A number of other taxes are assessed against businesses, such as mercantile taxes, business privilege taxes, and gross and net profit taxes (Fig. 12-3).

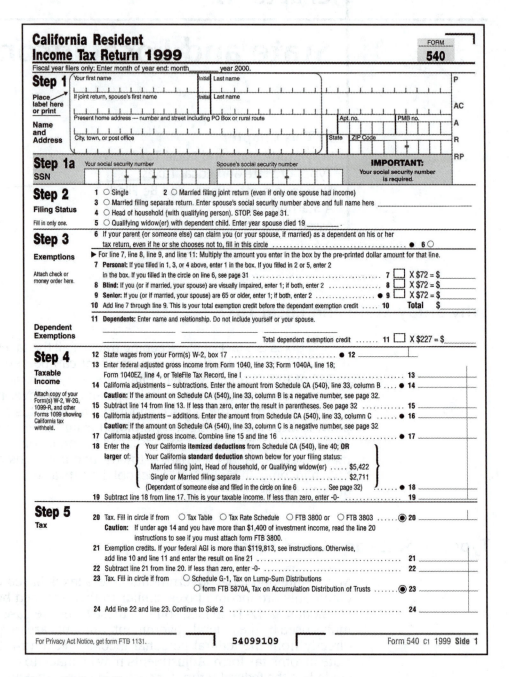

Figure 12-1   California income tax return form, page 1.

The amounts on which these taxes are based are generally a matter of local or state legislation and frequently show the ingenuity of local government officials in raising revenue.

Most people are familiar with the standard federal form 1040 and their own state equivalent form for the reporting of income by individuals.

PA-40 - 1999 (I) 9900110025

Pennsylvania Income Tax Return

PA Department of Revenue, Harrisburg, PA 17129-0006

OFFICIAL USE ONLY

PLEASE PRINT IN BLACK INK. ENTER ONE LETTER OR NUMBER IN EACH BOX. FILL IN OVALS COMPLETELY.

Your Social Security Number

Spouse s Social Security Number

Last Name

Your First Name MI

Spouse s First Name MI

Spouse s Last Name - Only if different from Last Name above

First line of address - P.O. Box; Apartment Number; Suite; RR No. - if applicable

Second line of address - Street Address

City or Post Office State ZIP Code

School Code Daytime Telephone Number

OVERSEAS MAIL - Use full return address to include city, country and Zip Codes in local formats.

Extension. See instructions.

Amended Return. Fill in this oval if you are amending your 1999 PA return.

Fiscal Year Filers, Fill in this oval.
FY beginning ___/___/99 & ending ___/___/___

Residency Status. Fill in only one oval.
- **R** Resident
- **N** Nonresident
- **P** Part-Year Resident from ___/___/99 to ___/___/99.

Type Filer. Fill in only one oval.
- **S** Single
- **J** Married, Filing Jointly
- **M** Married, Filing Separately
- **F** Final Return. Indicate reason:
- **D** Deceased. Date of death ___/___/99

Identification Label Change.
Fill in this oval if the label you received with this booklet is not completely correct, or if you did not file a 1998 PA tax return. Do not make corrections on the label -- **DISCARD IT.**

9900110025

Name of school district where you lived on 12/31/99. | County where you lived on 12/31/99. | Municipality where you lived on 12/31/99.

		Do not use cents. Enter whole dollars.
1a. Gross Compensation, from PA Schedule W-2S, or your Forms W-2, or other statements.	1a.	
1b. Unreimbursed Employee Business Expenses, from PA Schedule UE.	1b.	
1c. Net Compensation. Subtract Line 1b from Line 1a.	1c.	
2. Interest Income. Complete and enclose PA Schedule A, if over $2,500.	2.	
3. Dividend Income. Complete and enclose PA Schedule B, if over $2,500.	3.	
4. Net Income or Loss from the Operation of Business, Profession, or Farm. LOSS	4.	
5. Net Gain or Loss from the Sale, Exchange, or Disposition of Property. LOSS	5.	
6. Net Income or Loss from Rents, Royalties, Patents, or Copyrights. LOSS	6.	
7. Estate or Trust Income. Complete and enclose PA Schedule J.	7.	
8. Gambling and Lottery Winnings.	8.	
9. **Total PA Taxable Income.** Add only the positive income amounts from Lines 1c, 2, 3, 4, 5, 6, 7, and 8. DO NOT ADD any losses reported on Lines 4, 5, or 6.	9.	
10. **Contributions To Your Medical Savings Account.** See the instructions.	10.	
11. **Adjusted PA Taxable Income.** Subtract Line 10 from Line 9.	11.	
12. **PA Tax Liability. Multiply Line 11 by 2.8% (0.028). Also enter on Line 13, Side 2.**	12.	

Side 1

9900110025 EC OFFICIAL USE ONLY FC 9900110025

Figure 12-2 Pennsylvania income tax return form, page 1.

FIDUCIARY RETURN
A return filed on behalf of a trust or estate

A separate series of returns, **fiduciary returns**, are used for the reporting of income by estates and trusts. The federal fiduciary return is form 1041. These are not to be confused with similar forms, such as the federal 706 form, which is used to report the value of a decedent's estate and the transfer to beneficiaries. When the estate or trust earns income during the

CITY OF PHILADELPHIA
DUE BY APRIL 15, 1999

BUSINESS PRIVILEGE TAX RETURN

0699

BPT/BPT-EZ 1999

TAXPAYER'S NAME AND ADDRESS. PLACE LABEL HERE.

← Attach label and → Always enter your account number

CITY ACCOUNT NUMBER

0 1 2 3 4 5 6 7
■ PRINT YOUR NUMERALS LIKE THIS

Check if a change of address (✓) ☐

IF BUSINESS TERMINATED, GIVE DATE:

If there was a change in the business entity, refer to the instruction on the cover of this return.

Indicate if this is a seasonal business (✓) ☐

TAXPAYER'S DAYTIME PHONE NUMBER

TAXPAYER'S EVENING PHONE NUMBER

FEDERAL I.D. NUMBER

SOCIAL SECURITY NUMBER

COMPUTATION OF TAX DUE OR REFUND

LINE			Amount
1.	NET INCOME PORTION OF TAX (from Page 2, line 5 or Page 3, line 12 or Page 4, line 12). If there is no tax due, please enter "0"	1.	, , .00
2.	GROSS RECEIPTS PORTION OF TAX (from Page 2, line 8 or Page 6, line 8 or Page 7, line 18) If there is no tax due, please enter "0"	2.	, , .00
3.	TOTAL TAX DUE (Line 1 plus Line 2)	3.	, , .00
4.	ESTIMATED PAYMENTS MADE AND OTHER CREDITS		
	a. Credit from overpayment of 1998 NPT.	4a.	, , .00
	b. Credit from overpayment of 1998 Business Privilege Tax (Enter amount, if applicable from Line 8c of 1998 BPT or 8c of 1998 BPT-EZ)	4b.	, , .00
	c. Payment of 1999 BPT made with Application for Extension of Time to File	4c.	, , .00
	Total Payments and Credits (Line 4a plus 4b and 4c)	4.	, , .00
5.	TAX DUE. If line 3 is larger than line 4, enter difference here	5.	, , .00
6.	Interest and Penalty: (Refer to Instruction Sheet E for Cumulative %) (Cumulative % x line 5)	6.	, , .00
7.	TOTAL DUE including Interest and Penalty (Line 5 plus line 6). Make checks payable to "City of Philadelphia"	7.	, , .00
8.	If Line 4 is larger than line 3, Enter; a. Amount to be paid to taxpayer	8a.	, , .00
	b. Amount of overpayment to be applied up to the tax due to the 1998 Net Profits Tax	8b.	, , .00
	c. Amount of overpayment to be applied to 2000 Business Privilege Tax	8c.	, , .00

Under penalties of perjury, as set forth in 18 Pa. C.S. §§ 4902-4903 as amended, I swear that I have reviewed this return and accompanying statements and schedules, and to the best of my knowledge and belief, they are true and complete.

Taxpayer's Signature ____________ Date ____________

Preparer's Signature ____________ Preparer's Daytime Phone Number ____________

This Return must be filed and the AMOUNT DUE PAID IN FULL ON OR BEFORE 4/15/99

Page 1

Figure 12-3 Philadelphia mercantile tax return form, page 1.

administration of the estate or the operation of the trust, the income from the administration or operation is reported and an equivalent income tax is paid on an annual basis.

It is generally better to prepare the federal tax return forms before attempting the local or state tax forms. On some state and local returns, information that is necessary to complete the state or local return is carried over from the federal return. It is a common practice for state and local tax returns to require a copy of the federal tax return with the filing of the state return.

Determining the Returns to Be Filed

There is always some confusion in determining when and what returns are required to be filed for state and local purposes. The obligation for these taxes frequently can be determined by first ascertaining the domicile and residence of the individual and the location of the property owned by the taxpayer.

DOMICILE   That place to where a person intends to return and maintain as a permanent home in spite of frequent or long periods of absence

RESIDENCE   The current location where a person is living

Domicile is that place to where a person intends to return and maintain a permanent home in spite of frequent or long periods of absence. **Residence** is the current location where a person is living. With the increase in second-home families, the problem of making the decision as to which is the domicile and which is the residence can have a significant impact, not only on taxes, but on car insurance premiums and voting limitations. It is not uncommon for many taxpayers who own summer homes at a seashore or mountain area, or winter homes in a ski resort, where automobile insurance is substantially cheaper or tax rates substantially lower, to use this home as their residence for tax purposes as well. In reality, their intent is merely to save money, not to use this second home as a permanent domicile, but rather as a temporary seasonal residence.

State income taxes are normally assessed on residents of a state. The definition of a resident for state and local tax purposes may not be the same as traditional definitions of residence and domicile. Taxes may also be imposed on those who claim the state as their ultimate domicile even though they are temporarily residing outside the state, such as those in government or military service. Taxes on income are also frequently imposed on those who work in a jurisdiction either on a regular basis or only briefly (e.g., professional athletes, attorneys appearing in court, or doctors consulting at a hospital).

The location of the property may also create a tax obligation. Real estate taxes are the best example of taxes imposed on property based on its location and not that of the owner. In preparing state and local estate returns, this may also be important. Property owned by the decedent with a summer home at the shore or a winter home in Florida or Arizona may be exempt from inclusion in the home state but require inclusion in the state of the property's location.

A Starting Point

Determining the domicile, the residence, and the working locations, as well as the location of real property (real estate) owned by the client, will allow you to determine the potential tax obligations of the client and to obtain the needed tax forms and instructions for completion of the required returns.

☑ Jurisdiction Checklist

_____ Nationality
  _____ U.S. citizen
  _____ U.S. resident alien
  _____ U.S. nonresident citizen
  _____ Non-U.S. citizen/resident

_____ State
  _____ Domicile state
  _____ Primary home state
  _____ Secondary home state
  _____ Other home state

_____ County or parish

_____ City

_____ School district

_____ Other taxing district

_____ Work
  _____ Primary location
  _____ Secondary location
  _____ Spouse
    _____ Primary location
    _____ Secondary location

Most states make tax return forms and information available over the Internet, most forms can be downloaded directly to your printer. A list of Internet web sites is included in the appendix. Some local governments, such as the City of Philadelphia, also provide access to their tax forms over the Internet; forms may also be obtained by a fax from the number of revenue offices. The number of offices making these available increases every day.

The instructions should be carefully consulted after the determination that a tax applies because of domicile, work location, residence, or the type of income. In assembling the materials necessary, do not assume that the same definitions and rules apply across the board from jurisdiction to jurisdiction or even from tax form to tax form. Typical of these differences is the minimum before assessment of tax. For example, the federal estate tax only applies to estates with a value above a certain amount. Most state estate tax returns do not include any such exemption, with all value being taxed, usually after some allowance for deductions and allowances. Be especially careful when working with returns for a **foreign jurisdiction**, defined as those beyond your state border. The standard federal W-2 form also includes a section of the applicable amount for state or local tax purposes, which may be different than that for federal tax purposes. This may be a deduction from gross income for pension and profit-sharing deductions and similar items permitted by federal law but not

FOREIGN JURISDICTION A jurisdiction beyond the home jurisdiction, usually another state

permitted by a state tax law. Conversely, some items taxable for federal purposes, such as certain pension benefits, may be taxed for federal purposes, but exempt for state purposes. Since the rules change frequently, it is best to annually obtain current filing instructions from the applicable jurisdiction to determine changes from the previous year.

For example (Fig. 12-4) during the first three months of the year, the husband works in Maryland. For the last nine months of the year, he switches jobs and works in the City of Philadelphia in Pennsylvania. His wife works in Washington D. C. for the first six months of the year while living in Rockville, Maryland. The couple marries and moves to the State of Delaware in November of the tax year. Required tax returns would include the following.

1. The City of Washington D. C. levies a local tax on employment in the jurisdiction.

2. The City of Philadelphia imposes a wage tax on employment in the City.

3. The Commonwealth of Pennsylvania requires the filing of a state income tax return.

4. Maryland has a state income tax and the local government (county) collects a tax based on the Maryland state return, all of which is calculated on the state return form.

5. Delaware also has a state income tax and, unlike some jurisdictions, does not have a reciprocal relationship with adjacent states that would allow for direct credit for employment taxes paid in other jurisdictions, such as the city wage tax in Philadelphia and the state income tax of Pennsylvania.

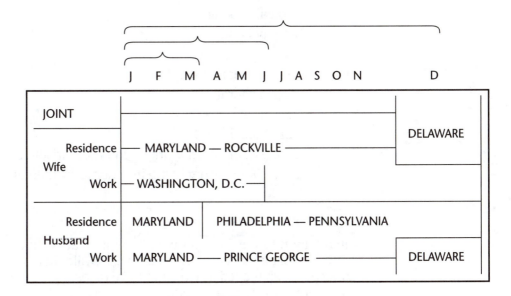

Figure 12-4   Tax return example timeline.

Assembling the Information

Document Checklist

_____ W-2 wage tax statements
    _____ Client
    _____ Spouse
_____ 1099 forms
    _____ 1099R, pensions
    _____ 1099G, unemployment benefits
    _____ 1099 MISC
    _____ 1099-SSA, Social Security benefits
_____ 1098 form
_____ K-1 forms, partnerships
_____ K-1 form, S corporations
_____ K-1 form, estates and trusts
_____ Previous year's state and local tax refunds
_____ Employee business expenses
_____ Form 1040 ES, estimated tax payments
_____ Brokerage account statements
_____ Multiple support agreements
_____ Sale of property information
    _____ Bill of sales
    _____ Real estate settlement sheets
_____ Charitable contributions
_____ Medical expenses
_____ Tax payments
_____ Interest payments
_____ Previous year's tax returns
    _____ Federal
    _____ State
    _____ Local
    _____ Others from working in other jurisdictions
    _____ Others from living in other jurisdictions

CHAPTER SUMMARY

In addition to the federal tax obligation, states, cities, counties, parishes, and school districts also impose taxes. While there may be some relationship between the federal tax and local taxes, the preparer should never assume that there is any relationship between the various taxes nor any common set of definitions, deductions, exclusions, or includable items of income. The responsibility is on the preparer to be certain that all required tax returns are prepared and filed in a timely manner.

GLOSSARY

Domicile   That place to where a person intends to return and maintain as a permanent home in spite of frequent or long periods of absence

Fiduciary return   A return filed on behalf of a trust or estate

Flat-rate tax   Generally, a tax computed without regard to deductions

Foreign jurisdiction   A jurisdiction beyond the home jurisdiction, usually another state

Residence   The current location where a person is living

REVIEW QUESTIONS

1. How many different taxes are imposed in the jurisdiction in which you reside?
2. For the taxes listed in your answer to question 1, what are the differences in the application of the tax and the tax rate?
3. If your jurisdiction imposes an income tax, what is the equivalent form to the federal form 1040 and what are the differences in the tax base and rate?
4. Why should the federal tax returns be prepared before the state and local tax returns?
5. Is your jurisdiction's use of the traditional definitions of domicile and residence used in determining state or local tax obligations?
6. What is the web site address for your state tax department for information and for tax forms?
7. Does your jurisdiction allow a credit for taxes paid to other jurisdictions?
8. What are the problems in determining which state and local taxes may be owed?
9. What are some of the different types of taxes imposed by state and local government?
10. Why should a new set of tax regulations be obtained each year?

Chapter 13

Fiduciary Taxation: Trusts and Decedents' Estates

In This Chapter
Why Study Fiduciary Taxation?
Trust Basics
Trust Taxation
Types of Trusts for Tax Purposes
Who Must File a Return?
When Must the Return Be Filed?
Preparing the Trust Tax Return—Form 1041
Ethical Issue

Why Study Fiduciary Taxation?

Inter vivos and testamentary trusts have become a popular way for clients to minimize taxes during their lifetime and in their estate, as well as a method for providing for the management of assets. The creation of trusts also creates a new tax entity that must file annual tax returns, both federal and state. Income earned during the administration of a decedent's estate must also be reported, and the applicable tax must be paid. It should be noted that this is a separate obligation from the filing of the *estate* tax return. In some cases, the provisions of the will provide for the long-term management of the estate assets before distribution to the ultimate beneficiaries, and a fiduciary return will be filed in the same manner as a trust.

Trust Basics

TRUST A legal entity created by a party in which property is transferred to a third party to be held and managed for the benefit of another party, called the beneficiary

GRANTOR A party setting up a trust; also called a settlor

A **trust** is a legal entity created by a party, called the **grantor** or settlor, in which property is transferred to a third party, called the **trustee**, to be held and managed for the benefit of another party, called the beneficiary. The trustee holds the property in a fiduciary capacity. A trustee is obligated to treat and handle the trust property in good faith for the beneficiaries, placing the interest of the beneficiaries above the trustee's own interests. A failure to act in a fiduciary manner may expose the trustee to personal liability for losses suffered by the trust.

TRUSTEE   A party to whom property has been transferred to be managed for the benefit of another

The validity of a trust is based on compliance with state law. While a trust may be set up for almost any lawful purpose, the federal taxability of the trust, separate and apart from the grantor, requires that the grantor give up dominion and control to the trustee. When the grantor maintains effective control of the trust, the income from the trust will be reported by the grantor and not by the trust.

During a person's lifetime, he or she will be required to file annual individual income tax returns, including the federal form 1040. Upon his or her death, depending on the size of his or her estate, a one-time filing must be made, the federal inheritance tax return form 709. Regardless of the need to file the federal inheritance return, there may be an obligation to file the estate fiduciary return to account for income earned by the estate during the administration of the estate. Many estates cannot be completely settled within a 12-month period and therefore require the filing of the annual federal fiduciary form 1041 (Fig. 13-1). In addition to the estate inheritance tax return, there may be an obligation to file fiduciary tax returns on an annual basis for any trust, whether inter vivos or testamentary, as set up by the decedent during his or her lifetime of or as part of his or her will.

JFMAMJJASOND	JFMAMJJASOND	JFMAMJJASOND	
INTERVIVOS TRUST FIDUCIARY Return 1041	INTERVIVOS TRUST FIDUCIARY Return 1041	INTERVIVOS TRUST FIDUCIARY Return 1041	⚡
Lifetime Tax Returns Form 1040 and possible Gift Tax Returns	ESTATE INHERITANCE Return 709 (one-time filing)		
	ESTATE FIDUCIARY Return 1041	ESTATE FIDUCIARY Return 1041	⚡
	TESTAMENTARY TRUST FIDUCIARY Return 1041	TESTAMENTARY TRUST FIDUCIARY Return 1041	TESTAMENTARY TRUST FIDUCIARY Return 1041

Figure 13-1   Lifetime tax return timeline.

INTER VIVOS TRUST
A trust set up during the life of the grantor

TESTAMENTARY TRUST   A trust set up after the death of the grantor, as part of the administration of the grantor's estate

IRREVOCABLE
Giving up all rights to take back the amount given or placed in trust

Establishing the Trust

A trust can be established at any time. If the trust is set up during a person's lifetime, it is called an **inter vivos trust**, or if set up after the grantor's death, as part of the administration of an estate, it is called a **testamentary trust**. Trusts may be set up as part of a person's tax or estate planning. By making the trust **irrevocable**, the grantor may be able to

SPLITTING OF INCOME Dividing of taxable income among separate tax entities to achieve a reduction in the total tax paid

achieve a tax savings by the **splitting of income** among multiple tax entities or minimize estate taxes by eliminating inclusion of assets from inclusion in the estate of the decedent.

Non-tax-related reasons for establishing trusts are varied. A professional trustee may better manage assets for minors or elderly persons. Or, there may be a concern that the beneficiary will not be able to manage large sums of money without spending or wasting it on unnecessary items.

Trust Taxation

A properly established trust is always a separate entity for tax purposes. The rules for trust tax computation are similar to those for individuals. One of the major differences, however, is the amount for the personal exemption. For a trust, this amount is limited to $300 for those estates required to distribute all of its income annually or $100 for those allowed to accumulate income from year to year.

Types of Trusts for Tax Purposes

SIMPLE TRUST Under the Internal Revenue Code, a trust that is required to distribute all of its income for the taxable year in that year and does not make or set aside funds for charitable purposes

COMPLEX TRUST Under the Internal Revenue Code, a trust that may distribute some or all of the income each year or may accumulate the income from year to year

Trusts may be set up for many purposes. The names associated with the trust may reflect the purpose for establishing the trust such as a marital deduction trust, grandchildren trust, or support trust. These are descriptions that describe the functional purpose of the settlor in setting up the trust.

For federal tax purposes, there are two types of trusts, simple and complex. A **simple trust** is one that is required to distribute all of its income for the taxable year in that year and does not make or set aside funds for charitable purposes. A **complex trust** is one that may distribute some or all of the income or may accumulate the income from year to year. The trust document determines the tax classification based on the obligations for the distribution of income and contributions. It is possible that under the trust document the trust may be treated as simple trust in one tax year and a complex trust in another tax year.

Who Must File a Return?

A federal form 1041 must be filed for a trust if it has any taxable income for the tax year, any income in excess of $600, or any other beneficiaries who are nonresident aliens. Some trusts do not have to file a return, even if they have income. These are trusts where the grantor has retained such dominion and control over the trust that it is not viewed as a separate legal entity. In these trusts, the income is taxed to the grantor on his or her personal income tax return.

In addition to the filing of the federal form 1041, the trust may also have to file the following: information returns such as form 1099, to report the payments of interest or dividends; if the trust has employees, the usual employment forms W-2 and W-3 to report wages and withholding, and forms 940 and 941 to report and pay employee withholding; and forms related to generation-skipping transfers.

The fiduciary, whether the trustee of the trust or the executor of the estate is liable under the Internal Revenue Code for the payment of the tax. This obligation does not end, even after discharge (the end of the fiduciary role), if the fiduciary had knowledge of the obligation before his or her discharge as trustee or executor.

When Must the Return Be Filed?

The trust return must be filed by the 15th day of the fourth month after the end of the trust tax year. Most trusts adopt the calendar year, hence the 15th of April is the annual filing deadline. The trust may be established at anytime during the year. Therefore, the first tax year may be a short year, starting from the date of creation of the trust and ending on December 31. An automatic extension of the time for filing of three months may be requested by filing form 8736 (Fig. 13-2) on or before the due date of the return. Although an extension for filing the return is available, the expected tax payment must be made on time to avoid interest and penalties.

Form **8736**
(Rev. October 2000)
Department of the Treasury
Internal Revenue Service

Application for Automatic Extension of Time To File U.S. Return for a Partnership, REMIC, or for Certain Trusts

▶ **File a separate application for each return.**

OMB No. 1545-1054

Please type or print.
File by the due date for filing the return for which an extension is requested. See instructions.

Name | **Employer identification number**

Number, street, and room or suite no. If a P.O. box, see instructions.

City or town, state, and ZIP code. If a foreign address, enter city, province or state, and country. Follow the country's practice for entering the postal code.

1 I request an automatic **3-month** extension of time to file (check only one):
☐ Form 1041 ☐ Form 1041-QFT ☐ Form 1065 ☐ Form 1065-B ☐ Form 1066

2 If the entity does not have an office or place of business in the United States, check this box . . . . ▶ ☐

3a For calendar year 20......, or other tax year beginning ...., 20......, and ending.................., 20......

b If this tax year is for less than 12 months, check reason:
☐ Initial return ☐ Final return ☐ Change in accounting period

4 If this extension is requested for Form 1041, Form 1041-QFT, Form 1065-B, or Form 1066, enter the following amounts:

a Tentative total tax from Form 1041, Form 1041-QFT, Form 1065-B, or Form 1066 (see instructions) . $ ________

b Refundable credits and estimated tax payments, including any prior year overpayment allowed as a credit, from Form 1041, Form 1041-QFT, or Form 1065-B (see instructions). REMICs, enter -0- . . $ ________

c **Balance due.** Subtract line 4b from line 4a. If zero or less, enter -0-. Enclose payment, if any, with Form 8736 (see instructions) . . . . ▶ $

Figure 13-2 Federal form 8736, Application for Automatic Extension of Time To File U.S. Return for a Partnership, REMIC, or for Certain Trusts.

Preparing the Trust Tax Return—Form 1041

The return is broken down into four main sections: Information, Income, Deduction, and Tax Calculation and Payments. Figure 13-3 shows tax forms linked to form 1041.

Basic Information

The basic information required includes the name of the trust and the name and address of the fiduciary filing the return on behalf of the trust. As with any taxable entity, a federal employer's identification number (EIN) must be secured from the Internal Revenue Service and used on all documents filed to identify the entity filing the returns. This may be obtained by the fiduciary by filing a form W-4. Returns filed without an EIN will have one assigned when the Internal Revenue Service receives the return. Failure to include the correct number or any number already assigned may result in multiple numbers being assigned. This can cause a great deal of confusion and wasted time eliminating the extra EIN from the system and many hours spent by the taxpayer responding to computer-generated letters from the IRS.

The type of entity, whether simple, complex, or a grantor trust, is determined from the document establishing the trust. As previously mentioned, this determination will depend on the grantor's control over the trust and whether all income is distributed annually during the trust tax year.

Determining Income

The determination of the income of a trust or estate is the same as that of an individual. All items of income received during the tax year are included in gross income. This includes dividends and interest, rents, and income from the sale of property. Income also includes "income in respective of a decedent." This is income earned by the decedent before death, but not paid until after death, which is paid to the trust or estate. This may also include a portion of the lump sum distribution of an individual retirement account, or IRA. In addition to the basic form 1041, additional schedules may be required that support the entry on the form 1041. Income from operations of a business is calculated on schedule C; gains and losses from capital transactions are reported on schedule D; rents, royalty, partnerships, and income from other estates and trusts are reported on schedule E; and farm income is reported on schedule F. Additional schedules and attachments may also be filed as support for entries on these forms.

Determining Expense Deductions

The trust or estate may take a deduction for the ordinary and necessary expenses associated with the generation of income, including ordinary business expenses. These expenses may include the fees paid to the trustee, and fees paid for the preparation of tax returns, investment advice, state and local income taxes, and interest expenses. As with individuals, there is a two percent floor for miscellaneous itemized deductions.

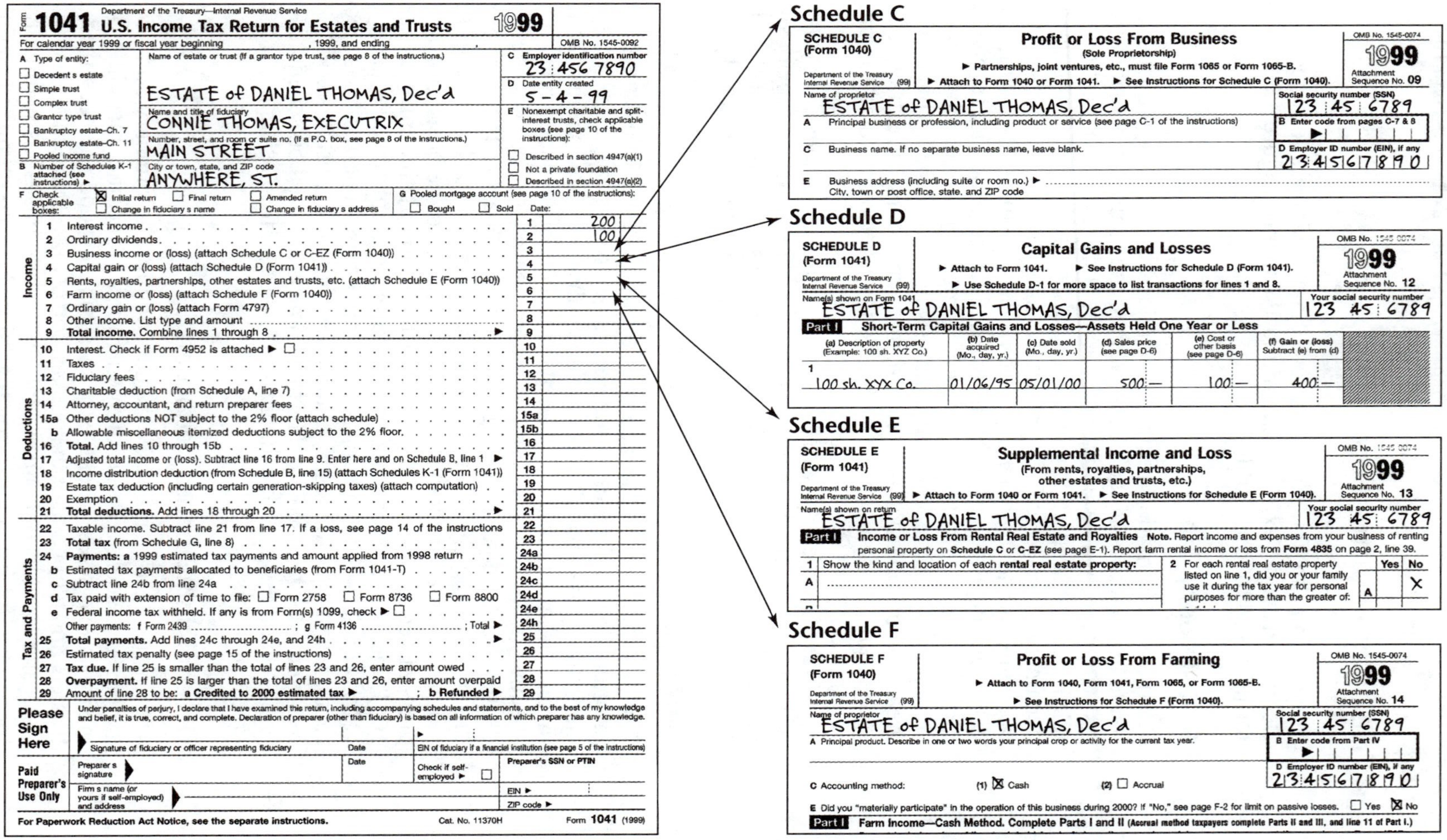

Figure 13-3 Federal form 1041 linked to supporting schedules.

Miscellaneous deductions must exceed two percent of adjusted gross income, or AGI. The trust or estate does not have an AGI. The trust or estate is permitted to calculate the equivalent of the AGI. Unlike the individual taxpayer computation, the trust or estate is permitted to take a deduction for expenses that would not otherwise be included in the two percent floor, for items that would not have been incurred if the property was not held in a trust or estate.

The Distribution Deduction

Normally, a trust or estate may take a deduction for distributions made to the beneficiaries. By definition, a simple trust is one that is required to distribute all of its net income in that year. The simple trust, subject to the distributable net income rules described below, will normally get a deduction for all of the income earned each year. A complex trust is, under the trust document, not required to distribute all of its income each year.

Distributable Net Income

DNI   Distributable net income is a calculation made by trusts and estates to determine the amount of the deduction from a trust's or estate's income for distributions made to the beneficiaries of the trust or estate

The term **distributable net income**, or **DNI**, is a concept limited to trusts and estates. It is a calculation that determines the maximum amount of the deduction from a trust's or estate's income for distributions made to the beneficiaries of the trust or estate. The calculation of DNI is also used to determine the character of the distribution to the beneficiaries. The beneficiaries are taxed on the lesser of the amount distributed to them or their share of the DNI (Fig. 13-4).

DNI is the fiduciary's taxable income before the distribution deduction or personal exemption is subtracted. Capital gains and losses from principal assets are not included or eliminated. Extraordinary dividends and taxable stock dividends are also not included, if from principal assets. Tax-exempt income is added, less any expenses associated with the earning of the exempt income.

Schedule B	Income Distribution Deduction		
1	Adjusted total income (from page 1, line 17) (see page 16 of the instructions)	1	
2	Adjusted tax-exempt interest	2	
3	Total net gain from Schedule D (Form 1041), line 16, column (1) (see page 16 of the instructions)	3	
4	Enter amount from Schedule A, line 4 (reduced by any allocable section 1202 exclusion). . .	4	
5	Capital gains for the tax year included on Schedule A, line 1 (see page 16 of the instructions)	5	
6	Enter any gain from page 1, line 4, as a negative number. If page 1, line 4, is a loss, enter the loss as a positive number	6	
7	**Distributable net income (DNI).** Combine lines 1 through 6. If zero or less, enter -0-.	7	
8	If a complex trust, enter accounting income for the tax year as determined under the governing instrument and applicable local law ⌊ 8 ⌋		
9	Income required to be distributed currently	9	
10	Other amounts paid, credited, or otherwise required to be distributed	10	
11	Total distributions. Add lines 9 and 10. If greater than line 8, see page 17 of the instructions	11	
12	Enter the amount of tax-exempt income included on line 11	12	
13	Tentative income distribution deduction. Subtract line 12 from line 11	13	
14	Tentative income distribution deduction. Subtract line 2 from line 7. If zero or less, enter -0-	14	
15	**Income distribution deduction.** Enter the smaller of line 13 or line 14 here and on page 1, line 18	15	

Figure 13-4   Distributable Net Income (DNI) schedule calculation.

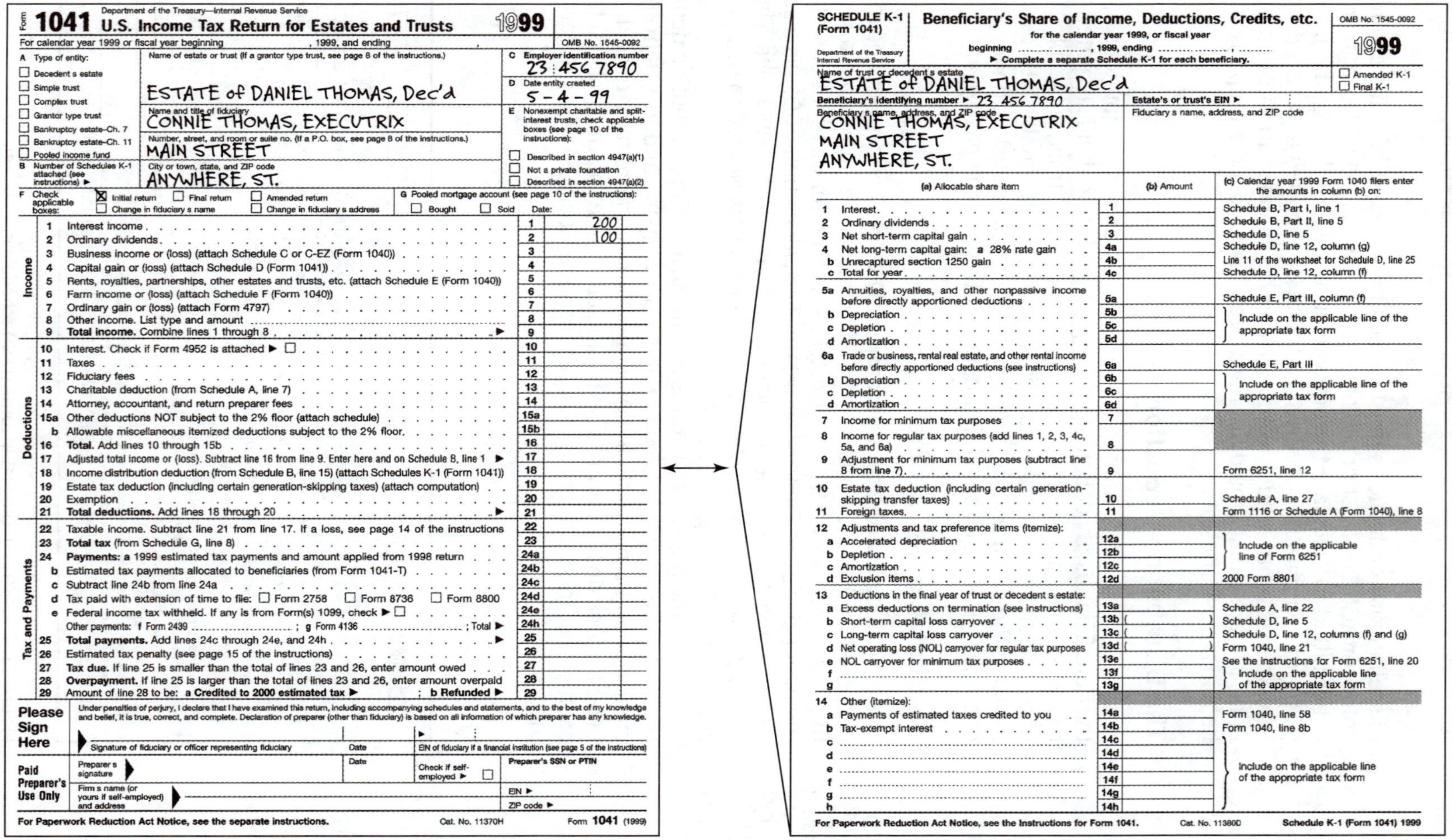

Form **1041** Department of the Treasury—Internal Revenue Service
U.S. Income Tax Return for Estates and Trusts 1999
For calendar year 1999 or fiscal year beginning , 1999, and ending , OMB No. 1545-0092

A Type of entity: ☐ Decedent's estate ☐ Simple trust ☐ Complex trust ☐ Grantor type trust ☐ Bankruptcy estate-Ch. 7 ☐ Bankruptcy estate-Ch. 11 ☐ Pooled income fund
B Number of Schedules K-1 attached (see instructions) ▶

Name of estate or trust (If a grantor type trust, see page 8 of the instructions.): ESTATE of DANIEL THOMAS, Dec'd
Name and title of fiduciary: CONNIE THOMAS, EXECUTRIX
Number, street, and room or suite no. (If a P.O. box, see page 8 of the instructions.): MAIN STREET
City or town, state, and ZIP code: ANYWHERE, ST.

C Employer identification number: 23 : 456 7890
D Date entity created: 5 - 4 - 99
E Nonexempt charitable and split-interest trusts, check applicable boxes (see page 10 of the instructions): ☐ Described in section 4947(a)(1) ☐ Not a private foundation ☐ Described in section 4947(a)(2)

F Check applicable boxes: ☒ Initial return ☐ Final return ☐ Amended return ☐ Change in fiduciary's name ☐ Change in fiduciary's address
G Pooled mortgage account (see page 10 of the instructions): ☐ Bought ☐ Sold Date:

Section	Line	Item	Box	Amount
Income	1	Interest income	1	200
	2	Ordinary dividends	2	100
	3	Business income or (loss) (attach Schedule C or C-EZ (Form 1040))	3	
	4	Capital gain or (loss) (attach Schedule D (Form 1041))	4	
	5	Rents, royalties, partnerships, other estates and trusts, etc. (attach Schedule E (Form 1040))	5	
	6	Farm income or (loss) (attach Schedule F (Form 1040))	6	
	7	Ordinary gain or (loss) (attach Form 4797)	7	
	8	Other income. List type and amount	8	
	9	**Total income.** Combine lines 1 through 8 ▶	9	
Deductions	10	Interest. Check if Form 4952 is attached ▶ ☐	10	
	11	Taxes	11	
	12	Fiduciary fees	12	
	13	Charitable deduction (from Schedule A, line 7)	13	
	14	Attorney, accountant, and return preparer fees	14	
	15a	Other deductions NOT subject to the 2% floor (attach schedule)	15a	
	b	Allowable miscellaneous itemized deductions subject to the 2% floor	15b	
	16	**Total.** Add lines 10 through 15b	16	
	17	Adjusted total income or (loss). Subtract line 16 from line 9. Enter here and on Schedule B, line 1 ▶	17	
	18	Income distribution deduction (from Schedule B, line 15) (attach Schedules K-1 (Form 1041))	18	
	19	Estate tax deduction (including certain generation-skipping taxes) (attach computation)	19	
	20	Exemption	20	
	21	**Total deductions.** Add lines 18 through 20 ▶	21	
Tax and Payments	22	Taxable income. Subtract line 21 from line 17. If a loss, see page 14 of the instructions	22	
	23	**Total tax** (from Schedule G, line 8)	23	
	24	**Payments: a** 1999 estimated tax payments and amount applied from 1998 return	24a	
	b	Estimated tax payments allocated to beneficiaries (from Form 1041-T)	24b	
	c	Subtract line 24b from line 24a	24c	
	d	Tax paid with extension of time to file: ☐ Form 2758 ☐ Form 8736 ☐ Form 8800	24d	
	e	Federal income tax withheld. If any is from Form(s) 1099, check ▶ ☐	24e	
		Other payments: f Form 2439 ; g Form 4136 ; Total ▶	24h	
	25	**Total payments.** Add lines 24c through 24e, and 24h ▶	25	
	26	Estimated tax penalty (see page 15 of the instructions)	26	
	27	**Tax due.** If line 25 is smaller than the total of lines 23 and 26, enter amount owed	27	
	28	**Overpayment.** If line 25 is larger than the total of lines 23 and 26, enter amount overpaid	28	
	29	Amount of line 28 to be: **a Credited to 2000 estimated tax** ▶ ; **b Refunded** ▶	29	

Please Sign Here Under penalties of perjury, I declare that I have examined this return, including accompanying schedules and statements, and to the best of my knowledge and belief, it is true, correct, and complete. Declaration of preparer (other than fiduciary) is based on all information of which preparer has any knowledge.
Signature of fiduciary or officer representing fiduciary | Date | EIN of fiduciary if a financial institution (see page 5 of the instructions)

Paid Preparer's Use Only Preparer's signature | Date | Check if self-employed ▶ ☐ | Preparer's SSN or PTIN
Firm's name (or yours if self-employed) and address | EIN ▶ | ZIP code ▶

For Paperwork Reduction Act Notice, see the separate instructions. Cat. No. 11370H Form **1041** (1999)

SCHEDULE K-1 (Form 1041) Department of the Treasury Internal Revenue Service
Beneficiary's Share of Income, Deductions, Credits, etc.
for the calendar year 1999, or fiscal year beginning , 1999, ending ,
▶ **Complete a separate Schedule K-1 for each beneficiary.**
OMB No. 1545-0092 1999

Name of trust or decedent's estate: ESTATE of DANIEL THOMAS, Dec'd ☐ Amended K-1 ☐ Final K-1
Beneficiary's identifying number ▶ 23 456 7890 | Estate's or trust's EIN ▶
Beneficiary's name, address, and ZIP code: CONNIE THOMAS, EXECUTRIX, MAIN STREET, ANYWHERE, ST. | Fiduciary's name, address, and ZIP code

(a) Allocable share item		(b) Amount	(c) Calendar year 1999 Form 1040 filers enter the amounts in column (b) on:
1 Interest	1		Schedule B, Part I, line 1
2 Ordinary dividends	2		Schedule B, Part II, line 5
3 Net short-term capital gain	3		Schedule D, line 5
4 Net long-term capital gain: a 28% rate gain	4a		Schedule D, line 12, column (g)
b Unrecaptured section 1250 gain	4b		Line 11 of the worksheet for Schedule D, line 25
c Total for year	4c		Schedule D, line 12, column (f)
5a Annuities, royalties, and other nonpassive income before directly apportioned deductions	5a		Schedule E, Part III, column (f)
b Depreciation	5b		Include on the applicable line of the appropriate tax form
c Depletion	5c		
d Amortization	5d		
6a Trade or business, rental real estate, and other rental income before directly apportioned deductions (see instructions)	6a		Schedule E, Part III
b Depreciation	6b		Include on the applicable line of the appropriate tax form
c Depletion	6c		
d Amortization	6d		
7 Income for minimum tax purposes	7		
8 Income for regular tax purposes (add lines 1, 2, 3, 4c, 5a, and 6a)	8		
9 Adjustment for minimum tax purposes (subtract line 8 from line 7)	9		Form 6251, line 12
10 Estate tax deduction (including certain generation-skipping transfer taxes)	10		Schedule A, line 27
11 Foreign taxes	11		Form 1116 or Schedule A (Form 1040), line 8
12 Adjustments and tax preference items (itemize):			
a Accelerated depreciation	12a		Include on the applicable line of Form 6251
b Depletion	12b		
c Amortization	12c		
d Exclusion items	12d		2000 Form 8801
13 Deductions in the final year of trust or decedent's estate:			
a Excess deductions on termination (see instructions)	13a		Schedule A, line 22
b Short-term capital loss carryover	13b	( )	Schedule D, line 5
c Long-term capital loss carryover	13c	( )	Schedule D, line 12, columns (f) and (g)
d Net operating loss (NOL) carryover for regular tax purposes	13d	( )	Form 1040, line 21
e NOL carryover for minimum tax purposes	13e		See the instructions for Form 6251, line 20
f	13f		Include on the applicable line of the appropriate tax form
g	13g		
14 Other (itemize):			
a Payments of estimated taxes credited to you	14a		Form 1040, line 58
b Tax-exempt interest	14b		Form 1040, line 8b
c	14c		
d	14d		Include on the applicable line of the appropriate tax form
e	14e		
f	14f		
g	14g		
h	14h		

For Paperwork Reduction Act Notice, see the Instructions for Form 1041. Cat. No. 11380D **Schedule K-1 (Form 1041) 1999**

Figure 13-5 Federal form 1041 with link to schedule K-1.

Preparing the K-1 for Beneficiaries

The K-1 is the form used to report the income, deductions, and nature of the amounts such as tax-exempt income to the beneficiaries of the estate (Fig. 13-5). After the fiduciary return is completed, the distribution to each beneficiary is allocated and reported on the individual K-1 form.

 Ethical Issue

> **ABA Model Code:**
>
> Guideline 7: "A lawyer should take reasonable measures to prevent conflicts of interest resulting from a legal assistance or other employment or interests insofar as such other employment or interests would present a conflict of interest if it were that of the lawyer."

> Should there be a conflict of interest for a legal assistant to purchase from a client's estate property such as a car or real estate?

CHAPTER SUMMARY

A trust may be considered an independent entity for tax purposes. To be treated as a separate legal entity for tax purposes, an inter vivos trust must be independent of the control of the grantor. Testamentary trusts are created as part of the administration of a decedent's estate as provided for in the deceased's will. During the period of administration, the testamentary trust, as well as the estate itself, is required to file a fiduciary return for federal tax purposes and may also be required to file a return for state and local tax purposes. While there are similarities between federal income taxation, fiduciary taxation is determined in large part by a different set of rules and regulations.

GLOSSARY

Complex trust   Under the Internal Revenue Code, a trust that may distribute some or all of the income each year or may accumulate the income from year to year

DNI   Distributable net income is a calculation made by trusts and estates to determine the amount of the deduction from a trust's or estate's income for distributions made to the beneficiaries of the trust or estate

Grantor   A party setting up a trust; also called a *settlor*

Inter vivos trust   A trust set up during the life of the grantor

Irrevocable   Giving up all rights to take back the amount given or placed in trust

Simple trust   Under the Internal Revenue Code, a trust that is required to distribute all of its income for the taxable year in that year and does not make or set aside funds for charitable purposes

Splitting of income   Dividing of taxable income among separate tax entities to achieve a reduction in the total tax paid

Testamentary trust   A trust set up after the death of the grantor, as part of the administration of the grantor's estate

Trust   A legal entity created by a party in which property is transferred to a third party to be held and managed for the benefit of another party, called the beneficiary

Trustee   A party to whom property has been transferred to be managed for the benefit of another

REVIEW QUESTIONS

1. What is an inter vivos trust?
2. What is a testamentary trust?
3. List all of the potential federal tax returns that the administrator or executor of an estate might be required to file?
4. What is the tax advantage for setting up trusts?
5. What are the non-tax-related reasons for setting up a trust?
6. How is a trust's status as simple or complex determined?
7. When is a federal form 1041 required to be filed?
8. What is meant by the "distribution deduction on"?
9. What is distributable net income?
10. Under what circumstances is a trust an independent tax entity?

Chapter 14

State Estate Tax

In This Chapter
Why Study State Estate Tax?
Inheritance and Estate Taxes
Preparing the State Returns
Estate Timetable

Why Study State Estate Tax?

AFFINITY OR CONSANGUINITY
The degree of relationship between people, usually blood relationships and relationships by marriage

The concept of the gross estate as determined for federal purposes is not followed by state probate law or tax rules. The amount of tax and the base used for determining the state's inheritance, estate, or gift tax vary widely from state to state. Some states apply a uniform tax rate while others levy multiple rates of tax, depending on the relationship of the beneficiary to the decedent. Others use a pickup method, collecting a tax that would otherwise be paid to another branch of government. For this reason, it may be necessary to determine the relationship between the decedent and the beneficiary. Generally, the lowest tax rates are reserved for surviving spouses and children, with the higher rates based on the degree of **affinity or consanguinity** of the parties.

Inheritance and Estate Taxes

INHERITANCE TAX
A tax imposed on the right to receive the assets from the estate of a decedent

The **inheritance tax**, imposed by some states, is a tax on the right to receive the assets from the estate and is therefore imposed not on the estate, but rather on the beneficiary. Since the executor or administrator of the estate usually pays the tax before distribution to the beneficiaries, this may seem a moot point; however, in some cases beneficiaries may be called on to pay their share before distribution. The estate tax is a tax on the transfer of property. The pickup tax is the third general form of tax at the state level. This is a tax equal to the tax credit that would be available on the federal estate tax return. It is referred to as a pickup tax because the state picks up the tax that would otherwise be paid to another governmental agency; in this case, the federal government as part of the federal estate tax.

The actual forms and tax regulations vary considerably from state to state and are constantly being updated and modified. Before commencing the preparation of any return, it is essential that the latest copy of the return and instructions be in hand. The general concept of each type of return is reasonably constant, but the details, including rate of tax, may vary. Those states that conform their taxes to the federal system, such as New York (Fig. 14-1), may be more subject to changes.

General Information

Introduction

Article 26 of the New York State Tax Law imposes an estate tax on the transfer of the New York **taxable assets** of a deceased individual. It is a tax levied, at graduated rates, on the entire taxable estate rather than on the distributive shares received by each recipient of property.

The New York estate tax law as amended on April 28, 1998, conforms, with modifications, to the estate tax provisions of the federal Internal Revenue Code (IRC) of 1986 and all amendments enacted on or before August 5, 1997.

The New York adjusted gross estate and total New York deductions are the same as the total federal gross estate and the total federal deductions, with certain modifications (see instructions for lines 63 through 74).

The New York adjusted gross estate is valued either as of the date of death or the alternate valuation date (see *Alternate Valuation* on page 6 of these instructions).

If the estate is required to file a federal estate tax return, a copy of the federal return, Form 706, must be submitted with Form ET-90, *New York State Estate Tax Return* (see *Completing Form ET-90* on page 5 of these instructions.)

The New York adjusted taxable estate is determined by subtracting the amount of deductions authorized by the statute from the value of the adjusted gross estate. Different provisions of the statute control the determination of the net tax liability for estates of New York residents and estates of nonresidents. The decedent's **domicile** is the controlling factor in determining residency.

Figure 14-1   New York federal conformity statement.

While most estates are not large enough to require filing a federal estate return, few will avoid some type of state filing. Even where the federal return is not required, most of the information needed for state tax purposes can be obtained from the federal inheritance tax form 706 (Fig. 14-2) and, where applicable, the federal gift tax form 709. When there is no need to prepare and file the federal return, the forms can be used as a checklist for preparing the state return. Many states use a form similar to the federal form, such as the Pennsylvania inheritance form (Fig. 14-3), the Connecticut gift tax form (Fig. 14-4), and the New York estate tax form (Fig. 14-5), requiring individual schedules with a summary or recapitulation.

The problem for the legal assistant is to be sure that all of the relevant information has been obtained, particularly making certain that all of the assets of the estate have been accounted for and properly valued as required by state law. Having a good checklist or questionnaire will avoid missing information. Even in those cases where there is no tax imposed on the estate or on a class of assets, an accounting to the beneficiaries with accurate and complete information is required. As with the preparation of the federal returns, a review of previous year's income tax returns and gift

Form 706
(Rev. July 1999)

Department of the Treasury
Internal Revenue Service

United States Estate (and Generation-Skipping Transfer) Tax Return

Estate of a citizen or resident of the United States (see separate instructions).
To be filed for decedents dying after December 31, 1998
For Paperwork Reduction Act Notice, see page 1 of the separate instructions.

OMB No. 1545-0015

Part 1.—Decedent and Executor

1a Decedent's first name and middle initial (and maiden name, if any) | 1b Decedent's last name | 2 Decedent's Social Security No.

3a Legal residence (domicile) at time of death (county, state, and ZIP code, or foreign country) | 3b Year domicile established | 4 Date of birth | 5 Date of death

6a Name of executor (see page 4 of the instructions) | 6b Executor's address (number and street including apartment or suite no. or rural route; city, town, or post office; state; and ZIP code)

6c Executor's social security number (see page 4 of the instructions)

7a Name and location of court where will was probated or estate administered | 7b Case number

8 If decedent died testate, check here ▶ ☐ and attach a certified copy of the will. | 9 If Form 4768 is attached, check here ▶ ☐

10 If Schedule R-1 is attached, check here ▶ ☐

Computation

1 Total gross estate less exclusion (from Part 5, Recapitulation, page 3, item 12) . . . . | 1
2 Total allowable deductions (from Part 5, Recapitulation, page 3, item 23) . . . . | 2
3 Taxable estate (subtract line 2 from line 1) . . . . | 3
4 Adjusted taxable gifts (total taxable gifts (within the meaning of section 2503) made by the decedent after December 31, 1976, other than gifts that are includible in decedent's gross estate (section 2001(b))) | 4
5 Add lines 3 and 4 . . . . | 5
6 Tentative tax on the amount on line 5 from Table A on page 12 of the instructions . . . . . . | 6
7a If line 5 exceeds $10,000,000, enter the lesser of line 5 or $17,184,000. If line 5 is $10,000,000 or less, skip lines 7a and 7b and enter -0- on line 7c . | 7a
b Subtract $10,000,000 from line 7a . . . . | 7b
c Enter 5% (.05) of line 7b . . . . | 7c
8 Total tentative tax (add lines 6 and 7c) . . . . | 8
9 Total gift tax payable with respect to gifts made by the decedent after December 31, 1976. Include gift taxes by the decedent's spouse for such spouse's share of split gifts (section 2513) only if the decedent was the donor of these gifts and they are includible in the decedent's gross estate (see instructions) | 9
10 Gross estate tax (subtract line 9 from line 8) . . . . | 10
11 Maximum unified credit (applicable credit amount) against estate tax . | 11

Figure 14-2 Form 706, United States Estate Tax Return.

REV-1500 EX (6-00)

COMMONWEALTH OF PENNSYLVANIA
DEPARTMENT OF REVENUE
DEPT. 280601
HARRISBURG, PA 17128-0601

REV-1500

INHERITANCE TAX RETURN
RESIDENT DECEDENT

OFFICIAL USE ONLY

FILE NUMBER

COUNTY CODE   YEAR   NUMBER

DECEDENT

DECEDENT'S NAME (LAST, FIRST, AND MIDDLE INITIAL) | SOCIAL SECURITY NUMBER

DATE OF DEATH (MM-DD-YEAR) | DATE OF BIRTH (MM-DD-YEAR) | THIS RETURN MUST BE FILED IN DUPLICATE WITH THE **REGISTER OF WILLS**

(IF APPLICABLE) SURVIVING SPOUSE'S NAME (LAST, FIRST, AND MIDDLE INITIAL) | SOCIAL SECURITY NUMBER

CHECK APPROPRIATE BLOCKS

☐ 1. Original Return | ☐ 2. Supplemental Return | ☐ 3. Remainder Return (date of death prior to 12-13-82)
☐ 4. Limited Estate | ☐ 4a. Future Interest Compromise (date of death after 12-12-82) | ☐ 5. Federal Estate Tax Return Required
☐ 6. Decedent Died Testate (Attach copy of Will) | ☐ 7. Decedent Maintained a Living Trust (Attach copy of Trust) | ☐ 8. Total Number of Safe Deposit Boxes
☐ 9. Litigation Proceeds Received | ☐ 10. Spousal Poverty Credit (date of death between 12-31-91 and 1-1-95) | ☐ 11. Election to tax under Sec. 9113(A) (Attach Sch O)

CORRESPONDENT

THIS SECTION MUST BE COMPLETED. ALL CORRESPONDENCE AND CONFIDENTIAL TAX INFORMATION SHOULD BE DIRECTED TO:

NAME | COMPLETE MAILING ADDRESS

FIRM NAME (If Applicable)

TELEPHONE NUMBER

RECAPITULATION

1. Real Estate (Schedule A) | (1)
2. Stocks and Bonds (Schedule B) | (2)
3. Closely Held Corporation, Partnership or Sole-Proprietorship | (3)
4. Mortgages & Notes Receivable (Schedule D) | (4)
5. Cash, Bank Deposits & Miscellaneous Personal Property (Schedule E) | (5)
6. Jointly Owned Property (Schedule F) ☐ Separate Billing Requested | (6)
7. Inter-Vivos Transfers & Miscellaneous Non-Probate Property | (7)

OFFICIAL USE ONLY

Figure 14-3 Pennsylvania form 1500, Inheritance Tax Return Resident Decedent.

STATE OF CONNECTICUT
DEPARTMENT OF REVENUE SERVICES
INHERITANCE TAX SECTION
P.O. BOX 2972, HARTFORD, CT 06104-2972

FORM CT-706

CONNECTICUT ESTATE TAX RETURN

For decedents dying on or after July 1, 1997

☐ **Amended Return**

Make checks payable to : Commissioner of Revenue Services

Decedent's name (last, first, middle initial)	Date of death	Probate court
Decedent's residence at date of death (street address)	Connecticut file number, if known	
City State ZIP	Social security number	

IMPORTANT: ORIGINAL RETURNS MUST BE FILED SEPARATELY WITH THE PROBATE COURT AND THE DEPARTMENT OF REVENUE SERVICES TO BE CONSIDERED DULY FILED. A COMPLETE COPY OF THE FEDERAL ESTATE TAX RETURN, FORM 706, WITH ATTACHMENTS, MUST ACCOMPANY THE RETURN FILED WITH THE DEPARTMENT OF REVENUE SERVICES. PLEASE READ THE GENERAL RETURN INFORMATION SECTION ON THE REVERSE BEFORE COMPLETING THIS RETURN.

Computation of Tax for a Resident Decedent

1	Credit for state death taxes (From federal 706)		1
2	Total death taxes paid to other states (From Schedule A on reverse)	2	
3	Gross value of property outside Connecticut (From federal 706)	3	
4	Total gross estate (From federal 706)	4	
5	Estate percentage outside Connecticut (Divide Line 3 by Line 4)	5 %	
6	Prorated credit (Multiply Line 1 by Line 5)	6	
7	Allowable deduction (Lesser of Line 2 or Line 6)		7
8	Tentative Connecticut estate tax due (Subtract Line 7 from Line 1)		8
9	Total amount of Connecticut succession taxes paid		9
10	Connecticut Estate Tax Due (Subtract Line 9 from Line 8. If less than zero, enter 0)		10
11	Prior estate tax payments made to Connecticut		11
12	If Line 11 is greater than Line 10, enter **overpayment** (Subtract Line 10 from Line 11)		12
13	If Line 10 is greater than Line 11, enter **tax due** (Subtract Line 11 from Line 10)		13
14	If late, enter penalty ________ plus interest ________ (See instructions on reverse)		14
15	Amount you owe with this return (Add Lines 13 and 14)		15

Figure 14-4 Connecticut estate tax form 709.

For office use only

New York State Department of Taxation and Finance

New York State Estate Tax Return **ET-706** (10/00)

For an estate of a decedent whose date of death is on or after February 1, 2000

Check here if this is an amended return ☐

Decedent's Last name	First name	Middle initial	Social security number	
Address of decedent at time of death *(number and street)*			Date of death	Check box if copy of death certificate is attached *(see inst.)* ☐
City, village or post office	State	ZIP code	County of residence	

On the date of death, decedent was a: ☐ Resident of New York State ☐ Nonresident of New York State *(attach completed Form ET-141, Estate Tax Domicile Affidavit)*

Executor – If you are submitting Letters Testamentary or Letters of Administration with this form, indicate in this box the type of letters. Enter ***L*** if regular, ***LL*** if limited letters. If you are not submitting letters with this form, enter ***N***.

Surrogate's court – If a proceeding for probate or administration has commenced in a surrogate's court in New York State, enter county.

Attorney's or authorized representative's Last name First name MI	Executor's Last name First name MI
In care of *(firm's name)* Check box if POA is attached ☐	If more than one executor, check box and see *Instructions* ☐
Address of attorney or authorized representative	Address of executor
City, village or post office State ZIP code	City, village or post office State ZIP code
Social security number of attorney or authorized rep. Telephone number ( )	Social security number of executor Telephone number ( )

If the decedent possessed a cause of action or was a plaintiff in any litigation at the time of death, check this box and complete *Schedule 3* on the back *(see instructions)*. ☐

Installment payments of tax for closely held business.
Do you elect to pay the tax in installments as described in IRC section 6166 (NY Tax Law section 997)? If *Yes*, attach Form ET-415 in duplicate. ☐ Yes ☐ No

Releases of lien are requested Attach Form(s) ET-117 *(see instructions)* *(Enter number of counties)*	Federal estate tax return required. If *Yes*, attach a completed copy. ☐ Yes ☐ No
Federal gross estate tax from line 10 of Form 706	Federal taxable estate from line 3 of Form 706

Tax Computation

Figure 14-5 Form ET-706, New York State Estate Tax Return.

Figure 14-6 Florida Preliminary Notice and Report form.

tax returns may indicate areas requiring further inquiry to discover includable assets and items, such as insurance policies that may be payable directly to beneficiaries if the proper documentation is processed, even if not included in the state tax base. In some cases, the information may need to be reported to the state, such as on the Florida Preliminary Notice and Report form (Fig. 14-6).

☑ **Checklist**

Basic Information
_____ Full name of decedent
_____ Social Security number
_____ Date of death
_____ Place of death
_____ Domicile address
_____ Other residence address
_____ Birth date
_____ Birth place

_____ Cause of death

_____ Duration of last Illness

_____ Surviving spouse

    _____ Social Security number

    _____ Address

_____ Children

    _____ Address

_____ Other heirs and beneficiaries

    _____ Names

    _____ Address

    _____ Social Security number

    _____ Relationship

_____ Executor(rix)

    _____ Address

    _____ Social Security number

_____ Trustee

    _____ Address

    _____ Social Security number

    _____ Nature of trust

_____ Beneficiaries of trust

_____ Date of trust

    _____ Type

    _____ Name

    _____ Federal ID number

Documents

_____ Will

_____ Codicil

_____ Death certificate

_____ Birth certificate

_____ Marriage license

_____ Gift tax returns

_____ Last lifetime income tax returns

    _____ Federal

    _____ State

    _____ Local

Property

_____ Real estate

    _____ Primary residence

_____ Secondary residence

_____ Other

_____ Location

_____ Joint or co-tenant

_____ Copy of deed

_____ Copy of mortgage

_____ Appraised value

_____ Copy of appraisal

_____ Personal property

_____ Inventory

_____ Appraisal

_____ Copy of appraisal

_____ Banks

_____ Bank

_____ Location

_____ Account numbers

_____ Safe deposit box

_____ Keys

_____ Checking accounts

_____ Saving accounts

_____ Other accounts

_____ Brokerage accounts

_____ Title location

Preparing the State Returns

Inheritance Tax Returns

The inheritance tax is imposed on the right to receive property and is imposed by 16 states. The rates of tax, the items included, and the deductions vary from state to state. In concept, the inheritance tax is very similar to the federal estate tax (i.e., Gross Estate less Deductions equals Taxable Estate). Then, depending on the state, a tax is assessed. In some states, such as Pennsylvania, the tax depends on the relationship of the beneficiary to the deceased (Fig. 14-7). Close relatives pay a lower rate than more distant relatives.

The Pennsylvania inheritance return, typical of many state returns, follows the pattern of the federal return. Page 1 of the return (see Fig. 14-3) summarizes the information from the attached supporting schedules. The details are provided in the attached schedules, shown in Figure 14-8.

REV-1502EX • (1-97) (I)

COMMONWEALTH OF PENNSYLVANIA
INHERITANCE TAX RETURN
RESIDENT DECEDENT

SCHEDULE A
REAL ESTATE

ESTATE OF   FILE NUMBER

All real property owned solely or as a tenant in common must be reported at fair market value. Fair market value is defined as the price at which property would be exchanged between a willing buyer and a willing seller, neither being compelled to buy or sell, both having reasonable knowledge of the relevant facts. Real property which is jointly-owned with right of survivorship must be disclosed on Schedule F.

ITEM NUMBER	DESCRIPTION	VALUE AT DATE OF DEATH
1.		

REV-1503 EX • (1-97) (I)

COMMONWEALTH OF PENNSYLVANIA
INHERITANCE TAX RETURN
RESIDENT DECEDENT

SCHEDULE B
STOCKS & BONDS

ESTATE OF   FILE NUMBER

All property jointly-owned with right of survivorship must be disclosed on Schedule F.

ITEM NUMBER	DESCRIPTION	VALUE AT DATE OF DEATH
1.		

REV-1504 EX • (1-97) (I)

COMMONWEALTH OF PENNSYLVANIA
INHERITANCE TAX RETURN
RESIDENT DECEDENT

SCHEDULE C
CLOSELY-HELD CORPORATION,
PARTNERSHIP or SOLE-PROPRIETORSHIP

ESTATE OF   FILE NUMBER

Schedule C-1 or C-2 (including all supporting information) must be attached for each closely-held corporation/partnership interest of the decedent, other than a sole-proprietorship. See instructions for the supporting information to be submitted for sole-proprietorships.

ITEM NUMBER	DESCRIPTION	VALUE AT DATE OF DEATH
1.		

REV-1505EX • (1-97) (I)

COMMONWEALTH OF PENNSYLVANIA
INHERITANCE TAX RETURN
RESIDENT DECEDENT

SCHEDULE C-1
CLOSELY-HELD CORPORATE
STOCK INFORMATION REPORT

ESTATE OF   FILE NUMBER

1. Name of Corporation _____   State of Incorporation _____
    Address _____   Date of Incorporation _____
    City _____ State _____ Zip Code _____ Total Number of Shareholders _____
2. Federal Employer I.D. Number   Business Reporting Year

REV-1506EX • (1-97) (I)

COMMONWEALTH OF PENNSYLVANIA
INHERITANCE TAX RETURN
RESIDENT DECEDENT

SCHEDULE C-2
PARTNERSHIP
INFORMATION REPORT

ESTATE OF   FILE NUMBER

1. Name of Partnership _____   Date Business Commenced _____
    Address _____   Business Reporting Year _____
    City _____ State _____ Zip Code _____
2. Federal Employer I.D. Number

REV-1507 EX • (1-97) (I)

COMMONWEALTH OF PENNSYLVANIA
INHERITANCE TAX RETURN
RESIDENT DECEDENT

SCHEDULE D
MORTGAGES & NOTES
RECEIVABLE

ESTATE OF   FILE NUMBER

All property jointly-owned with the right of survivorship must be disclosed on Schedule F.

ITEM NUMBER	DESCRIPTION	VALUE AT DATE OF DEATH
1.		

(continues)

Figure 14-7   Pennsylvania Rev. 1500 schedules.

COMMONWEALTH OF PENNSYLVANIA
INHERITANCE TAX RETURN
RESIDENT DECEDENT

SCHEDULE E
CASH, BANK DEPOSITS, & MISC. PERSONAL PROPERTY

ESTATE OF _____ FILE NUMBER _____

Include the proceeds of litigation and the date the proceeds were received by the estate. All property jointly-owned with the right of survivorship must be disclosed on Schedule F.

ITEM NUMBER	DESCRIPTION	VALUE AT DATE OF DEATH
1.		

REV-1509 EX • (1-97) (I)

COMMONWEALTH OF PENNSYLVANIA
INHERITANCE TAX RETURN
RESIDENT DECEDENT

SCHEDULE F
JOINTLY-OWNED PROPERTY

ESTATE OF _____ FILE NUMBER _____

If an asset was made joint within one year of the decedent s date of death, it must be reported on Schedule G.

SURVIVING JOINT TENANT(S) NAME	ADDRESS	RELATIONSHIP TO DECEDENT
A.		

REV-1510 EX • (1-97) (I)

COMMONWEALTH OF PENNSYLVANIA
INHERITANCE TAX RETURN
RESIDENT DECEDENT

SCHEDULE G
INTER-VIVOS TRANSFERS & MISC. NON-PROBATE PROPERTY

ESTATE OF _____ FILE NUMBER _____

This schedule must be completed and filed if the answer to any of questions 1 through 4 on the reverse side of the REV-1500 COVER SHEET is yes.

ITEM NUMBER	DESCRIPTION OF PROPERTY INCLUDE THE NAME OF THE TRANSFEREE, THEIR RELATIONSHIP TO DECEDENT AND THE DATE OF TRANSFER. ATTACH A COPY OF THE DEED FOR REAL ESTATE .	DATE OF DEATH VALUE OF ASSET	% OF DECD S INTEREST	EXCLUSION (IF APPLICABLE)	TAXABLE VALUE
1					

REV-1511 EX • (1-97) (I)

COMMONWEALTH OF PENNSYLVANIA
INHERITANCE TAX RETURN
RESIDENT DECEDENT

SCHEDULE H
FUNERAL EXPENSES & ADMINISTRATIVE COSTS

ESTATE OF _____ FILE NUMBER _____

Debts of decedent must be reported on Schedule I.

ITEM NUMBER	DESCRIPTION	AMOUNT
A.	FUNERAL EXPENSES:	

REV-1512 EX • (1-97) (I)

COMMONWEALTH OF PENNSYLVANIA
INHERITANCE TAX RETURN
RESIDENT DECEDENT

SCHEDULE I
DEBTS OF DECEDENT, MORTGAGE LIABILITIES, & LIENS

ESTATE OF _____ FILE NUMBER _____

Include unreimbursed medical expenses.

ITEM NUMBER	DESCRIPTION	AMOUNT
1.		

REV-1514 EX • (1-97) (I)

COMMONWEALTH OF PENNSYLVANIA
INHERITANCE TAX RETURN
RESIDENT DECEDENT

SCHEDULE K
LIFE ESTATE, ANNUITY & TERM CERTAIN
(Check Box 4 on Rev-1500 Cover Sheet)

ESTATE OF _____ FILE NUMBER _____

This schedule is to be used for all single life, joint or successive life estate and term certain calculations. For dates of death prior to 5-1-89, actuarial factors for single life calculations can be obtained from the Department of Revenue, Specialty Tax Unit. Actuarial factors can be found in IRS Publication 1457, Actuarial Values, Alpha Volume for dates of death on or after 5 -1-89.
Indicate the type of instrument which created the future interest below and attach a copy to the tax return.

☐ Will   ☐ Intervivos Deed of Trust   ☐ Other

Figure 14-7 *Continued.*

Figure 14-8 Pennsylvania schedule J, Beneficiaries.

Estate Tax Returns

ESTATE TAX A tax imposed on the transfer of property from a decedent's estate

The **estate tax** is imposed on the right to transfer property and is imposed by a small number of states, such as New York (Fig. 14-9).

Gift Tax

GIFT TAX A tax imposed on the lifetime transfer of a present interest in property

Most states that impose the estate or inheritance tax also impose a **gift tax**, such as Connecticut (see Fig. 14-10).

Pickup Tax Returns

PICKUP TAX A tax equal to the tax credit that would be available on the federal estate tax return

The majority of states impose a **pickup tax**. This is a tax equal to the credit that is allowed on the federal tax return.

For office use only

New York State Department of Taxation and Finance

New York State Estate Tax Return

ET-90 (9/98)

For estates of decedents whose date of death is after May 25, 1990

Decedent's last name | First | Middle initial | Social security number

Address of decedent at time of death (number and street) | Date of death | Check box if copy of death certificate is attached (see inst.)

City, village or post office | State | ZIP code | County of residence

On the date of death, decedent was a: ☐ Resident of New York State ☐ Nonresident of New York State (attach completed Form ET-141 Estate Tax Domicile Affidavit)

Executor - If you are submitting Letters Testamentary or Letters of Administration with this form, indicate in this box the type of letters. Enter **L** if regular, **LL** if limited letters. If you are not submitting letters with this form, enter N.

Attorney's or authorized representative's last name | First | MI | Check box if POA is attached | Executor's last name | First | Middle initial

In care of (firm's name) | If more than one executor, check box and see instructions ☐

Address of attorney or authorized representative | Address of executor

City, village or post office | State | ZIP code | City, village or post office | State | ZIP code

Social security number of attorney or authorized rep. | Telephone number ( ) | Social security number of executor | Telephone number ( )

☐ Waivers are requested Attach Form(s) ET-99 (see instructions) | Releases of lien are requested Attach Form(s) ET-117 (see instructions) (Enter number of counties)

If a proceeding for probate or administration has commenced in a Surrogate's Court in New York State, enter county | Was a copy of this return filed with the Surrogate's Court? ☐ Yes ☐ No

Federal estate tax return required ☐ Yes ☐ No Federal gross estate | Federal taxable estate

Tax Computation

1 New York adjusted gross estate (from page 2, line 34) ... 1
2 Total New York allowable deductions (from page 2, line 51) ... 2
3 New York adjusted taxable estate (subtract line 2 from line 1) ... 3
4 New York adjusted taxable gifts (from Worksheet I in the instructions) ... 4
5 Preliminary tentative tax base (add lines 3 and 4) ... 5
6 Preliminary tentative tax on the amount on line 5 (from Table A in the instructions) ... 6
7 Unified credit (from Table B in the instructions) ... 7
8 Net preliminary tentative tax (subtract line 7 from line 6) ... 8
9 Tax attributable to New York adjusted taxable gifts (line 4 divided by line 5; multiplied by line 8; see instructions) ... 9
10 Tax not attributable to New York adjusted taxable gifts (subtract line 9 from line 8) 10
11 Multiply line 10 by the decimal on line 37 ... 11
12 New York tentative tax (add lines 9 and 11) ... 12
13 Gift tax payable for gifts made after 1982 (from Worksheet II in the instructions) ... 13
14 New York estate tax before other credits (subtract line 13 from line 12) ... 14
15a Agricultural exemption credit (from Form ET-411) ... 15a
15b Closely held business credit (from Form ET-416) ... 15b
15c Add lines 15a and 15b ... 15c
16 Credit for New York estate tax on prior transfers (from Form ET-190) ... 16
17 Credit for New York gift tax paid on pre-1983 gifts (from Form ET-412) ... 17
18 Total other credits (add lines 15c, 16 and 17) ... 18
19a New York net estate tax (subtract line 18 from line 14) ... 19a
19b New York minimum tax (from Worksheet III in the instructions) ... 19b
19c New York estate tax (add lines 19a and 19b) ... 19c
20 Prior tax payments (attach a schedule of date(s) and amount(s) of payment(s)) ... 20
21 If line 20 is less than line 19c, subtract line 20 from line 19c. This is the **amount you owe** ... 21
22 If line 20 is more than line 19c, subtract line 19c from line 20. This is the amount to **be refunded to you** ... 22

Attach check or money order here.

Reminder: Sign this form on page 4. If there is an amount on line 21, make check payable to **Commissioner of Taxation and Finance.**
Mail your return and payment (if any) to: **NYS Estate Tax, Processing Center, PO Box 5556, New York NY 10087-5556**

See Instructions regarding your obligation to file a copy of this return with Surrogate's Court.

Page 2 ET-90 (9/98)

Recapitulation (Attach federal Form 706 if applicable)

Do you, the executor, elect alternate valuation in accordance with section 954(b) of the Tax Law? ☐ Yes ☐ No

Gross assets (see instructions) | Value at Date of Death or Alternate Value

23 Schedule A — Real Estate ... 23
24 Schedule B — Stocks and Bonds ... 24
25 Schedule C — Mortgages, Notes, Cash and Bank Deposits ... 25
26 Schedule D — Insurance on the Decedent's Life ... 26
27 Schedule E — Jointly Owned Property ... 27
28 Schedule F — Other Miscellaneous Property ... 28
29 Schedule G — Transfers During Decedent's Life ... 29
30 Schedule H — Powers of Appointment ... 30
31 Schedule I — Annuities ... 31
32 Total (add lines 23 through 31) ... 32
33a Enter the amount from Form ET-417, if any, for the exclusion for a family owned business ... 33a
33b Enter the amount from Form ET-418, if any, for the exclusion for land subject to a qualified conservation easement ... 33b
33c Enter the amount from Form ET-419, if any, for assets excludible from the New York gross estate for victims of Nazi persecution ... 33c
33d Total of exclusions (add lines 33a, b, and c) ... 33d
33e * Enter the net amount of additions (or subtractions) from page 3, line 69 ... 33e
33f Add or subtract line 33e to/from the amount on line 33d) ... 33f
34 **New York adjusted gross estate** (add or subtract line 33f to/from the amount on line 32) ... 34

Computations

35 For resident decedent (enter amount from page 3, line 70) ... 35
36a New York gross estate for resident decedent (subtract line 35 from line 34) ... 36a
36b New York gross estate for nonresident decedent (enter amount from page 3, line 71c) ... 36b
37 Divide line 36a or 36b by line 34 (carry the decimal to four places; cannot be more than 1.0) ... 37

Deductions (see instructions) **Note:** To claim a deduction for principal residence, complete Schedule 5 on page 4.

38 Schedule J — Funeral Expenses and Expenses Incurred in Administering Property Subject to Claims ... 38
39 Schedule K — Debts of Decedent, Including Mortgages and Liens ... 39
40 Schedule L — Net Losses During Administration ... 40
41 Add lines 38, 39, and 40 ... 41
42 * Federal estate tax on excess retirement accumulations (section 4980A(d) of the IRC), if any ... 42
43 Subtract line 42 from line 41 ... 43
44 Enter the amount from Form ET-90.4, Schedule M, line 9 or from federal Form 706, page 3, Schedule M ... 44
45 * Enter amount, if any, from page 4, line 72 ... 45
46 New York bequests to surviving spouse (line 44 and add or subtract line 45) ... 46
47 Enter the amount from Form ET-90.4, Schedule N, line 16 or from federal Form 706, page 3, Schedule O ... 47
48 * Enter amount, if any, from page 4, line 73 ... 48
49 New York charitable deduction (line 47 and add or subtract line 48) ... 49
50 Deduction for principal residence (from line 74) ... 50
51 Total New York allowable deductions (add lines 43, 46, 49, and 50; also enter on page 1, line 2) ... 51

*** For use only when a federal estate tax return, Form 706, is attached. Line 42 is applicable only if a deduction was taken on the federal return.**

52 Decedent's business or occupation | Occupation code (from Table C in instructions)

At time of death decedent was: ☐ Single ☐ Legally separated ☐ Divorced - Date ______
☐ Widow/Widower - Name of deceased spouse ______ SS# ______
Date of Death ______
☐ Married - Name of surviving spouse ______

Election of Marital Deduction for Noncitizen Spouse — If the surviving spouse is not a citizen of the United States and a marital deduction is elected for New York estate tax purposes, both the executor and the surviving spouse must signify by signing below:

Executor	Date	Surviving spouse	Date

ET-90 (9/98) Page 3

Estate of | Social security number

Check the Yes or No box for each question | Yes | No

53 Do you elect a marital deduction for qualified terminable interest property under section 955(c) (QTIP)? ... ☐ ☐
54 Are you making any of the following elections? (If yes, also check applicable box or boxes below) ... ☐ ☐
a Special use valuation under section 954-a of the Tax Law ... a ☐
b Exclusion for land subject to a qualified conservation easement under section 954-b of the Tax Law (complete and attach Form ET-418) ... b ☐
c Exclusion for a family-owned business under section 954-c of the Tax Law (complete and attach Form ET-417) ... c ☐
55 Do you elect to pay the tax in installments as described in IRC section 6166 (NY 997)? If Yes, attach Form ET-415 in duplicate ... ☐ ☐
56 Did the decedent, at the time of death, own any interest in a partnership or unincorporated business; own stock in an inactive or closely held business; or have an interest in any commercial property or incorporated business? ... ☐ ☐
57 Does the gross estate contain any IRC section 2044 property? ... ☐ ☐
58 Was there any insurance on the decedent's life, or were there any annuities or lump sum distributions that are not included on the return as part of the gross estate? ... ☐ ☐
59 Was the decedent a party to litigation within three years preceding death, or is there any pending or contemplated cause of action relative to decedent's death? ... ☐ ☐
60 Were there in existence at the time of the decedent's death any trusts created by the decedent during his or her lifetime or any trusts not created by the decedent under which the decedent possessed any power, beneficial interest or trusteeship? ... ☐ ☐
61 Are there any assets wholly or partially excluded from the gross estate other than jointly-held assets with the surviving spouse? ... ☐ ☐
62 Did the decedent at the time of death own any artwork, stamp collections, coin collections or other collections? ... ☐ ☐

Schedule 1 — Adjustments to Federal Gross Estate	Additions	Subtractions
63 Property subject to a limited power of appointment created before September 1, 1930, includable in the New York estate under section 957 of the Tax Law ...	63	
64 Federal gift tax, if any, included on Schedule G of federal Form 706 ...		64
65 New York State gift tax, if any, paid by decedent or decedent's estate for gifts made by decedent or spouse within three years of decedent's death ...	65	
66 Enter the **full** value of property included in the federal gross estate under the provisions of section 2044 of the Internal Revenue Code (QTIP) ...		66
67 Enter the **full** value of property includable in the New York gross estate under the provisions of section 954(a)(4) and (5) of the Tax Law ...	67	
68 Totals (add lines 63, 65, and 67 in Additions column and add lines 64 and 66 in Subtractions column) ...	68	
69 Net difference - plus or minus (enter here and on page 2, line 33e) ...	69	

Schedule 2 - Adjustment to Determine the New York Gross Estate of a Resident or Nonresident Decedent

For a resident decedent: List each item of real and tangible personal property located **outside** New York State, including the item number and the schedule on which it is listed (do not include bank accounts or other intangible assets located outside New York State). Attach additional sheets if necessary.

70 Total value of property located outside New York State (listed above) for a resident decedent (enter here and on page 2, line 35) ... 70

For a nonresident decedent: List each item of real property and tangible personal property located in New York State, that is required to be included in the New York gross estate. Indicate the item number and the schedule on which it is listed. **Do not include** bank accounts or other intangible assets located in or outside New York State. Property in a Q-TIP Trust that is not required to be included in the New York gross estate under the provisions of section 954(a)(4) and (5) of the Tax Law, should also be excluded.

71a Total value of property located in New York State listed above for a nonresident decedent ... 71a
71b Real property and tangible personal property within New York State, that is included in the amount on lines 33a, 33b, or 33c ... 71b
71c Total value of property includable in the New York gross estate of a nonresident (subtract line 71b from line 71a, enter here and on page 2, line 36b) ... 71c

Page 4 ET-90 (9/98)

Schedule 3 - Adjustment to Federal Marital Deduction

If an addition to, or subtraction from, the federal marital deduction is required:

List the property and indicate the federal schedule(s) on which it is listed. Also, indicate the amount of the adjustment (see instructions).
Note: If you are making adjustments to claim the marital deduction for a surviving spouse who is not a citizen of the United States, both the executor and the surviving spouse must sign in the space provided in item 52 on the bottom of page 2.
Also subtract the value of property reported on Form ET-419, Computation of Exclusion for a Victim of Nazi Persecution, that passed to the surviving spouse.

72 Total value of property listed on this schedule (if negative amount, enter minus; enter here and on page 2, line 45) ... 72

Schedule 4 - Adjustments to Federal Deduction for Charitable, Public and Similar Gifts and Bequests

If an addition to, or subtraction from, the federal marital deduction is required:

List the property and indicate the federal schedule(s) on which it is listed. Also, indicate the amount of the adjustment (see instructions). Include as an addition property passing under a limited power of appointment created before September 1, 1930, that passes or has passed to a qualified charitable organization, if such property is included in the amount on line 63, page 3 (Tax Law, section 957(c)). Subtract the value of property reported on Form ET-419, Computation of Exclusion for a Victim of Nazi Persecution, that passed to a qualified charitable organization.

73 Total value of property listed on this schedule (if negative amount, enter minus; enter here and on page 2, line 48) ... 73

Schedule 5 - Deduction for Principal Residence (for estates of decedents whose date of death is on or after June 8, 1995)

a. Value of principal residence as reported on Schedule A, B, E (Part II only) F, or G ... a
b. Mortgages and other deductions specifically attributable to principal residence as reported on Schedules J, K, L, M, and N:
Administration expenses (from Schedules J and L) ...
Debts of decedent (from Schedule K) ...
Bequests to spouse (marital deduction) (from Schedule M) ...
Charitable bequests (from Schedule N or federal Schedule O) ...
Total deductions (add items above) ... b
c. Net value of principal residence (subtract line b from line a) ... c
d. Maximum allowable deduction ... d 250,000 00
74 Deduction for principal residence (enter the lesser of line c or line d; enter here and on line 50) ... 74

If an attorney or authorized representative is listed on page 1, he or she must complete the following declaration:
I declare that I am a (check one or more) ☐ attorney; ☐ certified public accountant; ☐ enrolled agent; or ☐ public accountant enrolled with the New York State Education Department; and agree to represent the executor for the estate, and I am authorized to receive tax information regarding this estate.

Signature of authorized representative | Date

Under penalties of perjury, I declare that I have examined this return, including accompanying schedules and statements, and to the best of my knowledge and belief, it is true, correct, and complete. Declaration of preparer other than the executor is based on all information of which preparer has any knowledge. Furthermore, I/we, as executor(s) for this estate, authorize the person, if any, named as my/our representative on the front of this return to receive confidential tax information regarding this estate.

Signature of executor	Date	Signature of co-executor	Date
Signature of preparer other than executor			Date
Address of preparer	City	State	ZIP code

Figure 14-9 New York ET-90, pages 1–4.

STATE OF CONNECTICUT
DEPARTMENT OF REVENUE SERVICES

FORM CT-709

CONNECTICUT GIFT TAX RETURN

CT-709
CALENDAR YEAR
▶ **2000**

(Rev. 12/00)

Donor's First Name and Middle Initial ▶ 　　　　Last Name 　　　　Social Security Number

Address ▶ 　　Number and Street 　　PO Box 　　Date Received *(FOR DEPARTMENT USE ONLY)*

City, Town or Post Office ▶ 　　State 　　ZIP Code

Legal Residence (domicile) (county and state) ▶ 　　Citizenship if not U.S.

Check applicable box: 　Connecticut Resident ☐ 　Nonresident ☐ 　Check here if Amended Return ☐ *(Attach an explanation)*

IMPORTANT: FORM CT-709 *CANNOT* BE FILED AS A JOINT RETURN

SECTION 1

A. 1. If the donor died during the calendar year for which this return is filed, check here ▶☐ and enter date of death ▶ _____ 2000

2. If the donor died during the calendar year for which this return is filed and no federal estate tax return is required to be filed, check here ☐

B. If the donor died during the calendar year for which this return is filed and a federal estate tax return extension was requested on federal Form 4768, *Application for Extension of Time to File a Return and/or Pay U.S. Estate (and Generation-Skipping Transfer) Taxes*, check here ▶☐

C. 1. If the donor is claiming special valuation on a gift of farmland, check here ▶☐

2. If you elect under I.R.C. §529(c)(2)(B) to treat any transfers made this year to a qualified state tuition program as made ratably over a five-year period beginning this year, check here. (See instructions) ☐

	YES	NO
D. Is your spouse a U.S. citizen?	☐	☐
If **NO**, did you transfer any property to your spouse during the calendar year?	☐	☐
E. **Gifts by husband or wife to third parties** – Do you consent to have the gifts made by you and your spouse to third parties during the calendar year considered as made one-half by each of you? *(See instructions)*	☐	☐

(If the answer is NO, skip Lines F, G, and H and go to Schedule A. If the answer is YES, the following information must be furnished and your spouse must sign the consent shown below.)

F. Were you married to one another during the entire calendar year? *(See instructions)*	☐	☐

If the answer above is **NO**, check whether ☐ married ☐ divorced ☐ widowed 　Give date _____

G. Will your spouse file a gift tax return for this calendar year?	☐	☐

H. **Consent of Spouse** – I consent to have the gifts made by me and by my spouse to third parties during the calendar year considered as made one-half by each of us. We are both aware of the joint and several liability for tax created by the execution of this consent.

Name of consenting spouse ▶ _____ 　Social Security No. ▶ _____

Consenting spouse's signature _____ 　Date _____

SECTION 2　　**TAX COMPUTATION**

1. Total taxable gifts (Schedule A, Line 13) .... ▶	1	
2. Connecticut Gift Tax *(See instructions)* .... ▶	2	
3. Payments made with extension request .... ▶	3	
4. If Line 3 is greater than Line 2, enter **amount overpaid** (Subtract Line 2 from Line 3) .... ▶	4	
5. If Line 2 is greater than Line 3, enter balance of tax due (Subtract Line 3 from Line 2) .... ▶	5	
6. Interest (from due date of tax) .... ▶	6	
7. Penalty .... ▶	7	
8. Total amount **due** (Add Lines 5, 6, and 7) .... ▶	8	

Due Date: On or before April 15 following the close of the calendar year in which the gifts were made. The due date is April 17, 2001, for calendar year 2000. (For donors who died during the calendar year in which the gifts were made, see instructions.)
Make check or money order payable to: COMMISSIONER OF REVENUE SERVICES
Write the donor's Social Security Number and "2000 Form CT-709" on the check.

Mail to: Department of Revenue Services
PO Box 2978
Hartford CT 06104-2978

DECLARATION: I declare under the penalty of false statement that I have examined this return (including any accompanying schedules and statements) and, to the best of my knowledge and belief, it is true, complete, and correct. (The penalty for false statement is imprisonment not to exceed one year or a fine not to exceed two thousand dollars, or both.) Declaration of preparer (other than donor) is based on all information of which preparer has any knowledge.

Sign Here	Donor's Signature	Date	Telephone Number ( )
Keep a copy of this return for your records	Paid Preparer's Signature	Date	Preparer's PTIN or SSN
	Firm Name and Address ▶		Federal Employer ID Number

ATTACH A COMPLETE COPY OF FEDERAL FORM 709 AND THE NECESSARY SUPPLEMENTAL DOCUMENTS (SEE INSTRUCTIONS)

Figure 14-10　Connecticut Form 709, Gift Tax Return.

Estate Timetable

Immediate

Arrange entry into safe deposit box after checking state law
Prepare and file petition for letters of administration or file will
Advertise grant of letters of administration or probate, if required
Obtain federal ID number
Arrange mail forwarding, if necessary
Give notices to state/local agencies, where required
Give notice to beneficiaries, where required

SCHEDULE A - Computation of Taxable Gifts (Attach additional sheets if necessary)

A Item No.	B Gifts Subject to Gift Tax	C Donor's adjusted basis of gift	D Date of gift	E Value at date of gift
	Donee's name and address Donee's Social Security Number Relationship to donor (if any) Description of gift If the gift was made by means of a trust, enter trust's identifying number below If the gift was market securities, enter CUSIP number(s), if available If the gift was property, its fair market value at the date of the gift is considered the amount of the gift. See instructions for gifts of farmland.			
1				

1. Total gifts made by donor (*See instructions*) **1**

2. One-half of items (*Item No.(s)_____*) attributable to spouse (*See instructions*) **2**

3. Subtract Line 2 from Line 1 .... **3**

4. Gifts made by spouse to be included (From *Schedule A*, Line 2, of spouse's return) **4**

5. Total gifts (Add Line 3 and Line 4) **5**

6. Total annual exclusions for gifts listed on *Schedule A*, including Line 4 above (*See instructions*) **6**

7. Total included amount of gifts (Subtract Line 6 from Line 5) **7**

DEDUCTIONS

8. Gifts to spouse for which a marital deduction will be claimed, based on items (*Item No.(s)_____*) of *Schedule A* **8**

9. Exclusions attributable to gifts on Line 8 .... **9**

10. Marital deduction (Subtract Line 9 from Line 8) **10**

11. Charitable deduction (based on *Item No.(s)_____* less exclusions) **11**

12. Total deductions (Add Line 10 and Line 11) **12**

13. Taxable gifts (Subtract Line 12 from Line 7)
Enter here and also in Section 2, Line 1, on the front of this return **13**

Terminable Interest Marital Deduction (*See instructions*)

14. ☐ ◄ Check here if you elected, under the rules of I.R.C. §2523(f), to include gifts of qualified terminable interest property on Line 8 above. Enter the item numbers (from *Schedule A*, above) of the gifts for which you made this election. ➤ _____

15. ☐ ◄ Check here if you elect under I.R.C. §2523(f)(6) **NOT** to treat as qualified terminable interest property any joint and survivor annuities that are reported on *Schedule A* and would otherwise be treated as qualified terminable interest property under I.R.C. §2523(f). Enter the item numbers (from *Schedule A*) for the annuities for which you are making this election. ➤ _____

PLEASE ATTACH THE NECESSARY SUPPLEMENTARY DOCUMENTS (*SEE INSTRUCTIONS***)**

CT-709 Back (Rev. 12/00)

Figure 14-10   *Continued.*

Intermediate

Apply for death benefits
Apply for burial benefits
Determine dates for payment of taxes
File inventory, where required
Determine filing date for inventory and/or audit
Prepare proposed distribution schedule
Obtain last illness bills
Obtain funeral bill
Obtain copies of statements of debts owed at time of death
File state, local, and federal inheritance estate and/or gift tax returns
Prepare and file last lifetime tax returns

CHAPTER SUMMARY

Unlike the federal unified gift and estate tax system, the individual states impose a number of different taxes on gifts and estates. Each state is free to assess its own particular combination of taxes, independent of the federal taxes or other states' taxes. The executors and administrators for decedents with property located in different states may need to comply with the tax laws and regulations of multiple states. In some cases, the tax may be imposed based on the decedent's last domicile and, in others, on the physical location of the property itself. While in some jurisdictions there is similarity of the states' taxes to the federal return, the local and state rules and regulations must be consulted to ensure proper compliance.

GLOSSARY

Affinity or consanguinity   The degree of relationship between people, usually blood relationships and relationships by marriage

Estate tax   A tax imposed on the transfer of property from a decedent's estate

Gift tax   A tax imposed on the lifetime transfer of a present interest in property

Inheritance tax   A tax imposed on the right to receive the assets from the estate of a decedent

Pickup tax   A tax equal to the tax credit that would be available on the federal estate tax return

REVIEW QUESTIONS

1. Does your jurisdiction use the same definition of gross estate as used by the federal tax system?
2. What is a pickup tax?
3. What is the difference between an inheritance tax and an estate tax?
4. Does it follow that if no federal estate tax return is required, no state estate tax return will be required? Explain.
5. What kind of information can be obtained from lifetime income and gift tax returns that will assist in the preparation of the estate tax returns?
6. Why is knowing the relationship between the decedent and the beneficiary important in preparing estate tax returns?
7. What estate tax is imposed by your jurisdiction?
8. Is a gift tax imposed in your jurisdiction?
9. Is a pickup tax imposed in your jurisdiction?
10. What is the Internet address in your jurisdiction for obtaining necessary estate tax forms?

Chapter 15

Federal Estate and Gift Tax

In This Chapter
Why Study Federal Estate and Gift Tax?
Gift and Estate Taxes
The Gift Tax
Preparing the Federal Gift Tax Return—Form 709
The Estate Tax
Preparing the Federal Estate Tax Return—Form 706

Why Study Federal Estate and Gift Tax?

You have no doubt heard Ben Franklin's statement, "Nothing is certain but death and taxes," but even death does not end the tax obligation. The federal government imposes a tax on the transfer of assets in excess of certain amounts during a person's lifetime and at the time of his or her death. Most states also impose some form of tax on the assets transferred from a decedent to his or her beneficiaries. In some states, this is a tax on the estate and, in others, this tax is on the recipient of the transfer, with the obligation on the executor or administrator to file the required returns. The actual preparation of these returns is usually by the attorney's office handling the estate for the executor or administrator.

Gift and Estate Taxes

GIFT TAX   A tax imposed on certain transfers made during a person's lifetime

ESTATE TAX   A tax applied to the transfers of property after a person's death

The federal gift tax and the federal estate tax are wealth transfer taxes. The **gift tax** is imposed on certain transfers made during a person's lifetime. The federal **estate tax** is applied to the transfers after a person's death. These taxes at the federal level are imposed on the person making the gift and not on the recipient. In some states, the obligation to pay the tax may be on the recipient.

At the federal level, the gift tax and the estate tax are part of the unified transfer tax system. In 1976, these two separate tax systems were unified into one tax system that combines the amount of certain lifetime gifts with the amount of transfers after death in determining the rate of tax assessed.

**UNIFIED TRANSFER
TAX** A tax system
that combines the
amount of certain
lifetime gifts with the
amount of transfers
after death in deter-
mining the rate of tax
to be assessed

TAX CREDIT A
direct reduction in the
amount of tax to be paid

UNIFIED CREDIT
An offset against the tax
assessed on the com-
bined values of inter
vivos and testamentary
gifts and bequests

Special rules apply to gifts that were made prior to 1977. Congress exempted the gifts from the **unified transfer tax** made prior to the unified system's enactment in 1976. If any pre-1977 gifts are an element of a current estate, the rules on these gifts should be consulted.

A **credit** reduces the amount of the actual tax paid. Under the unified system, this **tax unified credit** against the tax has the effect of eliminating combined inclusive gift and estate taxes when the combined total does not exceed certain amounts. The combined total increases each year as shown below. This is subject to congressional action that may increase the amounts; therefore, the current amounts should be checked when preparing the returns.

Unified Credit	Applicable Exclusion Amount
For 1998 of $202,050	$625,000
For 1999 of $211,300	$650,000
For 2000 of $220,550	$675,000
For 2001 of $220,550	$675,000
For 2002 of $229,800	$700,000
For 2003 of $229,800	$700,000
For 2004 of $287,300	$850,000
For 2005 of $326,300	$950,000
After 2005, $345,800	$1,000,000

The Gift Tax

INTER VIVOS The
transfer of property
during the lifetime of
the donor

**ADEQUATE
CONSIDERATION**
The fair market value or
an amount that would
be paid by persons not
having a personal or
business relationship

PRESENT INTEREST
An interest in property
that vests immediately
right of use and
enjoyment

The federal gift tax is imposed on the **inter vivos** transfer of real and personal property without **adequate consideration**. Not every gift is included. Certain gifts and transfers may be excluded in calculating the amount. (See sec. 2503(b) of the IRS Code). Generally, gifts of a **present interest** of no more than $10,000 to any one donee per year do not have to be reported, subject to indexing for inflation after 1998. These gifts may be made to an unlimited number of donees. While the concept appears simple on the surface, as with most tax codes, there are many levels of rules, regulations, and interpretations that may affect the actual calculation. The legal assistant needs to make inquiries as to the nature and subject matter of these gifts, as well as the source of the gifts (Fig. 15-1).

Gifts by married persons may have more planning possibilities. Generally, married couples can make joint gifts of up to $20,000 of a present interest to an individual donee. A spouse may need to sign a consent to this gift to have it considered as made one half by each spouse. In some cases, each spouse may have to file a federal gift tax return. Unlike the individual income tax return, the gift tax return must be filed individually, not as a joint return. A gift tax return may also be required if the spouse is *not* a U.S. citizen and the total gifts to the spouse exceed $100,000 in one year.

Certain other transactions of a financial nature may require the filing of the gift tax return. Of the more common transactions, is the forgiveness of a debt that exceeds the $10,000 limitation for annual exclusion, or the

Form **709-A** (Rev. November 2000) Department of the Treasury Internal Revenue Service	**United States Short Form Gift Tax Return** Calendar year 20.........	OMB No. 1545-0021

1 Donor s first name and middle initial	2 Donor s last name	3 Donor's social security number

4 Address (number, street, and apartment number)		5 Legal residence (domicile)

6 City, state, and ZIP code		7 Citizenship

8 Did you file any gift tax returns for prior periods? . . . . ☐ Yes ☐ No

If "Yes," state when and where earlier returns were filed ▶

9 Name of consenting spouse	10 Consenting spouse's social security number

Note: *Do not use this form to report gifts of closely held stock, partnership interests, fractional interests in real estate, or gifts for which the value has been reduced to reflect a valuation discount. Instead, use Form 709.*

List of Gifts

(a) Donee s name and address and description of gift	(b) Donor s adjusted basis of gift	(c) Date of gift	(d) Value at date of gift

Figure 15-1   Consent portion of federal form 709A.

below-market rate of interest charge on a debt or an interest-free loan. Sales or exchanges of property at less than the real value of the property will also be treated as a gift for tax purposes.

Special rules also apply to the gifts defined as **generation-skipping gifts**. These are generally gifts that skip over the next generation to a third generation of donees called a skip person. Obviously, these areas require direct review, by the supervising attorney, of the facts assembled by the legal assistant. The interpretation of these rules is highly complex and in a constant state of flux. The legal assistant can, however, gather the background data for review and for the ultimate determination by the attorney in charge.

Preparing the Federal Gift Tax Return—Form 709

As with most tax returns, the first page of form 709 contains general information and a summary of the schedules. The schedules must be prepared first and the totals entered on page 1 (Fig. 15-2). A separate form 709 must be filed for each taxpayer; joint returns are not allowed. A spouse, however, may consent to have jointly made gifts treated as being made

Form **709**	**United States Gift (and Generation-Skipping Transfer) Tax Return**	OMB No. 1545-0020
	(Section 6019 of the Internal Revenue Code) (For gifts made during calendar year 1999)	**1999**
Department of the Treasury Internal Revenue Service	▶ See separate instructions. For Privacy Act Notice, see the Instructions for Form 1040.	

Part 1—General Information

1 Donor s first name and middle initial	2 Donor s last name	3 Donor's social security number
4 Address (number, street, and apartment number)		5 Legal residence (domicile) (county and state)
6 City, state, and ZIP code		7 Citizenship

		Yes	No
8	If the donor died during the year, check here ▶ ☐ and enter date of death................. , ...		
9	If you received an extension of time to file this Form 709, check here ▶ ☐ and attach the Form 4868, 2688, 2350, or extension letter		
10	Enter the total number of separate donees listed on Schedule A—count each person only once. ▶		
11a	Have you (the donor) previously filed a Form 709 (or 709-A) for any other year? If the answer is "No," do not complete line 11b ..		
11b	If the answer to line 11a is "Yes," has your address changed since you last filed Form 709 (or 709-A)?		
12	Gifts by husband or wife to third parties.—Do you consent to have the gifts (including generation-skipping transfers) made by you and by your spouse to third parties during the calendar year considered as made one-half by each of you? (See instructions.) (If the answer is "Yes," the following information must be furnished and your spouse must sign the consent shown below. **If the answer is "No," skip lines 13–18 and go to Schedule A.**)		
13	Name of consenting spouse **14 SSN**		
15	Were you married to one another during the entire calendar year? (see instructions)		
16	If the answer to 15 is "No," check whether ☐ married ☐ divorced or ☐ widowed, and give date (see instructions) ▶		
17	Will a gift tax return for this calendar year be filed by your spouse?		
18	**Consent of Spouse—**I consent to have the gifts (and generation-skipping transfers) made by me and by my spouse to third parties during the calendar year considered as made one-half by each of us. We are both aware of the joint and several liability for tax created by the execution of this consent.		

Consenting spouse's signature ▶   Date ▶

Part 2—Tax Computation

			Yes	No
1	Enter the amount from Schedule A, Part 3, line 15	1		
2	Enter the amount from Schedule B, line 3	2		
3	Total taxable gifts (add lines 1 and 2)	3		
4	Tax computed on amount on line 3 (see Table for Computing Tax in separate instructions). . .	4		
5	Tax computed on amount on line 2 (see Table for Computing Tax in separate instructions). . .	5		
6	Balance (subtract line 5 from line 4)	6		
7	Maximum unified credit (nonresident aliens, see instructions)	7	211,300	00
8	Enter the unified credit against tax allowable for all prior periods (from Sch. B, line 1, col. C) . .	8		
9	Balance (subtract line 8 from line 7)	9		
10	Enter 20% (.20) of the amount allowed as a specific exemption for gifts made after September 8, 1976, and before January 1, 1977 (see instructions)	10		
11	Balance (subtract line 10 from line 9)	11		
12	Unified credit (enter the smaller of line 6 or line 11)	12		
13	Credit for foreign gift taxes (see instructions)	13		
14	Total credits (add lines 12 and 13)	14		
15	Balance (subtract line 14 from line 6) (do not enter less than zero)	15		
16	Generation-skipping transfer taxes (from Schedule C, Part 3, col. H, Total)	16		
17	Total tax (add lines 15 and 16)	17		
18	Gift and generation-skipping transfer taxes prepaid with extension of time to file	18		
19	If line 18 is less than line 17, enter BALANCE DUE (see instructions)	19		
20	If line 18 is greater than line 17, enter AMOUNT TO BE REFUNDED	20		

Under penalties of perjury, I declare that I have examined this return, including any accompanying schedules and statements, and to the best of my knowledge and belief it is true, correct, and complete. Declaration of preparer (other than donor) is based on all information of which preparer has any knowledge.

Donor s signature ▶   Date ▶

Preparer s signature (other than donor) ▶   Date ▶

Preparer s address (other than donor) ▶

Attach check or money order here.

For Paperwork Reduction Act Notice, see page 8 of the separate instructions for this form.   Cat. No. 16783M   Form **709** (1999)

Figure 15-2   Federal form 709, gift tax return.

one half by each of them by signing the consent in part 1. If a split gift is made, a tax return must be filed, even if the amount is less than the $10,000 annual exclusion. The consenting spouse may use a simplified form 709A if that is the only reason for the filing of a return.

Computation of Taxable Gifts—Schedule A

DONEE The recipient of a gift

The computation of taxable gifts (Fig. 15-3) requires gifts to be divided into two categories: gifts only subject to gift tax, and those also subject to the generation-skipping tax. The information required is the same; the important difference is the characterization of the **donee** as a *skip person*.

Form 709 (1999)   Page **2**

| SCHEDULE A | Computation of Taxable Gifts (Including Transfers in Trust) |

A   Does the value of any item listed on Schedule A reflect any valuation discount? If the answer is "Yes," see instructions   . Yes ☐ No ☐

B   ☐ ◀ Check here if you elect under section 529(c)(2)(B) to treat any transfers made this year to a qualified state tuition program as made ratably over a 5-year period beginning this year. See instructions. Attach explanation.

Part 1—Gifts Subject Only to Gift Tax. *Gifts less political organization, medical, and educational exclusions—see instructions*

A Item number	B ● Donee s name and address ● Relationship to donor (if any) ● Description of gift ● If the gift was made by means of a trust, enter trust s identifying number and attach a copy of the trust instrument ● If the gift was of securities, give CUSIP number	C Donor s adjusted basis of gift	D Date of gift	E Value at date of gift
1				

Total of Part 1 (add amounts from Part 1, column E)   . . . . ▶

Part 2—Gifts That are Direct Skips and are Subject to Both Gift Tax and Generation-Skipping Transfer Tax. You must list the gifts in chronological order. *Gifts less political organization, medical, and educational exclusions—see instructions. (Also list here direct skips that are subject only to the GST tax at this time as the result of the termination of an "estate tax inclusion period." See instructions.)*

A Item number	B ● Donee s name and address ● Relationship to donor (if any) ● Description of gift ● If the gift was made by means of a trust, enter trust s identifying number and attach a copy of the trust instrument ● If the gift was of securities, give CUSIP number	C Donor s adjusted basis of gift	D Date of gift	E Value at date of gift
1				

Total of Part 2 (add amounts from Part 2, column E)   . . . . ▶

Part 3—Taxable Gift Reconciliation

1	Total value of gifts of donor (add totals from column E of Parts 1 and 2)	1	
2	One-half of items ....attributable to spouse (see instructions)	2	
3	Balance (subtract line 2 from line 1)	3	
4	Gifts of spouse to be included (from Schedule A, Part 3, line 2 of spouse s return—see instructions) .	4	

If any of the gifts included on this line are also subject to the generation-skipping transfer tax, check here ▶ ☐ and enter those gifts also on Schedule C, Part 1.

5	Total gifts (add lines 3 and 4)	5	
6	Total annual exclusions for gifts listed on Schedule A (including line 4, above) (see instructions) . . .	6	
7	Total included amount of gifts (subtract line 6 from line 5)	7	

Deductions (see instructions)

8	Gifts of interests to spouse for which a marital deduction will be claimed, based on items .... of Schedule A **8**		
9	Exclusions attributable to gifts on line 8 . . . . **9**		
10	Marital deduction—subtract line 9 from line 8 . . . . **10**		
11	Charitable deduction, based on items ....less exclusions . . **11**		
12	Total deductions—add lines 10 and 11	12	
13	Subtract line 12 from line 7	13	
14	Generation-skipping transfer taxes payable with this Form 709 (from Schedule C, Part 3, col. H, Total) .	14	
15	Taxable gifts (add lines 13 and 14). Enter here and on line 1 of the Tax Computation on page 1 . . .	15	

(If more space is needed, attach additional sheets of same size.)   Form **709** (1999)

(continues)

Figure 15-3   Federal form 709, schedule A.

Form 709 (1999)   Page **3**

SCHEDULE A   **Computation of Taxable Gifts** (continued)

16 Terminable Interest (QTIP) Marital Deduction. (See instructions for line 8 of Schedule A.)

If a trust (or other property) meets the requirements of qualified terminable interest property under section 2523(f), and

  a. The trust (or other property) is listed on Schedule A, and

  b. The value of the trust (or other property) is entered in whole or in part as a deduction on line 8, Part 3 of Schedule A,

then the donor shall be deemed to have made an election to have such trust (or other property) treated as qualified terminable interest property under section 2523(f).

If less than the entire value of the trust (or other property) that the donor has included in Part 1 of Schedule A is entered as a deduction on line 8, the donor shall be considered to have made an election only as to a fraction of the trust (or other property). The numerator of this fraction is equal to the amount of the trust (or other property) deducted on line 10 of Part 3, Schedule A. The denominator is equal to the total value of the trust (or other property) listed in Part 1 of Schedule A.

If you make the QTIP election (see instructions for line 8 of Schedule A), the terminable interest property involved will be included in your spouse s gross estate upon his or her death (section 2044). If your spouse disposes (by gift or otherwise) of all or part of the qualifying life income interest, he or she will be considered to have made a transfer of the entire property that is subject to the gift tax (see Transfer of Certain Life Estates on page 3 of the instructions).

17 Election Out of QTIP Treatment of Annuities

☐ ◄ Check here if you elect under section 2523(f)(6) **NOT** to treat as qualified terminable interest property any joint and survivor annuities that are reported on Schedule A and would otherwise be treated as qualified terminable interest property under section 2523(f). (See Instructions.) Enter the item numbers (from Schedule A) for the annuities for which you are making this election ►

Figure 15-3   *Continued.*

Gifts of Prior Periods—Schedule B

PROGRESSIVE TAX
A tax whose rates increase as the taxable amount increases

The gift tax is a **progressive tax**. The tax is based on the total of all lifetime taxable gifts. As the amount of gifts increases, the applicable tax rate also increases. To determine the current rate, the prior year's gifts must also be included. These earlier gifts added to the current gifts will determine the new higher rate of tax (Fig. 15-4).

SCHEDULE B   **Gifts From Prior Periods**

If you answered "Yes" on line 11a of page 1, Part 1, see the instructions for completing Schedule B. If you answered "No," skip to the Tax Computation on page 1 (or Schedule C, if applicable).

A Calendar year or calendar quarter (see instructions)	B Internal Revenue office where prior return was filed	C Amount of unified credit against gift tax for periods after December 31, 1976	D Amount of specific exemption for prior periods ending before January 1, 1977	E Amount of taxable gifts

1 Totals for prior periods (without adjustment for reduced specific exemption) **1**

2 Amount, if any, by which total specific exemption, line 1, column D, is more than $30,000 . . . . . **2**

3 Total amount of taxable gifts for prior periods (add amount, column E, line 1, and amount, if any, on line 2). (Enter here and on line 2 of the Tax Computation on page 1.) **3**

(If more space is needed, attach additional sheets of same size.)   Form **709** (1999)

Figure 15-4   Federal form 709, schedule B.

Tax Computation

The total of line 1 (schedule A) and line 2 (schedule B) determines the total tax at the current level of total lifetime taxable gifts. This total is reduced by the amount of tax on prior period gifts (schedule B) to determine the amount of tax due for the current year.

Generation-Skipping Tax

Schedule C of form 709 (Fig. 15-5) is used for determining the additional tax imposed on the type of gifts designated as generation skipping. The

---

Form 709 (1999) Page **4**

SCHEDULE C | **Computation of Generation-Skipping Transfer Tax**

Note: *Inter vivos direct skips that are completely excluded by the GST exemption must still be fully reported (including value and exemptions claimed) on Schedule C.*

Part 1—Generation-Skipping Transfers

A Item No. (from Schedule A, Part 2, col. A)	B Value (from Schedule A, Part 2, col. E)	C Split Gifts (enter ½ of col. B) (see instructions)	D Subtract col. C from col. B	E Nontaxable portion of transfer	F Net Transfer (subtract col. E from col. D)
1					
2					
3					
4					
5					
6					

If you elected gift splitting and your spouse was required to file a separate Form 709 (see the instructions for "Split Gifts"), you must enter all of the gifts shown on Schedule A, Part 2, of your spouse's Form 709 here.

In column C, enter the item number of each gift in the order it appears in column A of your spouse's Schedule A, Part 2. We have preprinted the prefix "S-" to distinguish your spouse's item numbers from your own when you complete column A of Schedule C, Part 3.

In column D, for each gift, enter the amount reported in column C, Schedule C, Part 1, of your spouse's Form 709.

	Split gifts from spouse's Form 709 (enter item number)	Value included from spouse's Form 709	Nontaxable portion of transfer	Net transfer (subtract col. E from col. D)
S-				
S-				
S-				
S-				
S-				
S-				
S-				

Part 2—GST Exemption Reconciliation (Section 2631) and Section 2652(a)(3) Election

Check box ▶ ☐ if you are making a section 2652(a)(3) (special QTIP) election (see instructions)

Enter the item numbers (from Schedule A) of the gifts for which you are making this election ▶ ....

1 Maximum allowable exemption (see instructions) . . . . | 1 |
2 Total exemption used for periods before filing this return . . . . | 2 |
3 Exemption available for this return (subtract line 2 from line 1) . . . . | 3 |
4 Exemption claimed on this return (from Part 3, col. C total, below) . . . . . . | 4 |
5 Exemption allocated to transfers not shown on Part 3, below. **You must attach a Notice of Allocation.** (See instructions.) . . . . | 5 |
6 Add lines 4 and 5 . . . . | 6 |
7 Exemption available for future transfers (subtract line 6 from line 3) . . . . . . | 7 |

Part 3—Tax Computation

A Item No. (from Schedule C, Part 1)	B Net transfer (from Schedule C, Part 1, col. F)	C GST Exemption Allocated	D Divide col. C by col. B	E Inclusion Ratio (subtract col. D from 1.000)	F Maximum Estate Tax Rate	G Applicable Rate (multiply col. E by col. F)	H Generation-Skipping Transfer Tax (multiply col. B by col. G)
1					55% (.55)		
2					55% (.55)		
3					55% (.55)		
4					55% (.55)		
5					55% (.55)		
6					55% (.55)		
					55% (.55)		
					55% (.55)		
					55% (.55)		
					55% (.55)		

Total exemption claimed. Enter here and on line 4, Part 2, above. May not exceed line 3, Part 2, above . . . . . . | | Total generation-skipping transfer tax. Enter here, on line 14 of Schedule A, Part 3, and on line 16 of the Tax Computation on page 1 . . . . | |

(If more space is needed, attach additional sheets of same size.) Form **709** (1999)

Figure 15-5   Federal form 709, schedule C.

relationship of the donor to the donee is used to determine if the gift is generation skipping (e.g., does the gift avoid the next generation, such as a child, and go to the next generation, such as a grandchild).

Examples of Transfers Subject to Gift Tax	**Examples of Transfers Not Subject**
Gratuitous transfer of any kind of property	Gifts to political organization
Sales or exchanges not in the ordinary course of business for less than full value	Gifts to educational organization
The exercise or release of a general power of appointment	Gifts for payment of medical care
Forgiveness of a debt	
Free of interest or below-market rate of interest on a loan	
Certain property settlements in a divorce	

The Estate Tax

A tax is imposed on the transfer of the taxable estate of every decedent who is a citizen or resident of the United States (see IRC sec. 2001). The taxable estate is the gross estate less allowable deductions. The estate tax on the taxable estate is reduced by any unified credit not used against the gift tax.

The tax is determined as shown in the following.

	Gross Estate	
less	deductions	$_____
	Taxable Estate	
plus	post-1976 gifts	$_____
	tax base for estate tax	
times	tax rate	
	Tentative Tax	$_____
less	adjustments for post-1976 gifts	
less	credits	
	Estate Tax Liability	$_____

✔ Checklist for Preparing Estate Returns

_____ Death certificate

    _____ Date of death

    _____ Social Security number

_____ Beneficiaries

    _____ Name

———— Address
———— Date of birth
———— Social Security number
———— Relationship to deceased
———— Will
  ———— Executor
  ———— Trustee
  ———— Beneficiaries named
  ———— Individuals
  ———— Charities
———— Codicils to will
  ———— Changes to underlying will
———— Trust agreements
  ———— Inter vivos
  ———— Testamentary
———— Jurisdictional information
  ———— Decedent's domicile
  ———— Decedent's residence
———— Income tax returns
  ———— Federal
  ———— State
  ———— Local
———— Gift tax returns
———— Assets
  ———— Real estate
  ———— Stocks and bonds
  ———— Banks
  ———— Insurance
  ———— Personal
———— Deductions

Preparing the Federal Estate Tax Return—Form 706

Page 1 of the federal estate return form 706 (Fig. 15-6) is primarily for the computation of the estate tax. The general information and summary of the attached schedules are on pages 2 and 3. As with most tax returns, the need to prepare and file the return may not be obvious until after the information has been gathered for the calculation of the gross estate and the related deductions.

Form 706
(Rev. July 1999)

Department of the Treasury
Internal Revenue Service

United States Estate (and Generation-Skipping Transfer) Tax Return

Estate of a citizen or resident of the United States (see separate instructions).
To be filed for decedents dying after December 31, 1998
For Paperwork Reduction Act Notice, see page 1 of the separate instructions.

OMB No. 1545-0015

Part 1.—Decedent and Executor

1a Decedent's first name and middle initial (and maiden name, if any)	1b Decedent's last name	2 Decedent's Social Security No.
3a Legal residence (domicile) at time of death (county, state, and ZIP code, or foreign country)	3b Year domicile established 4 Date of birth 5 Date of death
6a Name of executor (see page 4 of the instructions)	6b Executor's address (number and street including apartment or suite no. or rural route; city, town, or post office; state; and ZIP code)
6c Executor's social security number (see page 4 of the instructions)	
7a Name and location of court where will was probated or estate administered	7b Case number
8 If decedent died testate, check here ▶ ☐ and attach a certified copy of the will.	9 If Form 4768 is attached, check here ▶ ☐
10 If Schedule R-1 is attached, check here ▶ ☐	

Part 2.—Tax Computation

1 Total gross estate less exclusion (from Part 5, Recapitulation, page 3, item 12) **1**
2 Total allowable deductions (from Part 5, Recapitulation, page 3, item 23) **2**
3 Taxable estate (subtract line 2 from line 1) **3**
4 Adjusted taxable gifts (total taxable gifts (within the meaning of section 2503) made by the decedent after December 31, 1976, other than gifts that are includible in decedent's gross estate (section 2001(b))) **4**
5 Add lines 3 and 4 . . . . **5**
6 Tentative tax on the amount on line 5 from Table A on page 12 of the instructions **6**
7a If line 5 exceeds $10,000,000, enter the lesser of line 5 or $17,184,000. If line 5 is $10,000,000 or less, skip lines 7a and 7b and enter -0- on line 7c . **7a**
  b Subtract $10,000,000 from line 7a **7b**
  c Enter 5% (.05) of line 7b **7c**
8 Total tentative tax (add lines 6 and 7c) **8**
9 Total gift tax payable with respect to gifts made by the decedent after December 31, 1976. Include gift taxes by the decedent's spouse for such spouse's share of split gifts (section 2513) only if the decedent was the donor of these gifts and they are includible in the decedent's gross estate (see instructions) **9**
10 Gross estate tax (subtract line 9 from line 8) **10**
11 Maximum unified credit (applicable credit amount) against estate tax . **11**
12 Adjustment to unified credit (applicable credit amount). (This adjustment may not exceed $6,000. See page 4 of the instructions.) . . . **12**
13 Allowable unified credit (applicable credit amount) (subtract line 12 from line 11). **13**
14 Subtract line 13 from line 10 (but do not enter less than zero) **14**
15 Credit for state death taxes. Do not enter more than line 14. Figure the credit by using the amount on line 3 less $60,000. See Table B in the instructions and **attach credit evidence** (see instructions) .. **15**
16 Subtract line 15 from line 14 . . . . **16**
17 Credit for Federal gift taxes on pre-1977 gifts (section 2012) (attach computation) **17**
18 Credit for foreign death taxes (from Schedule(s) P). (Attach Form(s) 706-CE.) **18**
19 Credit for tax on prior transfers (from Schedule Q) **19**
20 Total (add lines 17, 18, and 19) **20**
21 Net estate tax (subtract line 20 from line 16) **21**
22 Generation-skipping transfer taxes (from Schedule R, Part 2, line 10) **22**
23 Total transfer taxes (add lines 21 and 22) **23**
24 Prior payments. Explain in an attached statement **24**
25 United States Treasury bonds redeemed in payment of estate tax . **25**
26 Total (add lines 24 and 25) **26**
27 Balance due (or overpayment) (subtract line 26 from line 23). **27**

Under penalties of perjury, I declare that I have examined this return, including accompanying schedules and statements, and to the best of my knowledge and belief, it is true, correct, and complete. Declaration of preparer other than the executor is based on all information of which preparer has any knowledge.

Signature(s) of executor(s)   Date

Signature of preparer other than executor   Address (and ZIP code)   Date

Cat. No. 20548R

Figure 15-6   Federal form 706, estate tax return, pages 1–3.

Determining the Value of the Gross Estate

A decedent's gross estate includes all property, real or personal, tangible or intangible over which the decedent had control and enjoyment at the time of death (see IRC sec. 2031). The right to receive income from or con-

Form 706 (Rev. 7-99)

Estate of:

Part 3—Elections by the Executor

Please check the "Yes" or "No" box for each question. (See instructions beginning on page 5.)		Yes	No
1 Do you elect alternate valuation? **1**			
2 Do you elect special use valuation? . . . . If "Yes," you must complete and attach Schedule A–1. **2**			
3 Do you elect to pay the taxes in installments as described in section 6166? . . . . If "Yes," you must attach the additional information described on page 8 of the instructions. **3**			
4 Do you elect to postpone the part of the taxes attributable to a reversionary or remainder interest as described in section 6163? **4**			

Part 4—General Information (Note: *Please attach the necessary supplemental documents.* **You must attach the death certificate.)**
(See instructions on page 9.)

Authorization to receive confidential tax information under Regs. sec. 601.504(b)(2)(i); to act as the estate's representative before the IRS; and to make written or oral presentations on behalf of the estate if return prepared by an attorney, accountant, or enrolled agent for the executor:

Name of representative (print or type)	State	Address (number, street, and room or suite no., city, state, and ZIP code)

I declare that I am the ☐ attorney/ ☐ certified public accountant/ ☐ enrolled agent (you must check the applicable box) for the executor and prepared this return for the executor. I am not under suspension or disbarment from practice before the Internal Revenue Service and am qualified to practice in the state shown above.

Signature	CAF number	Date	Telephone number

1   Death certificate number and issuing authority (attach a copy of the death certificate to this return).

2   Decedent's business or occupation. If retired, check here ▶ ☐ and state decedent's former business or occupation.

3   Marital status of the decedent at time of death:
   ☐ Married
   ☐ Widow or widower—Name, SSN, and date of death of deceased spouse ▶ ....

   ☐ Single
   ☐ Legally separated
   ☐ Divorced—Date divorce decree became final ▶

4a Surviving spouse's name	4b Social security number	4c Amount received (see page 9 of the instructions)

5   Individuals (other than the surviving spouse), trusts, or other estates who receive benefits from the estate (do not include charitable beneficiaries shown in Schedule O) (see instructions). For Privacy Act Notice (applicable to individual beneficiaries only), see the Instructions for Form 1040.

Name of individual, trust, or estate receiving $5,000 or more	Identifying number	Relationship to decedent	Amount (see instructions)

All unascertainable beneficiaries and those who receive less than $5,000 . . . . ▶

Total . . . .

Please check the "Yes" or "No" box for each question.	Yes	No
6 Does the gross estate contain any section 2044 property (qualified terminable interest property (QTIP) from a prior gift or estate) (see page 9 of the instructions)?		

(continued on next page)   **Page 2**

(continues)

Figure 15-6   *Continued.*

trol over property previously transferred before death is included. For example, the value of a bank account for which the decedent retained the income for life. The difficulty in many estates is in finding all the assets. A good starting point is a review of the prior years federal, state, and local tax returns. Information on dividends and interest reported in prior years

Form 706 (Rev. 7-99)

Part 4—General Information (continued)

Please check the "Yes" or "No" box for each question.

	Yes	No
7a Have Federal gift tax returns ever been filed?		
If "Yes," please attach copies of the returns, if available, and furnish the following information:		

7b Period(s) covered	**7c** Internal Revenue office(s) where filed

If you answer "Yes" to any of questions 8–16, you must attach additional information as described in the instructions.

		Yes	No
8a	Was there any insurance on the decedent's life that is not included on the return as part of the gross estate?		
b	Did the decedent own any insurance on the life of another that is not included in the gross estate?		
9	Did the decedent at the time of death own any property as a joint tenant with right of survivorship in which **(a)** one or more of the other joint tenants was someone other than the decedent's spouse, and **(b)** less than the full value of the property is included on the return as part of the gross estate? If "Yes," you must complete and attach Schedule E		
10	Did the decedent, at the time of death, own any interest in a partnership or unincorporated business or any stock in an inactive or closely held corporation?		
11	Did the decedent make any transfer described in section 2035, 2036, 2037, or 2038 (see the instructions for Schedule G beginning on page 11 of the separate instructions)? If "Yes," you must complete and attach Schedule G		
12	Were there in existence at the time of the decedent's death:		
a	Any trusts created by the decedent during his or her lifetime?		
b	Any trusts not created by the decedent under which the decedent possessed any power, beneficial interest, or trusteeship?		
13	Did the decedent ever possess, exercise, or release any general power of appointment? If "Yes," you must complete and attach Schedule H		
14	Was the marital deduction computed under the transitional rule of Public Law 97-34, section 403(e)(3) (Economic Recovery Tax Act of 1981)?		
	If "Yes," attach a separate computation of the marital deduction, enter the amount on item 20 of the Recapitulation, and note on item 20 "computation attached."		
15	Was the decedent, immediately before death, receiving an annuity described in the "General" paragraph of the instructions for Schedule I? If "Yes," you must complete and attach Schedule I		
16	Was the decedent ever the beneficiary of a trust for which a deduction was claimed by the estate of a pre-deceased spouse under section 2056(b)(7) and which is not reported on this return? If "Yes," attach an explanation.		

Part 5—Recapitulation

Item number	Gross estate		Alternate value	Value at date of death
1	Schedule A—Real Estate	1		
2	Schedule B—Stocks and Bonds	2		
3	Schedule C—Mortgages, Notes, and Cash	3		
4	Schedule D—Insurance on the Decedent's Life (attach Form(s) 712)	4		
5	Schedule E—Jointly Owned Property (attach Form(s) 712 for life insurance) . .	5		
6	Schedule F—Other Miscellaneous Property (attach Form(s) 712 for life insurance)	6		
7	Schedule G—Transfers During Decedent's Life (att. Form(s) 712 for life insurance)	7		
8	Schedule H—Powers of Appointment	8		
9	Schedule I—Annuities	9		
10	Total gross estate (add items 1 through 9).	10		
11	Schedule U—Qualified Conservation Easement Exclusion	11		
12	Total gross estate less exclusion (subtract item 11 from item 10). Enter here and on line 1 of Part 2—Tax Computation	12		

Item number	Deductions		Amount
13	Schedule J—Funeral Expenses and Expenses Incurred in Administering Property Subject to Claims	13	
14	Schedule K—Debts of the Decedent	14	
15	Schedule K—Mortgages and Liens	15	
16	Total of items 13 through 15	16	
17	Allowable amount of deductions from item 16 (see the instructions for item 17 of the Recapitulation) . .	17	
18	Schedule L—Net Losses During Administration	18	
19	Schedule L—Expenses Incurred in Administering Property Not Subject to Claims	19	
20	Schedule M—Bequests, etc., to Surviving Spouse	20	
21	Schedule O—Charitable, Public, and Similar Gifts and Bequests	21	
22	Schedule T—Qualified Family-Owned Business Interest Deduction	22	
23	Total allowable deductions (add items 17 through 22). Enter here and on line 2 of the Tax Computation	23	

Page 3

Figure 15-6 *Continued.*

will give a clue as to the holdings at death. Review of the schedule D of form 1040 will show what was sold and, therefore, what should be looked for in the estate. Frequently, stock brokerage accounts will pay interest and can be checked for accounts. Similarly, those that charge fees are usually listed in the deduction section of the personal tax return for fees paid for account services. Bank accounts and insurance policies can also be discovered because of the interest paid and included on the lifetime returns. Real estate can be found from the listing of real estate taxes on the personal schedule A deductions or from the rental income portion of schedule E.

A review of the bank and brokerage statements may also give an indication of taxable gifts received prior to death. A review of copies of notes and loan documents may indicate interest-free or below-market interest that may need to be reviewed.

The following listing indicates the filing requirement for an estate for a person who died after 1997; prior to 1997, the amount was $600,000.

Year of Death	Estate Value
1998	$625,000
1999	$650,000
2000	$675,000
2001	$675,000
2002	$700,000
2003	$700,000
2004	$850,000
2005	$950,000
After 2005	$1,000,000

Valuation

One of the first questions in preparing estate returns is what value should be used for the assets listed in the return. Cash is not usually a problem; the dollar amount is the dollar amount, unless the cash is in the form of collectible coins or script. In these cases, the asset is not really cash but is included with other collectibles.

For stocks and bonds that are publicly traded, the value used is usually that listed in the stock listings of *The Wall Street Journal* or other major paper that reports the stock and bond closing prices on the decedent's date of death. Unlisted and privately traded stocks can present some unusual valuation issues. If the stock is the controlling interest in a small business, it may well have greater value than the minority interest on a per share basis. Before the per share value can be determined, the value of the business itself may first need to be calculated or established by an appraisal.

FAIR MARKET VALUE
The price a willing buyer would pay a willing seller, neither being required nor forced to sell or purchase the item

Real estate is usually listed at the **fair market value**. The fair market value is the price a willing buyer would pay a willing seller. In an ordinary case, this is determined by the price paid for comparable property in the area. It may also be set by the actual price paid and received by the estate in an arms-length transaction. An arms-length transaction is one in which there is no collusion between the buyer and seller, such as might exist between friendly relatives or close personal friends trying to do each other a favor.

Collectibles and antiques present the biggest problem in valuation. The first issue is determining if something is really a collectible or just some trinket that the deceased thought was of value, usually more sentimental than monetary. Artwork is always a hard call. What is considered art to one individual may not be to another. There are no absolutes. Unless there is a preexisting market for an item, such as a Tiffany lamp or a Picasso painting, even an appraisal may have limited value and be somewhat questionable.

In cases of items not easily subject to appraisal, an auction may be the method used to establish the value. This is usually the method used when the item has no sentimental value or other special interest to any of the beneficiaries and when it is not an item specially bequeathed to a beneficiary. What the estate receives from the auction is the value. When an appraisal is required, and the item is of general interest only and not a true collectible, the auctioneer may well be the best source of a written appraisal. The appraisal may be required if the return and the values are questioned in an audit.

Alternate Valuation Date

ALTERNATE VALUATION DATE
The value of an asset at a date other than the date of the death of the testator

The executor of the estate may elect, under IRC sec. 2032, to value the gross estate at the value of the property six months after the decedents death, if this has the effect of reducing the gross estate and the estate tax liability. The election must apply to the entire estate and cannot be applied only to selected assets. The value is the fair market value of the asset—the price that a willing buyer would pay and a willing seller would accept. Since this is not always obvious, it is helpful to obtain an independent valuation from a qualified appraiser. In selecting an appraiser, it is wise to consider his or her reputation and qualifications for the type of property to be appraised. It is not unusual for the Internal Revenue Service, state revenue agents, and, in many cases, beneficiaries to question the competency of the appraiser selected by the executor or the attorney representing the executor.

Deductions in Calculating Adjusted Gross Estate

The Internal Revenue Code provides four classes of deductible items.

1. Expenses and debts, including funeral expenses and the cost of administering the estate (sec. 2053; see Figs. 15-7 and 15-8)
2. Casualty and theft losses (sec. 2054)
3. Transfers to the surviving spouse (sec. 2056)
4. Transfers to charity (sec. 2055).

Deductions in Calculating the Taxable Estate

Certain gifts made during the lifetime of the decedent are added into the calculation for determining the taxable estate. Generally, gifts that exceed the annual limits per donee are added back at the value of the property or gift at the time of the gift. For example, if a gift of $15,000 to one donee by an individual exceeds the annual limit by $5,000, the $5,000 will be added back.

Form 706 (Rev. 7-99)

Estate of:

SCHEDULE J—Funeral Expenses and Expenses Incurred in Administering Property Subject to Claims

Note: *Do not list on this schedule expenses of administering property not subject to claims. For those expenses, see the instructions for Schedule L.*

If executors' commissions, attorney fees, etc., are claimed and allowed as a deduction for estate tax purposes, they are not allowable as a deduction in computing the taxable income of the estate for Federal income tax purposes. They are allowable as an income tax deduction on Form 1041 if a waiver is filed to waive the deduction on Form 706 (see the Form 1041 instructions).

Item number	Description	Expense amount	Total amount
1	**A. Funeral expenses:**		
	Total funeral expenses . . . . ▶		
	B. Administration expenses:		
1	Executors' commissions—amount estimated/agreed upon/paid. (Strike out the words that do not apply.)		
2	Attorney fees—amount estimated/agreed upon/paid. (Strike out the words that do not apply.) . .		
3	Accountant fees—amount estimated/agreed upon/paid. (Strike out the words that do not apply.)		
4	Miscellaneous expenses:	Expense amount	
	Total miscellaneous expenses from continuation schedules (or additional sheets) attached to this schedule		
	Total miscellaneous expenses . . . . ▶		
	TOTAL. (Also enter on Part 5, Recapitulation, page 3, at item 13.) . . . . ▶		

(If more space is needed, attach the continuation schedule from the end of this package or additional sheets of the same size.)
(See the instructions on the reverse side.)

Schedule J—Page 23

Figure 15-7   Federal form 706, schedule J.

Form 706 (Rev. 7-99)

Estate of:

SCHEDULE K—Debts of the Decedent, and Mortgages and Liens

Item number	Debts of the Decedent—Creditor and nature of claim, and allowable death taxes	Amount unpaid to date	Amount in contest	Amount claimed as a deduction
1				

Total from continuation schedules (or additional sheets) attached to this schedule . . . .

TOTAL. (Also enter on Part 5, Recapitulation, page 3, at item 14.) . . . .

Item number	Mortgages and Liens—Description	Amount
1		

Total from continuation schedules (or additional sheets) attached to this schedule . . . .

TOTAL. (Also enter on Part 5, Recapitulation, page 3, at item 15.) . . . .

(If more space is needed, attach the continuation schedule from the end of this package or additional sheets of the same size.)
(The instructions to Schedule K are in the separate instructions.)   **Schedule K—Page 25**

Figure 15-8 Federal form 706, schedule K, Debts of the Decedent, and Mortgages and Liens.

Tax Rates

The combined rates are progressive as shown in Figure 15-9.

Table A—Unified Rate Schedule

Column A	Column B	Column C	Column D
Taxable amount over	Taxable amount not over	Tax on amount in column A	Rate of tax on excess over amount in column A
			(Percent)
0	$10,000	0	18
$10,000	20,000	$1,800	20
20,000	40,000	3,800	22
40,000	60,000	8,200	24
60,000	80,000	13,000	26
80,000	100,000	18,200	28
100,000	150,000	23,800	30
150,000	250,000	38,800	32
250,000	500,000	70,800	34
500,000	750,000	155,800	37
750,000	1,000,000	248,300	39
1,000,000	1,250,000	345,800	41
1,250,000	1,500,000	448,300	43
1,500,000	2,000,000	555,800	45
2,000,000	2,500,000	780,800	49
2,500,000	3,000,000	1,025,800	53
3,000,000	....	1,290,800	55

Table B Worksheet

Federal Adjusted Taxable Estate

1 Federal taxable estate (from Tax Computation, Form 706, line 3) $_____

2 Adjustment   60,000

3 Federal adjusted taxable estate. Subtract line 2 from line 1. Use this amount to compute maximum credit for state death taxes in **Table B**.   _____

Table B

Computation of Maximum Credit for State Death Taxes

(Based on Federal adjusted taxable estate computed using the worksheet above.)

(1) Adjusted taxable estate equal to or more than—	(2) Adjusted taxable estate less than—	(3) Credit on amount in column (1)	(4) Rate of credit on excess over amount in column (1)	(1) Adjusted taxable estate equal to or more than—	(2) Adjusted taxable estate less than—	(3) Credit on amount in column (1)	(4) Rate of credit on excess over amount in column (1)
			(Percent)				(Percent)
0	$40,000	0	None	2,040,000	2,540,000	106,800	8.0
$40,000	90,000	0	0.8	2,540,000	3,040,000	146,800	8.8
90,000	140,000	$400	1.6	3,040,000	3,540,000	190,800	9.6
140,000	240,000	1,200	2.4	3,540,000	4,040,000	238,800	10.4
240,000	440,000	3,600	3.2	4,040,000	5,040,000	290,800	11.2
440,000	640,000	10,000	4.0	5,040,000	6,040,000	402,800	12.0
640,000	840,000	18,000	4.8	6,040,000	7,040,000	522,800	12.8
840,000	1,040,000	27,600	5.6	7,040,000	8,040,000	650,800	13.6
1,040,000	1,540,000	38,800	6.4	8,040,000	9,040,000	786,800	14.4
1,540,000	2,040,000	70,800	7.2	9,040,000	10,040,000	930,800	15.2
				10,040,000	....	1,082,800	16.0

Examples showing use of Schedule B

Example where the alternate valuation is not adopted; date of death, January 1, 1999

Item number	Description including face amount of bonds or number of shares and par value where needed for identification. Give CUSIP number.	Unit value	Alternate valuation date	Alternate value	Value at date of death
1	$60,000-Arkansas Railroad Co. first mortgage 4%, 20-year bonds, due 2001. Interest payable quarterly on Feb. 1, May 1, Aug. 1 and Nov. 1; N.Y. Exchange, CUSIP No. XXXXXXXXX	100	....	$............	$ 60,000
	Interest coupons attached to bonds, item 1, due and payable on Nov. 1, 1998, but not cashed at date of death	....	....	....	600
	Interest accrued on item 1, from Nov. 1, 1998, to Jan. 1, 1999 . ..	....	....	....	400
2	500 shares Public Service Corp., common; N.Y. Exchange, CUSIP No. XXXXXXXXX	110	....	....	55,000
	Dividend on item 2 of $2 per share declared Dec. 10, 1998, payable on Jan. 10, 1999, to holders of record on Dec. 30, 1998	....	....	....	1,000

Page 12   **Instructions for Schedules**

Figure 15-9   Unified tax rates schedule.

✔ Checklist for Preparing the Federal Estate Tax Return

_____ Obtain a tax identification number

_____ Notification of

    _____ Beneficiaries

    _____ Tax authorities

    _____ Creditors

_____ Collection of assets

    _____ Inventory and appraisal of assets

    _____ Location of assets

        _____ Home safe

        _____ Banks

        _____ Insurance companies

        _____ Credit unions

        _____ Safe deposit boxes

    _____ Real estate

        _____ Home

        _____ Vacation

        _____ Rental property

        _____ Commercial

        _____ Time share

    _____ Stocks

        _____ Publicly traded

        _____ Close corporation

    _____ Bonds

        _____ Corporate

        _____ Federal

        _____ State

    _____ Private notes receivable

    _____ Vehicles

    _____ Airplanes

    _____ Boats

Timetable
Federal timetable
State timetable

CHAPTER SUMMARY

The federal government historically imposed a tax on the transfer of property, without consideration, during one's lifetime (inter vivos gifts) and after death (testamentary). The two taxes were unified effective 1977, with a unified tax and unified tax credit. The unified tax credit permits a number of taxable inter vivos gifts and testamentary gifts to be made without taxation up to a certain amount, indexed to increase over a number of years. The gift tax still permits some gifts to individuals without tax. Generally, a person may make an unlimited number of tax-free gifts of not more than $10,000 per donee per year. A married couple may combine their gifts by the execution of a consent form, thereby permitting a $20,000 gift to each donee in each year. The excess inter vivos gift amounts are added to the taxable value of the estate for purposes of determining the unified tax.

GLOSSARY

Adequate consideration   The fair market value or an amount that would be paid by persons not having a personal or business relationship

Alternate valuation date   The value of an asset at a date other than the date of the death of the testator

Donee   The recipient of a gift

Estate tax   A tax applied to the transfers of property after a person's death

Fair market value   The price a willing buyer would pay a willing seller, neither being required nor forced to sell or purchase the item

Generation-skipping gifts   A gift that avoids the next generation (the skipped generation, such as a child) and goes to the following generation, such as a grandchild

Gift tax   A tax imposed on certain transfers made during a person's lifetime

Inter vivos   The transfer of property during the lifetime of the donor

Present interest   An interest in property that vests immediately right of use and enjoyment

Progressive tax   A tax whose rates increase as the taxable amount increases

Tax credit   A direct reduction in the amount of tax to be paid

Unified credit   An offset against the tax assessed on the combined values of inter vivos and testamentary gifts and bequests

Unified transfer tax   A tax system that combines the amount of certain lifetime gifts with the amount of transfers after death in determining the rate of tax to be assessed

REVIEW QUESTIONS

1. Why is the federal gift and estate tax referred to as a wealth transfer tax?
2. When were the federal gift and the federal estate taxes combined?
3. What is the effect of a tax credit?
4. What is the effect of the annual gift tax exclusion?
5. Can a husband and wife file a joint gift tax return?

6. What is a skip person?
7. What is meant by a progress tax?
8. Give an example of a gift not subject to gift tax?
9. What is one method of determining potential stockholdings at the time of a person's death?
10. What is the difference between value and worth?

Chapter 16

Using the Internet

In This Chapter

Why Study about the Internet?

The use of the computer in the law office has been increasing, not just in its traditional use for document preparation, but also for maintenance of accounting records and for the preparation of tax returns. Computers are also increasingly being used for the sharing of information in digital form between remote offices, courthouse government agencies, and clients. Computer files are easily shared today in the form of CDs, floppy disks, and tape cartridges, and by dial-up or Internet connection. Where in the past paper had to be copied and sent, frequently by messenger or express mail service, today, large files can be quickly exchanged electronically without any paper (hard copy) almost instantly to any point in the world.

The Internet

In its most basic form, the Internet, or the World Wide Web, may be thought of as nothing more than a group of computers linked together with the added ability to search all the connections for information. If you work in an office that has all of its computers networked together, you have a small version of the Internet (Fig. 16-1). Everyone's computer is connected

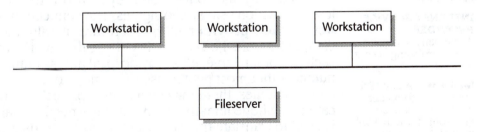

Figure 16-1   Graphic representation of a network system.

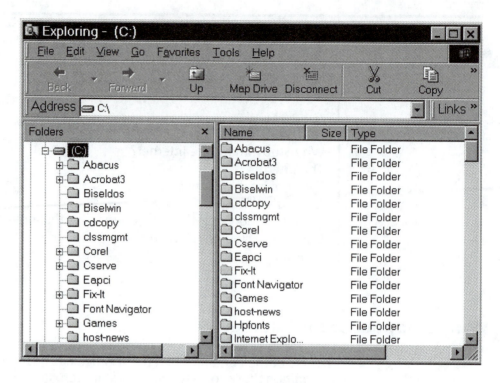

Figure 16-2   Microsoft Windows Explorer screen.

FILE SERVER   The central computer in a network computer system upon which the operating system rests; controls the flow of information between computers on the system and usually acts as storage unit for data

BACKBONE   The connecting line used by other computer systems to communicate with each other

INTERNET SERVICE PROVIDER
A company or organization providing access to the Internet

MODEM   A device for converting computer information into an electronic form that will allow it to be transferred over telephone lines and radio waves

to another person's computer, generally with a main computer in which resides the frequently shared data files and the software (network operating system) that controls the connections, and handles and directs requests from each computer. This main control computer is usually referred to as the **file server**. The search tool is usually a program such as Microsoft Windows Explorer that permits files to be found by location or other characteristics (Figs. 16-2 and 16-3).

If you think of your small network as being connected to other similar office networks, and all these other offices together with many other companies and government agencies around the world linked on some connecting line (a **backbone**), you have the World Wide Web (Fig. 16-4).

Generally, the connection is by some form of telephone line or wireless connection using radio signals. The connection is usually to an **internet service provider** (ISP). There are literally thousands of these ISP companies from the very small to those that are international in character, such as CompuServe. ISPs provide local access numbers or toll-free access numbers that most people use to connect to their service. In large offices and companies, there may be a direct connection (hard wired or by dedicated telephone line) that eliminates the need to dial up the ISP. A device is used to translate the electrical signals for transmission over these connections so the computers can "talk" to each other. This device is called a **modem**. A modem converts (modulates) the information from your key-

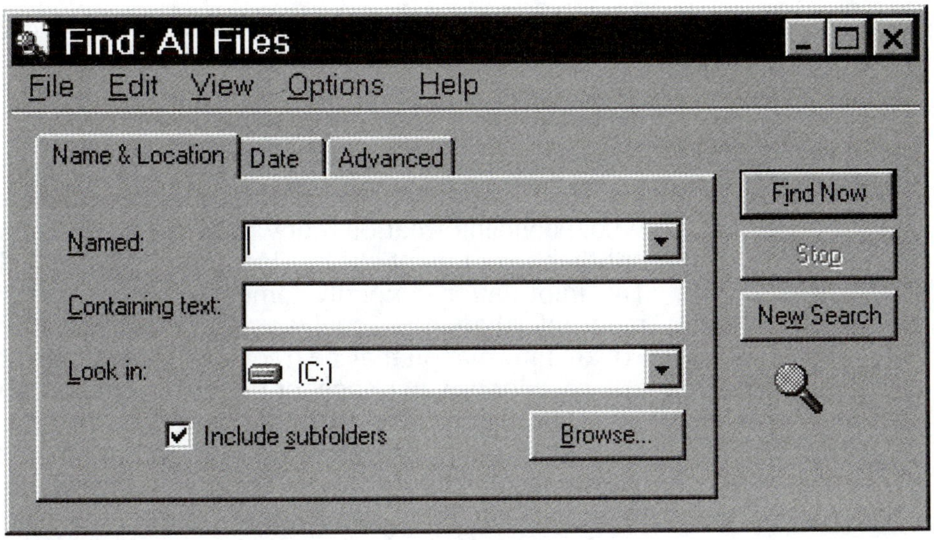

Figure 16-3   A Find screen.

board and computer into a form that can be electronically transferred over telephone lines and radio waves. At the receiving end of the signal is another modem that reconverts (demodulates) the signal into a usable form by the computer; hence, the term *mo* (modulate) *dem* (demodulate).

Depending on the modem and the ISP service, speeds of transmission may vary widely. The slower the connection provided by the modem and the service, the longer it takes to transmit and receive information, and, as with most services, the greater the speed, the higher the cost. It is easy to see that a multipage document will take longer to transmit or receive than a single-page document. The reasonableness of the cost of a high-speed connection depends on the volume and the number of pages regularly sent or received. Perhaps less obvious considerations are the size of the files and whether they are in graphic format. Most tax forms are available in a graphic form as opposed to a text form. A single tax form in graphic format may be the equivalent of a ten-page text document. Again,

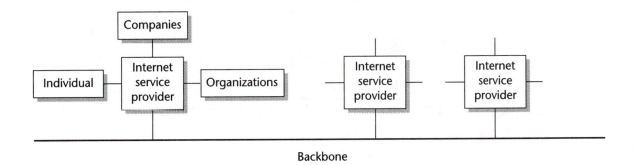

Figure 16-4   Backbone of World Wide Web.

depending on the frequency of tax form downloads, especially during tax season, it might be more productive to upgrade to a high-speed line.

Information, Forms, and Files

One of the biggest potential time-savers for the paralegal is the ready availability of information, forms, and files on the Internet or World Wide Web. Public information that would have required a trip to the courthouse or other government office is instantly available without leaving the office. This information generally comes from public or private sources. Government information is usually available without cost or at minimum cost. Private information may be free to all, such as the IBM patents Web site, or at a cost per use, per page, or per time period, such as a month.

Unless you have a direct connection to a computer database, you will be working with a software program known as a browser. The two most popular Web browsers are the Microsoft Internet Explorer and the Netscape Communicator. These browsers are typically used with Internet service providers, which act as intermediaries between the user and the World Wide Web, but who do not provide content. Some services (e.g., America Online (AOL) and CompuServe; Fig. 16-5) provide content, such as news and weather and specialty sections for the sharing of information, as well as providing the traditional Internet connections and e-mail.

Figure 16-5   CompuServe screen.

All of the browsers basically provide two main windows; one window to display e-mail (Fig. 16-6) and window one to display Internet search results (Fig. 16-7).

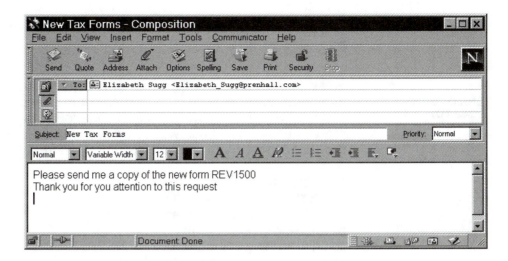

Figure 16-6   An e-mail window.

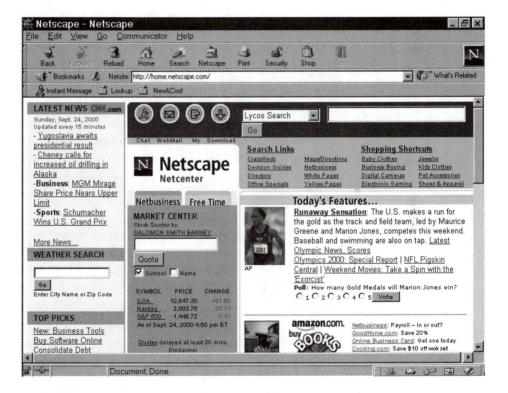

Figure 16-7   A Web window.

Search Engines

An Internet search engine is a program that is designed to take a word or set of words and search Web sites on the Internet. There are a number of different Internet search engines. Each of these searches in a different fashion, with many of the engines producing totally different results from the same search request. The number of search engines is constantly expanding. Some of these engines are far more suitable to legal and taxation searches than others. Other search engines, designed for use by children and families, may not return the same results needed in the professional areas. It is useful to create a search query and run the query through a number of different search engines to compare the results. For example, you may wish to search the topic "regulation of paralegals." Each of the search engines listed below may be accessed by entering their **uniform resource locator**, or **URL**, their Internet "address" in your Web browser.

UNIFORM RESOURCE LOCATOR The "address" used to access sites on the Internet

Alta Vista: **www.altavista.com**
Ask Jeeves: **www.askjeeves.com**
Dogpile: **www.dogpile.com**
Excite: **www.excite.com**
Google: **www.google.com**
Metacrawler: **www.metacrawler.com**
Yahoo: **www.yahoo.com**

Constructing a Search Query

Single words may be used in any of the search engines. However, frequently, you will be looking for more detailed information. Advanced queries may be constructed using words known as operators. Examples of operators are the words AND, OR, and NOT. For example, paralegal AND regulation. This would search for combinations of those two words together. If you want to find all the information about paralegal, but do not want anything related to regulation, then you might use the search query phrased, "paralegal NOT regulation." When two words are equally acceptable, you might request paralegal OR legal AND regulation.

In some search engines, the further operator NEAR may also be used; for example, paralegal NEAR regulation. Searches in databases such as WESTLAW and Lexis-Nexis allow you to search for words near each other by specifying the number of words apart that is acceptable (e.g., within 25 words).

Search Results

Some of the information you will find on the Web will be shown on the screen and will not need any additional effort to access. Some data, such as a phone number, address, or other limited amounts of information will appear and can then be copied manually or printed out using the print option to capture the displayed page. Other information may be in the form of large text or graphic files. These files may be many pages long or involve the use of graphic display programs, such as the popular Adobe series. Typical of the graphic images are the tax forms available from the Internal Revenue Service.

Addresses and Locations

Obviously, finding something usually requires knowing where it resides. We find people by looking for their homes or business addresses, or telephone numbers. The modern equivalent of a person's telephone number is his or her e-mail address. Computers on the Internet also have addresses known as **uniform resource locators**, also known as **URLs**. The URL is made up of three parts:

PROTOCOL ://COMPUTER/PATH.

The protocol is usually the http, or hypertext transfer protocol. The computer refers to the Internet computer name, such as **www.bucks.edu**. And the path refers to the directory or subdirectory on the computer where the information can be found. This may also be thought of as a file cabinet, with the protocol as the name of the file cabinet, the computer as the particular drawer in the file cabinet, and the path as the file folder in the drawer. Note: not all URLs have a path as part of the address.

As part of the naming protocol there is what is called a domain nomenclature. At the top of the domain are the extensions such as the edu in **www.bucks.edu**. Some of the most common extensions are listed below.

.org	organizations
.edu	educational institutions
.com	commercial operations
.gov	government agencies

In determining the authenticity of information, it is sometimes useful to know if the computer is a commercial site (.com) or a government site (.gov). For example, the official Internal Revenue Service site has the extension .gov. A sound-alike site uses the same IRS prefix but with the extension .com, an unofficial commercial site. In addition, there may be further extensions, such as .jp, .fr, or .uk. These designations refer to the country of origin of the computer, such as Japan, France, and United Kingdom. The combination of these various parts may be viewed as the address and zip code of the computer.

The official URL for the Internal Revenue Service is **www.irs.gov**. This is not to be confused with an unofficial private Web site, **irs.com**. To obtain official Internal Revenue Service forms and information, be sure to use the official site, **irs.gov**. A popular unofficial Web site, with direct links to official federal and state tax information and forms, is **www.taxsites.com**.

A word of caution: addresses of Web sites tend to change frequently. It is a good idea to keep a list of frequently used Web sites and update it regularly.

Format of Available Information

Single-Page Items. Most of the items that are displayed can be printed to a laser or inkjet printer attached to a computer. At the top of most Internet Web browsers is a printer icon, or a Print command in the file icon on the top of the page. Clicking on the icon or word Print in the file pull-down menu will cause the print process to begin. Note: this may require the computer to access the original source of the information, so be patient.

ATTACHMENTS
Files, text or graphic,
that are sent as part of
an e-mail

File Attachments. A popular method for transmitting text files and, occasionally, graphic images is to attach the text file or graphic file to an e-mail. This is really much easier than it sounds. Today, almost everyone has an e-mail address, whether at home or at work or both. To send or receive any e-mail requires the use of an Internet service provider and software program, such as Internet Explorer or Netscape Communicator, or one of the other specialty e-mail programs. With traditional e-mail, text is entered by the keyboard, transmitted to the e-mail account of a receiver, and read online. Virtually any file on the computer can be attached (linked) to be sent with the e-mail. The receiver needs only to click the mouse on the attachment, which may appear as an icon containing a paper clip. In most cases, the file will open up using the same program from which it was created, such as Microsoft Word or Corel WordPerfect. Occasionally, a file may be transmitted in a format that the receiver does not have the software to open. This is particularly true with regard to graphic images, pictures, and drawings.

Receiving and Downloading Files and Attachments

The same method is used for downloading both files and attachments. You should first determine if your computer has a directory (a folder) into which you can download these files. In Windows, this is usually a folder called My Download Files or My Files. If there is no existing folder, use your Windows Explorer to create a file with a name, such as Download. The Windows Explorer is a program in your Start Directory under Programs. Note: Windows Explorer is not the same as the Windows Internet Explorer, which is an Internet browser.

Most of the files attached as part of e-mail will be document files created and saved as either Microsoft Word or WordPerfect documents. You may want to save these files directly into your Word directory or the WordPerfect directory. Saving them in your computer download directory is one option, as is opening the file on the screen immediately, instead of saving it for later use.

Normally, text files and graphic images are considered static files. That is, by themselves, they do not perform any function, but contain data usable within another program, such as a word processor or graphic image viewer. However, it has become common to send as attachments, files that have miniprograms within them (e.g., macros that perform functions when activated, such as those used to calculate sums in worksheets). Others are self-contained software programs, such as screen savers that contain animation and some of the more popular animated cartoons. Most of these program files will have an extension of either **.exe**, or in some cases, for a particularly large file, **.zip**. Files with the .exe extension can be run immediately after downloading and saving. Files with the .zip extension are in a compressed form. Very large files, such as spreadsheets, photographs, diagrams, and some program files can take a long time to transmit over the Internet. This ties up the line, may increase the cost if the service is on a charge per minute, and can result in bad transmission if the line accidentally disconnects or suffers electrical interference.

.EXE FILES Files that are programs that will run immediately after downloading

.ZIP FILES Files that have been compressed to permit more rapid transfer of information, or to save computer disk space

To minimize these problems and out of courtesy, large files are run through a program that will compress them. After the compressed file is downloaded, it then will need to be uncompressed. A number of programs are available to un-compress files. Some of these require multiple steps to open the files, while others will perform the task automatically. For occasional use, the manual method is acceptable. But, with the increase in the number of compressed files, it may be more time efficient to purchase one of the automatic un-compress or "unzip" file programs.

Types of Image Formats

More and more frequently, the Internet is being used to obtain needed forms. These may be tax forms or court forms. Even the best-equipped office will need a form not found in the office supply room to complete a file. This may be an unusual federal tax form or a form from your or another state. These forms are usually made available in some form of image file. The most popular format for the Internal Revenue Service forms are in portable document format, or PDF, form, which many state agencies also use for document delivery. Other options may be presented for selection before obtaining the files desired. Knowing which option will work on your computer and with your printer will save time.

PDF

PORTABLE DOCUMENT FORMAT
One of the most popular of the file formats for viewing and retrieving graphic images (also referred to as PDF format)

Portable document format (PDF) is one of the most popular of the file formats. Most of the forms available for downloading are in this format. Your computer must have a program called Adobe Reader to retrieve these files. Adobe Reader is readily available as a free download from Adobe Systems. If it is not on your computer, you will generally receive an on-screen message alerting you and giving you the directions on where to obtain this program. After you have downloaded this program, the files will automatically open on your computer screen and be available for download as a file or directly to your printer.

PCL

PRINTER CONTROL LANGUAGE
A computer language used with Hewlett Packard and other compatible printers (also known as PCL)

Printer control language (PCL) is the computer language used with Hewlett Packard (HP) and compatible HP printers. It is not as widely used because of the size of the files and the frequent need to un-compress them before use. The required reader for this format is available from Page Technology Marketing.

PS

POSTSCRIPT LANGUAGE FORMAT
A programming language with instructions for printers that detail how the document is to be printed (also known as PS)

Postscript language format (PS) is a programming language that contains all the page characteristics that tell the printer with this programming language how to print out the document. This format requires large files, which usually must be uncompressed before use.

SGML

Standard Generalized Markup Language (SGML) is a federal and international standard that requires a commercially available software program to view and print.

Computer Viruses

Unfortunately, there are some computer-knowledgeable persons who develop and disseminate programs that attack and destroy computer programs, internal computer-operating systems, and, occasionally, the hard-disk drives of computers. These programs are known as computer viruses. There are numerous types of viruses, from those that create minor inconvenience to those that can destroy data and cause computer shutdowns. Some simple precautions can prevent disaster. A virus protection program, such as one of those sold by Norton, McAfee, and others, is as important to have on your computer as the computer-operating system itself. It is recommended that this be the first program loaded on a new computer. These programs will scan the computer to identify the presence of viruses, with the better programs able to eliminate the virus. Every disk should be scanned with a virus program before being used. Files that are downloaded from other computers or over the Internet should also be checked. As good as these programs are, they quickly go out of date as new viruses are created and unleashed. It is essential that these programs be updated regularly.

Downloading Copies of Tax Returns over the Internet

Most tax return forms are available over the Internet as portable document format, or PDF, files. To view or download forms in PDF format requires the use of Adobe Acrobat Reader. Adobe Acrobat Reader is free software that lets you view and print PDF files. This program is usually included with Web browsers and many other graphic programs. It is also available for free download from the Adobe Systems Web site, **www.adobe.com**.
To retrieve and download a form, use the following procedure.

- Select a file format
- Select the file(s) you wish to receive; to select multiple items, hold the control button down while selecting
- Press the Review Selected Files button; a results page will be displayed with links to the file(s) you requested
- Select the file title to retrieve

Unlike the federal web site, which offers alternative formats, most states and local governments use the Adobe PDF format. The Adobe Reader is updated on a regular basis. It is worth the investment of time to periodically update your computer program with the most current version from the Adobe Web site.

Electronic Filing of Tax Returns

The Internal Revenue Service and some states have combined in a joint effort to allow the electronic filing of both the federal and state individual income tax returns. Federal tax returns are transmitted directly to the Internal Revenue Service. The local or state tax authority then retrieves the information from the Internal Revenue Service. A feature of this service, known as IRS e-file, is the return receipt when the federal and state governments receive the form.

 **Ethical Issue**

NALA Code:

Canon 7: "A legal assistant must protect the confidences of a client and must not violate any rule or statute now in effect or hereafter enacted controlling privileged communications."

Privacy is a major issue in the use of the Internet for communications. Email has replaced the fax machine for communications between client and attorneys and between attorneys and other attorneys. Does this development raise an issue with regard to the protection of the confidences of a client?

CHAPTER SUMMARY

The use of the computer and the World Wide Web can make the life of a paralegal easier and more productive. Information that was previously available only by on-site visits to courthouses, libraries, and agencies is now available worldwide through the use of the computer and a modem or direct connection. Documents can now be easily sent to virtually anywhere in the world electronically and almost instantaneously. Print-quality graphic images, including reproducible tax forms, can also be transferred and retrieved. The use of a standardized format for graphic images, a portable document format (PDF), and the free availability of the program for reading these images offered by Adobe Systems, has made mass availability of tax forms by state or local government a reality.

GLOSSARY

Attachments   Files, text or graphic, that are sent as part of an e-mail
Backbone   The connecting line used by other computer systems to communicate with each other
.exe files   Files that are programs that will run immediately after downloading

File server   The central computer in a network computer system upon which the operating system rests; controls the flow of information between computers on the system and usually acts as storage unit for data

Internet service provider   A company or organization providing access to the Internet

Modem   A device for converting computer information into an electronic form that will allow it to be transferred over telephone lines and radio waves

Portable document format   One of the most popular of the file formats for viewing and retrieving graphic images (also referred to as PDF format)

Postscript language format   A programming language with instructions for printers that detail how the document is to be printed (also known as PS)

Printer control language   A computer language used with Hewlett Packard and other compatible printers (also known as PCL)

Uniform resource locator   The "address" used to access sites on the Internet

.zip files   Files that have been compressed to permit more rapid transfer of information, or to save computer disk space

REVIEW QUESTIONS

1. What is a computer virus?
2. How can one protect oneself against computer viruses?
3. What are the steps after connecting with the Internal Revenue Service for downloading desired tax forms?
4. What is the Adobe Reader, and how can one obtain a free copy?
5. What are zip files and why are they used?
6. What is a Web browser?
7. What is the difference between Microsoft Internet Explorer and Microsoft Windows Explorer?
8. What is an Internet service provider?
9. What does downloading mean?
10. How can the computer and the Internet increase a paralegal's productivity?

Appendix A

Accounting and Tax Web Sites

Why?

Accounting rules and tax regulations change frequently. The forms needed to complete tax returns also change as the laws change. Current federal and state tax forms are generally available for download over the Web. Current tax rules and regulations can be obtained over the Web on a daily basis. Forms and information from other states are available over the Web. With the ability to download required tax return forms immediately, deadlines that would pass if one had to rely on mail to obtain the required forms can be met.

Web sites change on a regular basis. The following web sites were accurate at the time of preparation.

Accounting Organizations

American Accounting Association
www.rutgers.edu/accounting/raw/aaa

Financial Accounting Standards Board
www.rutgers.edu/accounting/raw/fasb

American Institute of Certified Public Accountants
www.aicpa.com

Federation of Tax Administrators
Home page: **www.taxadmin.org**
Directory of State tax forms **www.taxadmin.org/fta/forms.ssi**

National Association of State Boards of Accountancy
www.nasba.org

Legal and Paralegal Organizations

National Federation of Paralegal Associations
www.paralegals.org

The National Association of Legal Assistants
www.nala.org

American Bar Association
www.abanet.org

Stock Exchanges

New York Stock Exchange
www.nyse.com

American Stock Exchange
www.amex.com

NASDAQ
www.nasdaq.com

Financial Newspapers

Financial Times
www.ft.com

The Wall Street Journal
Update.wsj.com

CNN Finance
www.cnnfn.com

Government Information

Federal

General Information
U.S. Federal Government Agencies Directory
www.lib.lsu.edu/gov/fedgov.html

Federal Government Resources on the Web
www.lib.eumich.edu/libhome/documents.center/federalnew.html

Federal Agencies Web Sites
Securities and Exchange Commission
www.sec.gov

General Accounting Office
www.gao.gov

General Services Administration
www.gsa.gov

Internal Revenue Service
www.irs.gov

US. Government Printing Office
www.access.gpo.gov

US Department Of Commerce
204.193.246.62/public.nsf

Simplified Tax and Wage Reporting System
www.tax.gov/1stop.htm

Pension Benefit Guarantee Corporation
www.pbgc.gov

U.S. Census Bureau
www.census.gov

U.S. Railroad Retirement Board
www.rrb.gov

Code of Federal Regulations
www.access.gpo.gov/nara/cfr/indx.html

U.S. Code
www.access.gpo.gov/congress/cong013.html

Small Business Administration
www.sba.gov

Social Security Administration
www.ssa.gov

State

Directory of State tax forms: **www.taxadmin.org/fta/forms.ssi**

Links to State and Local Sites
www.piperinfo.com/state/index.cfm

Legal Resources on the Net

Findlaw: Internet Legal Resources
www.findlaw.com

Lawrunner: A legal research tool
www.lawrunner.com

Internet Legal Resource Guide
www.ilrg.com

Cornell University Legal Information
www.law.cornell.edu

Yale University
www.yale.edu/lawweb

Appendix B

Alternative Ways to Obtain Federal Forms and Instructions

In addition to Internet access for retrieving forms and information, the Internal Revenue service provides forms and instructions by fax, in paper form, and on CD-ROM.

Phone. Obtain forms, publications, instructions and tax information by calling:

Forms and Publications (1-800-829-3676) to order current and prior year forms, instructions, and publications.

TeleTax Information (1-800-829-4477) to listen to prerecorded messages covering the TeleTax topics.

Fax. Tax Fax Service (1-703-368-9694) from your fax machine to get up to three items per call.

CD-ROM. A CD ROM containing current tax forms, instructions, and publications, as well as prior year tax forms and instructions, popular tax forms that may be filled in electronically, and Internal Revenue Bulletins may be obtained by ordering IRS publication 1796, Federal Tax Products, on CD-ROM. It may also be purchased online at **www.irs.gov/cdorders** from the national technical information service, or by calling 1-877-233-6767.

The forms listed in Figure B-1 are available by fax. Figure B-2 lists TeleTax topics, prerecorded messages covering tax information.

Forms Available by Fax

The following forms and instructions are available through our *Tax Fax* service by calling **703-368-9694** from the telephone connected to the fax machine. When you call, you will hear instructions on how to use the service. Select the option for getting forms. Then, enter the **Catalog No.** shown below for each item you want. When you hang up the phone, the fax will begin.

Name of Form or Instructions	Title of Form or Instructions	Catalog No.	No. of Pages
Form SS-4	Application for Employer Identification Number	16055	4
Form SS-8	Determination of Employee Work Status for Purposes of Federal Employment Taxes and Income Tax Withholding	16106	4
Form W-2c	Corrected Wage and Tax Statement	61437	8
Form W-3c	Transmittal of Corrected Wage and Tax Statements	10164	2
Instr. W-2c & W-3c		25978	4
Form W-4	Employee's Withholding Allowance Certificate	10220	2
Form W-4P	Withholding Certificate for Pension or Annuity Payments	10225	4
Form W-5	Earned Income Credit Advance Payment Certificate	10227	4
Form W-7	Application for IRS Individual Taxpayer Identification Number	10229	3
Form W-7A	Application for Taxpayer Identification Number for Pending U.S. Adoptions	24309	2
Form W-7P	Application for Preparer Tax Identification Number	26781	1
Form W-9	Request for Taxpayer Identification Number and Certification	10231	2
Instr. W-9	Instructions for Requestor of Form W-9	20479	2
Form W-9S	Request for Students or Borrower's Taxpayer Identification Number and Certification	25240	2
Form W-10	Dependent Care Provider's Identification and Certification	10437	1
Form 709	U.S. Gift (and Generation-Skipping Transfer) Tax Return	16783	4
Instr. 709		16784	8
Form 709A	U.S. Short Form Gift Tax Return	10171	2
Form 843	Claim for Refund and Request for Abatement	10180	1
Instr. 843		11200	2
Form 940	Employer's Annual Federal Unemployment (FUTA) Tax Return	11234	2
Instr. 940		13660	6
Form 940-EZ	Employer's Annual Federal Unemployment (FUTA) Tax Return	10983	2
Instr. 940-EZ		25947	4
Form 941	Employer's Quarterly Federal Tax Return	17001	3
Instr. 941			
Form 941c	Supporting Statement To Correct Information	11242	4
Form 990	Return of Organization Exempt From Income Tax	11282	6
Instr. 990 & 990EZ	General Instructions for Forms 990 and 990-EZ	22386	14
Instr. 990	Specific Instructions for Form 990	50002	16
Schedule A (Form 990)	Organization Exempt Under Section 501(c)(3)	11285	6
Instr. Sch. A		11294	8
Form 990EZ	Short Form Return of Organization Exempt From Income Tax	10642	2

Name of Form or Instructions	Title of Form or Instructions	Catalog No.	No. of Pages
Form 1040	U.S. Individual Income Tax Return	11320	2
Instr. 1040	Line Instructions for Form 1040	11325	28
Instr. 1040 (Base)	General Information for Form 1040	24811	26
Tax Table and Tax Rate Sch.	Tax Table and Tax Rate Schedules (Form 1040)	24327	13
Schedules A&B (Form 1040)	Itemized Deductions & Interest and Ordinary Dividends	11330	2
Instr. Sch. A&B		24328	8
Schedule C (Form 1040)	Profit or Loss From Business (Sole Proprietorship)	11334	2
Instr. Sch. C		24329	9
Schedule C-EZ (Form 1040)	Net Profit From Business (Sole Proprietorship)	14374	2
Schedule D (Form 1040)	Capital Gains and Losses	11338	2
Instr. Sch. D		24331	7
Schedule D-1 (Form 1040)	Continuation Sheet for Schedule D	10424	2
Schedule E (Form 1040)	Supplemental Income and Loss	11344	2
Instr. Sch. E		24332	6
Schedule EIC (Form 1040A or 1040)	Earned Income Credit	13339	2
Schedule F (Form 1040)	Profit or Loss From Farming	11346	2
Instr. Sch. F		24333	7
Schedule H (Form 1040)	Household Employment Taxes	12187	2
Instr. Sch. H		21451	8
Schedule J (Form 1040)	Farming Income Average	25513	2
Instr. Sch. J		25514	4
Schedule R (Form 1040)	Credit for the Elderly or the Disabled	11359	2
Instr. Sch. R		11357	4
Schedule SE (Form 1040)	Self-Employment Tax	11358	2
Instr. Sch. SE		24334	4
Form 1040A	U.S. Individual Income Tax Return	11327	2
Schedule 1 (Form 1040A)	Interest and Ordinary Dividend Income for Form 1040A Filers	12075	1
Schedule 2 (Form 1040A)	Child and Dependent Care Expenses for Form 1040A Filers	10749	2
Schedule 3 (Form 1040A)	Credit for the Elderly or the Disabled for Form 1040A Filers	12064	2
Instr. Sch. 3		12059	4
Form 1040-ES	Estimated Tax for Individuals	11340	7
Form 1040EZ	Income Tax Return for Single and Joint Filers With No Dependents	11329	2
Form 1040NR	U.S. Nonresident Alien Income Tax Return	11364	5
Instr. 1040NR			
Form 1040NR-EZ	U.S. Income Tax Return for Certain Nonresident Aliens With No Dependents	21534	2
Instr. 1040NR-EZ		21718	12
Form 1040X	Amended U.S. Individual Income Tax Return	11360	2
Instr. 1040X		11362	6

Page 6

Figure B-1

Name of Form or Instructions	Title of Form or Instructions	Catalog No.	No. of Pages	Name of Form or Instructions	Title of Form or Instructions	Catalog No.	No. of Pages
Form 1116	Foreign Tax Credit	11440	2	Form 6252	Installment Sale Income	13601	1
Instr. 1116		11441	10	Instr. 6252		64262	2
Form 1310	Statement of Person Claiming Refund Due a Deceased Taxpayer	11566	2	Form 6781	Gains and Losses From Section 1256 Contracts and Straddles	13715	3
Form 2106	Employee Business Expenses	11700	2	Form 8271	Investor Reporting of Tax Shelter Registration Number	61924	2
Instr. 2106		64188	4				
Form 2106-EZ	Unreimbursed Employee Business Expenses	20604	2	Form 8283	Noncash Charitable Contributions	62299	2
				Instr. 8283		62730	4
Form 2120	Multiple Support Declaration	11712	1	Form 8300	Report of Cash Payments Over $10,000 Received in a Trade or Business	62133	4
Form 2210	Underpayment of Estimated Tax by Individuals, Estates, and Trusts	11744	3				
Instr. 2210		63610	5	Form 8332	Release of Claim to Exemption for Child of Divorced or Separated Parents	13910	1
Form 2290	Heavy Highway Vehicle Use Tax Return	11250	2				
Instr. 2290		27231	8	Form 8379	Injured Spouse Claim and Allocation	62474	2
Form 2441	Child and Dependent Care Expenses	11862	2	Form 8582	Passive Activity Loss Limitations	63704	3
				Instr. 8582		64294	12
Instr. 2441		10842	3	Form 8586	Low-Income Housing Credit	63987	2
Form 2553	Election by a Small Business Corporation	18629	2	Form 8606	Nondeductible IRAs (Contributions, Distributions, and Basis)	63966	2
Instr. 2553		49978	2	Instr. 8606		25399	8
Form 2555	Foreign Earned Income	11900	3				
Instr. 2555		11901	4	Form 8615	Tax for Children Under Age 14 Who Have Investment Income of More Than $1,400	64113	2
Form 2555-EZ	Foreign Earned Income Exclusion	13272	2				
Instr. 2555-EZ		14623	3				
Form 2688	Application for Additional Extension of Time To File U.S. Individual Income Tax Return	11958	2	Form 8718	User Fee for Exempt Organization Determination Letter Request	64728	1
Form 2848	Power of Attorney and Declaration of Representative	11980	2	Form 8801	Credit for Prior Year Minimum Tax—Individuals, Estates, and Trusts	10002	2
Instr. 2848		11981	4	Form 8809	Request for Extension of Time To File Information Returns	10322	2
Form 3903	Moving Expenses	12490	2	Form 8812	Additional Child Tax Credit	10644	2
Form 4136	Credit for Federal Tax Paid on Fuels	12625	4	Form 8814	Parents' Election To Report Child's Interest and Dividends	10750	2
Form 4137	Social Security and Medicare Tax on Unreported Tip Income	12626	2				
Form 4506	Request for Copy or Transcript of Tax Form	41721	2	Form 8815	Exclusion of Interest From Series EE U.S. Savings Bonds Issued After 1989	10822	2
Form 4562	Depreciation and Amortization	12906	2	Form 8822	Change of Address	12081	2
Instr. 4562		12907	11	Form 8824	Like-Kind Exchanges	12311	2
Form 4684	Casualties and Thefts	12997	2	Instr. 8824		12597	2
Instr. 4684		12998	4	Form 8829	Expenses for Business Use of Your Home	13232	1
Form 4797	Sales of Business Property	13086	2				
Instr. 4797		13087	4	Instr. 8829		15683	3
Form 4835	Farm Rental Income and Expenses	13117	2	Form 8839	Qualified Adoption Expenses	22843	2
Form 4868	Application for Automatic Extension of Time To File U.S. Individual Income Tax Return	13141	4	Instr. 8839		23077	4
				Form 8850	Pre-Screening Notice and Certification Request for the Work Opportunity and Welfare-to-Work Credits	22851	2
Form 4952	Investment Interest Expense Deduction	13177	2				
Form 4972	Tax on Lump-Sum Distributions	13187	2	Instr. 8850		24833	2
Instr. 4972		13188	4	Form 8853	Medical Savings Accounts and Long-Term Care Insurance Contracts	24091	2
Form 5329	Additional Taxes Attributable to IRAs, Other Qualified Retirement Plans, Annuities, Modified Endowment Contracts, and MSAs	13329	2				
				Instr. 8853		24188	8
				Form 8857	Request for Innocent Spouse Relief	24647	4
Instr. 5329		13330	4	Form 8859	District of Columbia First-Time Homebuyer Credit	24779	2
Form 6198	At-Risk Limitations	50012	1				
Instr. 6198		50013	7	Form 8862	Information To Claim Earned Income Credit	25145	2
Form 6251	Alternative Minimum Tax—Individuals	13600	2	Instr. 8862		25343	2
				Form 8863	Education Credits	25379	4
Instr. 6251		64277	8	Form 9465	Installment Agreement Request	14842	2

Page 7

Figure B-1   *Continued.*

TeleTax Topics—To listen to pre-recorded messages covering tax information, call **1-800-829-4477**.

Topic No.	Subject
	IRS Help Available
101	IRS services—Volunteer tax assistance, toll-free telephone, walk-in assistance, and outreach programs
102	Tax assistance for individuals with disabilities and the hearing impaired
103	Small Business Tax Education Program (STEP)—Tax help for small businesses
104	Taxpayer Advocate Program—Help for problem situations
105	Public libraries—Tax information tapes and reproducible tax forms
	IRS Procedures
151	Your appeal rights
152	Refunds—How long they should take
153	What to do if you haven't filed your tax return (Nonfilers)
154	Form W-2—What to do if not received
155	Forms and Publications—How to order
156	Copy of your tax return—How to get one
157	Change of address—How to notify the IRS
	Collection
201	The collection process
202	What to do if you can't pay your tax
203	Failure to pay child support and other Federal obligations
204	Offers in compromise
205	Innocent spouse relief
	Alternative Filing Methods
251	Form 1040PC tax return
252	Electronic filing
253	Substitute tax forms
254	How to choose a tax preparer
255	TeleFile
	General Information
301	When, where, and how to file
302	Highlights of tax changes
303	Checklist of common errors when preparing your tax return
304	Extensions of time to file your tax return
305	Recordkeeping
306	Penalty for underpayment of estimated tax
307	Backup withholding
308	Amended returns
309	Roth IRA Contributions
310	Education IRA Contributions
311	Power of attorney information
	Filing Requirements, Filing Status, and Exemptions
351	Who must file?
352	Which form—1040, 1040A, or 1040EZ?
353	What is your filing status?
354	Dependents
355	Estimated tax
356	Decedents
	Types of Income
401	Wages and salaries
402	Tips
403	Interest received
404	Dividends
405	Refunds of state and local taxes
406	Alimony received
407	Business income
408	Sole proprietorship

Topic No.	Subject
409	Capital gains and losses
410	Pensions and annuities
411	Pensions—The general rule and the simplified method
412	Lump-sum distributions
413	Rollovers from retirement plans
414	Rental income and expenses
415	Renting vacation property and renting to relatives
416	Farming and fishing income
417	Earnings for clergy
418	Unemployment compensation
419	Gambling income and expenses
420	Bartering income
421	Scholarship and fellowship grants
422	Nontaxable income
423	Social security and equivalent railroad retirement benefits
424	401(k) plans
425	Passive activities—Losses and credits
426	Other income
427	Stock options
428	Roth IRA Distribution
	Adjustments to Income
451	Individual retirement arrangements (IRAs)
452	Alimony paid
453	Bad debt deduction
454	Tax shelters
455	Moving expenses
456	Student loan interest deduction
	Itemized Deductions
501	Should I itemize?
502	Medical and dental expenses
503	Deductible taxes
504	Home mortgage points
505	Interest expense
506	Contributions
507	Casualty losses
508	Miscellaneous expenses
509	Business use of home
510	Business use of car
511	Business travel expenses
512	Business entertainment expenses
513	Educational expenses
514	Employee business expenses
515	Disaster area losses
	Tax Computation
551	Standard deduction
552	Tax and credits figured by the IRS
553	Tax on a child's investment income
554	Self-employment tax
555	Five- or ten-year tax options for lump-sum distributions
556	Alternative minimum tax
557	Tax on early distributions from traditional and Roths
558	Tax on early distribution from retirement plans
	Tax Credits
601	Earned income credit (EIC)
602	Child and dependent care credit
603	Credit for the elderly or the disabled
604	Advance earned income credit
605	Education credits
606	Child tax credits
608	Excess social security and RRTA tax withheld
	IRS Notices
651	Notices—What to do
652	Notice of underreported income— CP 2000
653	IRS notices and bills and penalty and interest charges

Topic No.	Subject
	Basis of Assets, Depreciation, and Sale of Assets
701	Sale of your home—After May 6, 1997
702	Sale of your home—Before May 7, 1997
703	Basis of assets
704	Depreciation
705	Installment sales
	Employer Tax Information
751	Social security and Medicare withholding rates
752	Form W-2—Where, when, and how to file
753	Form W-4—Employee's Withholding Allowance Certificate
754	Form W-5—Advance earned income credit
755	Employer identification number (EIN)—How to apply
756	Employment taxes for household employees
757	Form 941—Deposit requirements
758	Form 941—Employer's Quarterly Federal Tax Return
759	Form 940/940-EZ—Deposit requirements
760	Form 940/940-EZ—Employer's Annual Federal Unemployment Tax Return
761	Tips—Withholding and reporting
762	Independent contractor vs. Employee
	Magnetic Media Filers— 1099 Series and Related Information Returns (For electronic filing of individual returns, use topic 252.)
801	Who must file magnetically
802	Applications, forms, and information
803	Waivers and extensions
804	Test files and combined Federal and state filing
805	Electronic filing of information returns
	Tax Information for Aliens and U.S. Citizens Living Abroad
851	Resident and nonresident aliens
852	Dual-status alien
853	Foreign earned income exclusion— General
854	Foreign earned income exclusion— Who qualifies?
855	Foreign earned income exclusion— What qualifies?
856	Foreign tax credit
857	Individual taxpayer identification number— Form W-7
858	Alien Tax Clearance
	Tax Information for Puerto Rico Residents (in Spanish)
901	Who must file a U.S. income tax return in Puerto Rico
902	Deductions and credits for Puerto Rico filers
903	Federal employment taxes in Puerto Rico
904	Tax assistance for Puerto Rico residents

Topic numbers are effective January 1, 2000.

Page 8

*U.S. Government Printing Office: 1999 — 456-038

Figure B-2

Appendix C

Model Executor's Account and Model Trustee's Account

MODEL EXECUTOR'S ACCOUNT

FIRST AND FINAL ACCOUNT OF
William C. Doe, Executor
For
ESTATE OF John Doe, Deceased

Date of Death:	November 14, 1988
Date of Executor's Appointment:	November 24, 1988
Accounting for the Period:	November 24, 1988 to November 30, 1989

Purpose of Account: William C. Doe, Executor, offers this account to acquaint interested parties with the transactions that have occurred during his administration.

*The account also indicates the proposed distribution of the estate.

It is important that the account be carefully examined. Requests for additional information or questions or objections can be discussed with:

[Name of Executor, Counsel, or other appropriate person]

[address and telephone number]

*Optional — for use if applicable.

(*continues*)

SUMMARY OF ACCOUNT

	Page	Current Value	Fiduciary Acquisition Value
*Proposed Distribution to Beneficiaries	[36]	<u>$102,974.56</u>	<u>$ 90,813.96</u>
Principal			
Receipts	[31-32]		$160,488.76
Net Gain (or Loss) on Sales or Other Disposition	[32]		<u>2,662.00</u>
			$163,150.76
Less Disbursements:			
Debts of Decedent	[33]	$ 485.82	
Funeral Expenses	[33]	1,375.00	
Administration Expenses	[33]	194.25	
Federal and State Taxes	[33]	5,962.09	
Fees and Commissions	[33]	<u>11,689.64</u>	<u>19,706.80</u>
Balance before Distributions			$143,443.96
Distributions to Beneficiaries	[33]		52,630.00
Principal Balance on Hand	[34]		$ 90,813.96
For Information:			
Investments Made	[34]		
Changes in Investment Holdings	[34]		
Income			
Receipts	[35]		$ 2,513.40
Less Disbursements	[35]		<u>178.67</u>
Balance Before Distributions			$ 2,334.73
Distributions to Beneficiaries	[35]		<u>2,334.73</u>
Income Balance on Hand			0
Combined Balance on Hand			<u>$ 90,813.96</u>

———————————

*Optional — for use if applicable.

Receipts of Principal

Assets Listed in Inventory (Value as of Date of Death)		Fiduciary Acquisition Value
Cash:		
First National Bank—checking account	$ 516.93	
Prudent Saving Fund Society—savings account	2,518.16	
Cash in possession of decedent	42.54	$ 3,077.63
Tangible Personal Property:		
Jewelry —		
1 pearl necklace		515.00
Furniture —		
1 antique highboy	$ 2,000.00	
1 antique side table	60.00	
1 antique chair	55.00	2,115.00
Stocks:		
200 shs. Home Telephone and Telegraph Co., common	$25,000.00	
50 shs. Best Oil Co., common	5,000.00	
1,000 shs. Central Trust Co., capital	50,850.00	
151 shs. Electric Data Corp., common	1,887.50	
50 shs. Fabulous Mutual Fund	1,833.33	
200 shs. XYZ Corporation, common	6,000.00	90,570.83
Realty:		
Residence—86 Norwood Road, West Hartford, CT		50,000.00
Total Inventory		$146,278.46

Note: To facilitate preparation, the accountant may prefer to detail the starting balance by attaching a copy of the inventory as an exhibit. (This would be inappropriate if the inventory is prepared in a form that includes substantial extraneous material or does not list assets in an orderly manner). The opening entry would then read:

"Assets Listed in Inventory per copy attached $146,278.48."

(continues)

Receipts Subsequent to Inventory
(Value When Received)

2/22/89	Proceeds of Sale—Best Oil Co., rights to subscribe received 2/15/89	$ 50.00*	
3/12/89	Fabulous Mutual Fund, capital gains dividend received in cash	32.50	
5/11/89	Refund of overpayment of 1988 U.S. individual income tax	127.80	
9/25/89	From Richard Roe, Ancillary Administrator, net proceeds on sale of oil and gas leases in Jefferson Parish, Louisiana	10,000.00	$ 10,210.30

Adjustment to Carrying Values
Increased value of 200 shs. XYZ Corporation,
common stock upon audit of Federal Estate Tax Return:

Adjusted value upon audit	$10,000.00	
Value per Inventory	6,000.00	$ 4,000.00
Total Receipts of Principal		$160,488.76

---

*Proceeds of sale of rights may be treated as an additional receipt, as illustrated here, or may be applied in reduction of carrying value as illustrated on page [43] of the Model Trustee's Account. Either method, consistently applied, is acceptable.

Gains and Losses on Sales or Other Dispositions

2/7/89	100 shs. Home Telephone & Telegraph Co., common			
	Net Proceeds	$14,025.00		
	Fiduciary Acquisition Value	12,500.00	$ 1,525.00	
3/15/89	1,000 shs. Central Trust Co., capital			
	Net Proceeds	27,467.00		
	Fiduciary Acquisition Value	25,425.00	2,042.00	
3/15/89	200 shs. XYZ Corporation, common			
	Fiduciary Acquisition Value	10,000.00		
	Net Proceeds	9,000.00		$ 1,000.00
5/21/89	35 shs. Electric Data Corp., common			
	Net Proceeds	530.00		
	Fiduciary Acquisition Value	437.50	92.50	
7/20/89	$10,000 U.S. Treasury Bonds 3%, due 7/1/92			
	Net Proceeds	10,000.00		
	Fiduciary Acquisition Value	9,997.50	2.50	
	Total Gains and Losses		$ 3,662.00	$ 1,000.00
	Less Loss		1,000.00	
	Net Gain		$ 2,662.00	

Disbursements of Principal

Debts of Decedent

1/25/89	John T. Hill, M.D., professional services	$ 250.00	
4/12/89	State Tax Commissioner, 1988 state capital gains tax	156.00	
1/25/89	Thomas Pharmacy, prescriptions	23.82	
2/1/89	Sanders Hardware, purchases per bill dated 12/15/88	56.00	$ 485.82

Funeral Expenses

1/10/89	Smith Funeral Home, services	1,200.00	
2/15/89	Jones Memorials, grave marker	175.00	1,375.00

Administration Expenses

11/14/88	Clerk of Court, probate costs	72.00	
2/22/89	Henry Smith, appraisal of jewelry and antiques	50.00	
11/16/89	Arden, Miles & Solomon, disbursements	56.00	
	Various miscellaneous affidavits, registered mail, toll telephone charges and other costs	16.25	194.25

Federal and State Taxes

8/13/89	State Tax Commissioner, state death tax		2,501.33	
8/13/89	Internal Revenue Service, federal estate tax		2,663.29	
11/15/89	Internal Revenue Service, U.S. fiduciary income tax for fiscal year ending 7/31/89 (attributable to capital gains)		283.84	
11/23/89	Internal Revenue Service, deficiency in Federal Estate Tax interest 8/14/89 to 11/24/89	$505.24 8.39	513.63	5,962.09

Fees and Commissions

11/16/89	Albert Schryver, Esq., fee as Guardian ad litem	375.00	

11/16/89	William C. Doe,
	Executor's principal commission
	   5% on $50,000
	   4% on $50,000
	   3% on $60,488
		6,314.64	

11/16/89	Arden, Miles & Solomon, attorney's fee	5,000.00	11,689.64
			$19,706.80

Disbursements of Principal to Beneficiaries

TO: Janet Doe, in satisfaction of gift under Article FIRST of Will

12/1/88	1 pearl necklace	$ 515.00	
	1 antique highboy	2,000.00	
	1 antique side table	60.00	
	1 antique side chair	55.00	$ 2,630.00

TO: Janet Doe, in satisfaction of gift under Article SECOND of Will

12/1/88	Residence—86 Norwood Road, West Hartford, CT	50,000.00
	Total Distributions of Principal to Beneficiaries	$52,630.00

(continues)

Principal Balance on Hand

	Current Value 12/10/89 or as noted	Fiduciary Acquisition Value
Cash	$ 5,305.63	$ 5,305.63
Stocks:		
50 shs. Best Oil Co., common	4,500.00	5,000.00
1,000 shs. Central Trust Co., capital—value at most recent sale, 9/18/89	32,168.76	25,425.00
116 shs. Electric Data Corp., common—not traded, value per company books, 12/29/88	1,684.00	1,450.00
50 shs. Fabulous Mutual Fund	4,016.17	1,833.33
200 shs. Home Telephone & Telegraph Co., common	16,000.00	12,500.00
$40,000 U.S. Treasury Bills due 12/14/89	$102,974.56	$90,813.96

Information Schedules — Principal

			Cost
Investments Made			
2/1/89	$10,000 U.S. Treasury Bonds, 3%	$10,022.50	
	Less accrued interest collected 6/29/89	25.00	$ 9,997.50
9/14/89	$40,000 U.S. Treasury Bills, due 12/14/89		39,300.00
Changes in Investment Holdings			
Central Trust Co.			
11/14/88	1,000 shs. Capital stock, par $5 inventoried		$50,850.00
1/15/89	1,000 shs. additional received in 2-1 split, _____ par reduced to $2.50		
	2,000 shs. par $2.50 carried at		50,850.00
3/15/88	1,000 shs. sold, carried at		25,425.00
	1,000 shs. remaining, carried at		$25,425.00
Home Telephone & Telegraph Co.			
11/14/88	200 shs. common par $10, inventoried		$25,000.00
2/7/89	100 shs. sold, carried at		12,500.00
	100 shs. remaining, carried at		12,500.00
3/30/89	100 shs. additional received in 2-1 split, _____ par reduced to $5		
	200 shs. par $5 carried at		12,500.00

Receipts of Income

Dividends

Best Oil Co., common 1/2/89 to 10/2/89—50 shs.		$ 20.00	
Central Trust Co., common			
1/15/89—2,000 shs.	$600.00		
4/13/89 to 10/15/89—1,000 shs.	900.00	1,500.00	
Electric Data Corp., common			
12/29/88 to 3/30/89—151 shs.	30.20		
6/29/89 to 9/28/89—116 shs.	23.20	53.40	
Fabulous Mutual Fund			
3/12/89 to 9/12/89—50 shs.		140.00	
Home Telephone & Telegraph Co., common			
2/1/89—200 shs.	225.00		
5/1/89 to 11/1/89—200 shs. (after stock split)	450.00	675.00	$2,388.40

Interest

U.S. Treasury Bonds, 3% due 7/1/92			
6/29/89—$10,000	150.00		
Less: accrued interest paid on purchase 2/1/89	(25.00)	125.00	125.00
Total			$2,513.40

Disbursements of Income

11/15/89	U.S. Fiduciary Income Tax for fiscal year ended 7/31/89 (allocable to income)	$ 53.00	
	To be paid:		
	William C. Doe—Executor's Income commission 5% on $2,513.40	125.67	
		$ 178.67	

Distributions of Income to Beneficiaries

	TO: William C. Doe, Trustee under Article FOURTH (A) for Walter Doe		
11/16/89	Cash	$1,167,37	
	TO: Sharon Doe		
11/16/89	Cash		
	Total	$2,334.73	

(continues)

Proposed Distributions to Beneficiaries

	Current Value 12/10/89 or as noted	Fiduciary Acquisition Value
Per Article FOURTH (A) of Will:		
TO: Walter C. Doe, Trustee for Walter Doe		
25 shs. Best Oil Co., common	$ 2,250.00	$ 2,500.00
500 shs. Central Trust Co., capital	16,084.38*	12,712.50
58 shs. Electric Data Corp., common	842.00*	725.00
25 shs. Fabulous Mutual Fund	2,008.09	916.67
100 shs. Home Telephone & Telegraph Co., common	8,000.00	6,250.00
$20,000 U.S. Treasury Bills, due 12/14/89	19,650.00	19,650.00
Cash	2,652.81	2,652.81
Per Article FOURTH (B) of Will:		
TO: Sharon Doe		
25 shs. Best Oil Co., common	$ 2,250.00	$ 2,500.00
500 shs. Central Trust Co., capital	16,084.38*	12,712.50
58 shs. Electric Data Corp., common	842.00*	725.00
25 shs. Fabulous Mutual Fund	2,008.09	916.67
100 shs. Home Telephone & Telegraph Co., common	8,000.00	6,250.00
$20,000 U.S. Treasury Bills, due 12/14/89	19,650.00	19,650.00
Cash	2,652.81	2,652.81
	$ 51,687.28	$45,406.98
Total	$102,974.56	$90,813.96

*Central Trust Co. — valued at most recent sale, 9/18/89.

*Electric Data Corp. — not traded, valued per company books 12/29/88.

MODEL TRUSTEE'S ACCOUNT

FIRST AND FINAL ACCOUNT
For the "Marital Trust" Established under the Will of John H. Doe, Deceased

Stated by UPSTANDING TRUST COMPANY, Surviving Trustee

and

Mary W. Doe (Deceased Trustee, Died December 30, 1987)
presently on her behalf by UPSTANDING TRUST COMPANY,
as Executor of her Will,

John H. Doe, Died	January 30, 1975
Date of Trustee's first receipt of funds	February 11, 1977
Account Stated for the Period	February 11, 1977 to June 15, 1979

Purpose of Account: William C. Doe, Executor, offers this account to acquaint interested parties with the transactions that have occurred during his administration.

*The account also indicates the proposed distribution of the estate.

It is important that the account be carefully examined. Requests for additional information or questions or objections can be discussed with:

[Name of Executor, Counsel, or other appropriate person]

[address and telephone number]

(continues)

SUMMARY OF ACCOUNT

	Page	Current Value	Fiduciary Acquisition Value
*Proposed Distribution to Beneficiaries	[47]	$293,572.79	$261,006.44
Principal			
Receipts	[40]		$158,259.02
Net Gain (or Loss) on Sales or Other Disposition	[41]		113,549.47
			$271,808.49
General Disbursements	[42]	77.36	
Fees	[42]	4,300.00	4,377.36
Balance before Distributions			$267,431.13
Distributions to Beneficiaries	[42]		10,703.79
Principal Balance on Hand	[42]		$256,727.34
For Information:	[43-45]		
Investments Made	[43]		
Changes in Investment Holdings	[43-45]		
Income			
Receipts (see note on Page [46] about waiver)	[46]		$ 5,907.25
Less Disbursements	[46]		227.96
Balance before Distributions			$ 5,679.29
Distributions to Beneficiaries	[46]		1,400.19
Income Balance on Hand	[46]		$ 4,279.10
Combined Balance on Hand			$261,006.44

Receipts of Principal

Assets Awarded trustees by adjudication dated January 30, 1977, of Smith, J., Upon the First Account of the executors and the schedule of distribution pursuant thereto:

1.	Premises 789 Main Street, Media, PA	$10,000.00	
2.	$7,000 face value, Bethlehem, PA General Bonds 1.75%, due 4/1/78	6,965.00	
3.	$20,000 face value, Ohio Turnpike Commission Project One bonds 3.25%, due 6/1/2010	18,025.00	
4.	352 shs. American Telephone & Telegraph Co., capital	54,340.00	
5.	703 shs. XYZ & Co., common	67,663.75	
6.	5 shs. Southwest Rodeo Oil Co., common	1.00	
7.	Checking account, Upstanding Trust Company	264.27	$157,259.02

Other Receipts:

3/15/77 Adjustment of Sewer Assessment	1,000.00	$158,259.03

Note: To facilitate preparation the accountant may prefer to detail the starting balance by attaching as an exhibit a copy of the closing balance from the last account, schedule of assets in the deed, etc., as appropriate. The opening entry would then read:

"Assets awarded by adjudication dated January 30, 1977, of Smith, J., upon the First Account of the executors per schedule of distribution pursuant thereto, copy attached $157,259.02."

(continues)

Gains and Losses on Sales or Other Dispositions

			Gain	Loss
7/2/77	103 shs. XYZ & Co., common			
	Net Proceeds	$25,614.54		
	Fiduciary Acquisition Value	9,913.75	$15,700.79	
7/11/77	5 shs. Southwest Rodeo Oil Co., common			
	Company declared bankrupt	0.00		
	Fiduciary Acquisition Value	1.00		$1.00
4/6/78	100 shs. XYZ & Co., common			
	Net Proceeds	22,226.25		
	Fiduciary Acquisition Value	9,625.00	12,601.25	
12/29/84	$20,000 face value, Ohio Turnpike commission Project One bonds due 6/1/2010			
	Net Proceeds	18,450.00		
	Fiduciary Acquisition Value	18,025.00	425.00	
6/19/88	500 shs. XYZ & Co., common			
	Net Proceeds	56,337.21		
	Fiduciary Acquisition Value	1.00	56,336.21	
8/9/88	$50,000 Commercial Credit Co. demand note			
	Repaid	50,000		
	Fiduciary Acquisition Value	50,000		
9/22/88	852 shs. American Telephone & Telegraph Co., capital			
	Net Proceeds	39,503.92		
	Fiduciary Acquisition Value	19,816.70	19,687.22	
11/17/88	$70,000 U.S. Treasury Bills			
	Matured	70,000.00		
	Fiduciary Acquisition Value	70,000.00		
11/17/88	Premises:			
	789 Main Street, Media, PA			
	Sold receiving			
	Purchase Money Mortgage	15,000.00		
	Cash	5,000.00		
	Total	20,000.00		
	Less expense of			
	Sale:			
	Broker's Commission 1,000.00			
	Transfer Tax 200.00	1,200.00		
	Balance	18,800.00		
	Fiduciary Acquisition Value	10,000.00	8,800.00	
	Total Gains and Losses		$113,550.47	$1.00
	Less Loss		1.00	
	Net Gain		$113,549.47	

Disbursements of Principal

General Disbursements

5/15/88	Fire Insurance, 789 Main Street, Media, PA		$ 50.00
6/15/89	Reimbursement to Smith, Jones and Brown, Esquires, for Miscellaneous expenses, 2/11/77 to date:		
	Postage and Insurance	$26.21	
	Telephone	1.15	27.36
	Total		$ 77.36

Fees

6/15/89	Smith, Jones, and Brown, Esquires, Attorneys' Fee	$ 4,300.00
		$ 4,377.36

Distributions of Principal to Beneficiaries

TO: Mary W. Doe

7/1/77	$7,000 face value Bethlehem, PA. General bonds, 1.75%, due 4/1/85	$ 6,965.00	
7/2/77	Cash	238.79	$ 7,203.79

TO: XYZ Charity

5/4/89	Advance distribution, case	3,500.00
	Total Distributions of Principal to Beneficiaries	$10,703.79

Principal Balance on Hand

	Current Value	Fiduciary Acquisition Value
$20,000 face value, Indiana Toll Road Commission East/West Revenue Bonds, 3.5%, due 1/1/2012	$ 13,600.00	$ 17,275.00
1,260 shs. American Telephone & Telegraph Company, capital	57,015.00	29,306.40
680 shs. ABC Corp., common	56,355.00	48,124.00
Mortgage, 789 Main Street, Media, PA, face amount $15,000 reduced to	14,750.00	14,750.00
$120,000 face value, ABC Corp. demand note	120,000.00	120,000.00
Checking account, Upstanding Trust Company	27,271.94	27,271.94
Total	$288,991.94	$256,727.34

(continues)

Information Schedules — Principal

	Investments Made			*Cost*
12/28/94	$20,000 Indiana Toll Rd. Comm. East/West Revenue Bonds, 3.5%, due 1/1/2012			
	Bought at face value			$ 17,275.00
6/29/88	$50,000 Commercial Credit Co., demand note			50,000.00
8/18/88	$70,000 U.S. Treasury Bills due 11/19/88			68,000.00
9/28/88	$120,000 A B C Corp., demand note			120,000.00
	Changes in Investment Holdings			
2/11/77	American Telephone & Telegraph Company, common			
2/11/77	352 shs. awarded		$54,340.00	
4/24/77	704 shs. received in three for one split		0.00	
	1,056 shs. carried at		54,340.00	
3/22/79	1,056 rights to subscribe to additional stock sold for		1,484.41*	
			52,855.59	
3/12/82	1,056 rights to subscribe to additional stock sold for		2,507.00	
			50,348.59	
6/22/82	1,056 shs. received in two for one split		0.00	
	2,112 shs. carried at		50,348.59	
5/5/88	2,112 rights to subscribe to additional stock sold for		1,225.49*	
			49,123.10	
9/22/88	852 shs. sold for	$39,503.92		
	Less Gain on Sale	19,687.22	19,816.70	
	1,260 shs. carried at		$29,306.40	

---

*Proceeds of sale may be applied in reduction of carrying value as illustrated here, or may be treated as on additional receipt, as illustrated on page [32] of the Model Executor's Account. Either method, consistently applied, is acceptable.

XYZ & Co., common

2/11/77	703 shs. awarded		$67,663.75
7/2/77	103 shs. sold for	$25,614.54	
	Less gain on sale	15,700.79	9,913.75
	600 shs. carried at		$57,750.00
4/6/78	100 shs. sold for	$22,226.25	
	Less gain on sale	12,601.25	9,625.00
	500 shs. carried at		$48,125.00
7/9/80	250 shs. A B C Corp., common received @ 47.6875 in one-half for one divestment distribution		11,921.88
			$36,203.12
1/6/82	180 shs. A B C Corp., common received @ 79 in a 0.36 share for one divestment distribution		14,220.00
			$21,983.12
1/4/83	*250 shs. A B C Corp., common received @ 96.0625 in a one-half for one divestment distribution, normally $24,015.62, of which the following was applied to account value		$21,982.12
			1.00
6/19/88	500 shs. sold for	$56,337.21	
	Less gain on sale	56,336.21	1.00
	0 No Longer held		$ 0.00

---

*This example is included to illustrate treatment of a case where the value of distribution exceeds carrying value.

A B C Corp., common

7/9/80	250 shs. received in distribution on 500 shs. X Y Z & Co., common		$11,921.88
1/6/82	180 shs. received in similar distribution		14,220.00
	430 shs. carried at		26,141.88
1/4/83	250 shs. received in similar distribution		21,982.12
6/15/89	_____ 34 shs. received as 5% stock dividend, transferred to income		
	680 shs. carried at		$48,124.00

789 Main Street, Media, PA

2/11/77	Awarded		$10,000.00
11/17/88	Sold for purchase money mortgage of $15,000 and cash of $5,000	20,000.00	
	Less settlement costs itemized in principal account	1,200.00	
	Balance	18,800.00	
	Less Gain on Sale	8,800.00	10,000.00
	No Longer Held		$ 0.00

Mortgage on 789 Main Street, Media, PA

11/17/88	$15,000 mortgage received on sale of said premises	$15,000.00
6/15/89	250 principal received on account	250.00
	$14,750 balance remaining	$14,750.00

Southwest Rodeo Oil Co., common

12/11/77	5 shs. Awarded	$ 1.00
7/11/77	_____ Company Declared Bankrupt	1.00
	0	0.00

Receipts of Income

Waiver of Income Accounting

An income accounting having been waived for the period February 11, 1977 to May 30, 1989, a limited schedule of receipts income follows:

6/1/89	Balance per last income statement rendered	$ 1,773.25
	Dividend	
6/8/89	A B C Corp. on 680 shs.	578.00
6/15/89	34 shs. A B C Corp. — 5% stock dividend @ $79.00	
	Interest	
6/1/89	Indiana Toll Road Commission	350.00
6/15/89	A B C Corp., demand note	520.00
	Total Income Receipts	$ 5,907.25

Disbursements of Income

6/1/89	Patrick Green, tax collector, 1989 personal property tax	$155.56	
6/15/89	Upstanding Trust Co.—5% commission on income collected 3/30/89–5/31/89	72.40	$ 227.96

Distributions of Income to Beneficiaries

6/1/89	TO: Upstanding Trust Co., executor under the will of Mary W. Doe, deceased, on income arising before 1/1/88		
	Cash	$ 650.19	
6/15/89	TO: XYZ Charity		
	Cash	750.00	$ 1,400.19

Balance of Income on Hand

		Current Value	Fiduciary Acquisition Value
6/15/89	Cash	$1,593.10	$1,593.10
6/15/89	34 shs. A B C Corp., common	2,987.75	2,686.00
		$4,580.85	$4,279.10

(continues)

Proposed Distributions to Beneficiaries

Per Article FIFTH of Will:

Mary W. Doe not having exercised her general power of appointment granted to her over the assets of the Marital Trust, the entire fund on hand is to be distributed pursuant to the terms of Article FIFTH of the Will by XYZ charity.

Principal

	Current Value	Fiduciary Acquisition Value
$20,000 face value, Indiana Toll Road Commission East/West Revenue Bonds, 3.5%, due 1/1/2002	$ 13,600.00	$ 17,275.00
1,260 shs. American Telephone & Telegraph Company, capital	57,015.00	29,306.40
680 shs. A B C Corp., common	56,355.00	48,124.00
Mortgage, 789 Main Street, Media, PA, face amount $15,000 reduced to	14,750.00	14,750.00
$120,000 face value, ABC Corporation demand note	120,000.00	120,000.00
Checking Account, Upstanding Trust Company	27,271.94	27,271.94
Total Principal	$288,991.94	$256,727.34

Income

		Current Value	Fiduciary Acquisition Value
6/15/89	Cash	$ 1,593.10	$ 1,593.10
6/15/89	34 shs. ABC Corp.	2,987.75	2,686.00
	Total Income	$ 4,580.85	$ 4,279.10
	Combined Total	$293,572.79	$261,006.44

WALTER TRUST, Vice President of Upstanding Trust Company, Surviving Trustee under the Will of JOHN E. DOE and Executor under the Will of Mary C. Doe, Deceased, Trustee under the Will of John H. Doe, hereby declares under (oath)* (penalties of perjury) that said Trustees have fully and faithfully discharged the duties of their office; that the foregoing First and Final Account is true and correct, and fully discloses all significant transactions occurring during the accounting period; that all known claims against the trust have been paid in full; that, to his knowledge, there are no claims now outstanding against the Trust; and that all taxes presently due from the Trust have been paid.

_____

WALTER TRUST

Subscribed and sworn to
by WALTER TRUST before me
this _____ day of _____, 19____.

_____
           Notary Public

_____

*Execution under oath before a notary or under penalties of perjury is optional, depending on rules of the local jurisdiction.

Index